The Preserving Book

Soil Association

The Preserving Book

Editor-in-chief Lynda Brown

With Carolyn Humphries and Heather Whinney

LONDON, NEW YORK, MELBOURNE,
MUNICH, AND DELHI

Photography Bill Reavell
Editor Susannah Steel
Designers Louise Dick, Simon Murrell

FOR DORLING KINDERSLEY

Project Editor Andrew Roff
Project Art Editor William Hicks
Senior Presentations Creative Caroline de Souza
Managing Editors Dawn Henderson, Angela Wilkes
Managing Art Editors Christine Keilty,
Marianne Markham
Production Editor Ben Marcus
Senior Production Controller Alice Sykes
Creative Technical Support Sonia Charbonnier

First published in Great Britain in 2010
by Dorling Kindersley Limited
80 Strand, London WC2R 0RL

Penguin Group (UK)
Copyright © 2010 Dorling Kindersley Limited

2 4 6 8 10 9 7 5 3

This edition produced for The Book People Ltd, Hall Wood Avenue,
Haydock, St Helens, WA11 9UL

ISBN 978 1 4053 5985 6

Colour reproduction by Colourscan, Singapore
Printed and bound in Tien Wah Press, Singapore

Discover more at
www.dk.com

www.soilassociation.org

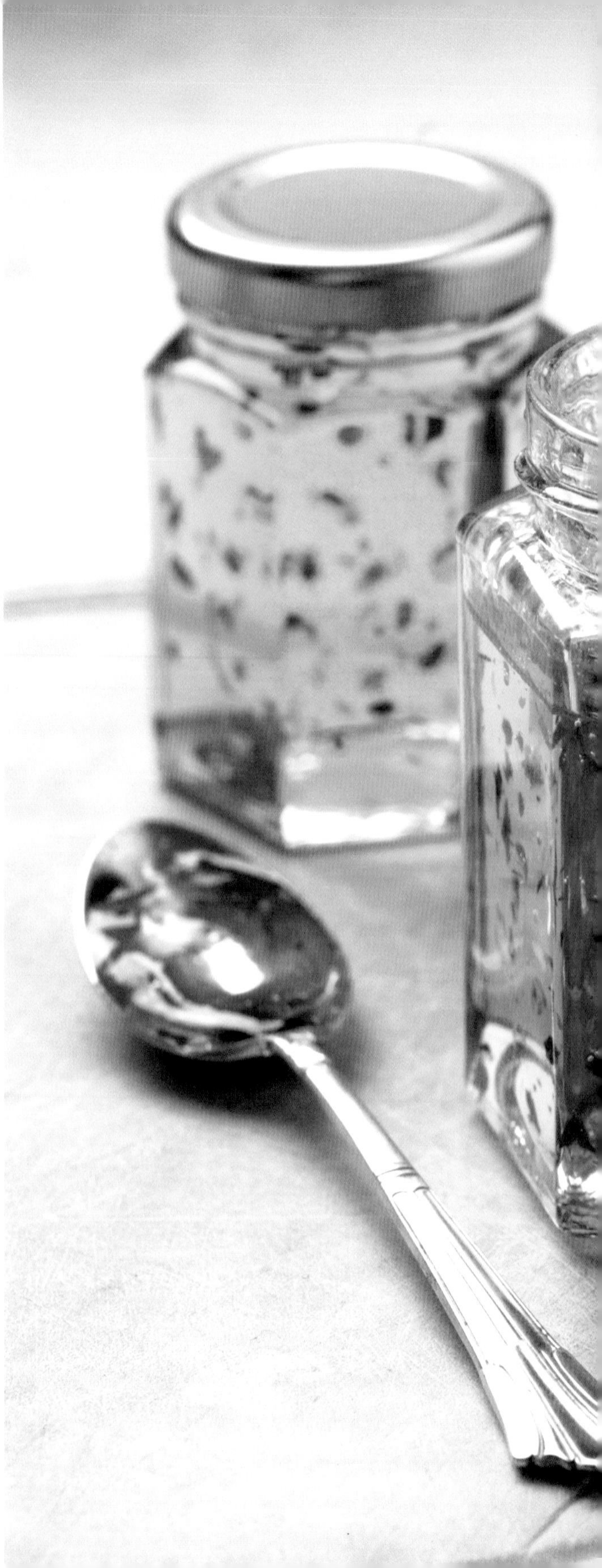

Contents

Foreword

Welcome to a brand new preserving book, a subject that is dear to my heart and which I hope will become dear to yours, too.

Preserving your own foods brings untold rewards, is immensely satisfying to do, and produces delicious results. It enables you to make the best use of organic, free-range, local, seasonal, and home-grown produce, and is very much at the centre of the current move to a more sustainable approach to our lives and the food we eat. Choosing, for example, organic foods, sustainably sourced fish, and organic fairtrade sugar to make preserves means your produce has an extra value, and contributes in more ways than one to helping make the environment and the world a better place. I'm a big fan, too, of home-grown fruits and vegetables. They're a great foundation for a sustainable lifestyle, and, as more and more people are discovering, there is nothing more pleasurable than enjoying a pot of home-made jam made with your own fruit.

Though preserving may be a time-honoured skill, this is very much a modern book. The recipes (a mix of traditional favourites and new) are the kind modern cooks will want to make using ingredients to be proud of, and with flavourings that will whet your interest as well as your appetite. Here and there we've also tried to update this great tradition. You don't have to turn the kitchen into a processing factory, make large quantities of preserves, or even use the traditional amounts of sugar if you don't want to. We've also included a few quick and easy modern interpretations of old techniques (freezer jams and freezer pickles, for example), introduced you to domestic smokers, and made sure you can tackle all the techniques confidently in your own kitchen.

So preserving is something to be embraced and celebrated. It opens many culinary doors and brings the promise of a lifetime's quiet pleasure. Best of all, every season brings something new and exciting to preserve; how good is that!

Lynda Brown

Contributors

Various professionals have given their recipes and valuable expertise to this book:

Carolyn Humphries

A journalist and food writer for over 30 years, Carolyn enjoys preserving everything from fruit to fish. For this book she has acted as a consultant and contributed freezing, bottling, and curing recipes.

Heather Whinney

A trained home economist and freelance food editor and writer, Heather has always had an enthusiasm and excitement about cooking with the seasons and preserving; chutney- and jam-making, in particular, are her real passions.

Trealy Charcuterie

Graham Waddington specializes in traditional quality British and European charcuterie using local free-range and organic meat. In 2010 the company received the BBC Radio 4 Food and Farming Awards Food Producer award.
www.trealyfarm.com

Organic Smokehouse

This multi-award-winning artisan smokehouse is the only purely organic production smokehouse in the UK, and uses an open chimney to smoke food. It was recently awarded the Royal Warrant to the Prince of Wales.
www.organicsmokehouse.com

The Old Smokehouse

Richard Muirhead is a chef by training, a passionate artisan smoker by profession, and proprietor of Brougham Foods in Cumbria. He supplies domestic smokers and wood chips, and runs food smoking courses.
www.the-old-smokehouse.co.uk

Andrew Hamilton

Brewing experts Andy and Dave Hamilton are the authors of *The Selfsufficientish Bible*. Andy is also the founder of the Bristol Brewing Circle, and is currently writing a book on home brewing.
www.selfsufficientish.com

The science of preserving

All foods have a natural shelf life, after which deterioration and decay – from internal ageing and invasion by bacteria, yeasts, and fungi (moulds) – set in. Effective preserving methods, often combined, can successfully halt or slow these processes to make foods safe to eat.

Cooling and freezing

Foods deteriorate faster in warm conditions, so the colder food is, the slower its rate of deterioration. At freezer temperatures below -18°C (0°F), micro-organisms can't function. Enzymes (organic catalysts, which speed up chemical reactions in cells) are not destroyed completely, however, which is why frozen food loses its flavour and texture over time. Once food is thawed, enzyme and micro-organism activity accelerate again. See section 1 for cold storage and section 3 for freezing.

Frozen beans Vegetables retain most of their flavour when frozen.

Removing moisture

Micro-organisms need moisture to grow; remove the moisture and they wither and die. There are two ways to remove moisture from food: drying with heat; or using a concentrated solution of salt or sugar (osmosis). The salt or sugar kills or severely inhibits the growth of microbes through dehydration. Dried food needs to be kept moisture-free while being stored; if not, new moulds will grow. See sections 2, 4, and 8 for drying, and salt and sugar preservation.

Dried apples Fruits must be dried throughly to remove all moisture.

MICRO-ORGANISMS

Bacteria, yeasts, and fungi (moulds) are universally present in the air, on our bodies, and on the food we eat. As these micro-organisms invade food, the food gradually spoils and becomes unpalatable and unsafe to eat. Micro-organisms generally thrive in warm, moist, airy, pH-friendly (alkaline) environments, and in the right conditions they multiply quickly. Food preservation is designed to create inhospitable environments for these micro-organisms and so makes food safe to eat (almost all micro-organisms are destroyed quickly at temperatures of 74–100°C/165–212°F and above). Although they cause spoilage of food, most micro-organisms are not harmful, and some are even beneficial.

Three sorts of micro-organisms that do cause concern, however, are Salmonella bacteria, which are destroyed by heat, and Staphylococci toxins and Clostridia bacteria spores, which are resistant to cooking and can cause food poisoning. Clostridia bacteria, including Clostridium botulinum (which causes botulism), thrive in warm, airless conditions, so special care always needs to be taken when preserving meat, fish, or vegetables under oil.

Strong concentrations

Micro-organisms cannot survive in alcohol, acidic conditions, or high concentrations of salt and sugar. Fruits are naturally acidic, but, as their acid content alone is not enough to prevent spoilage they are usually preserved in sugar or alcohol. Vegetables, by contrast, are more alkaline (which favours micro-organisms), so they are usually preserved in acidic vinegar, or salt, or a mixture of the two. See sections 4, 5, 6, and 8 for sugar, vinegar, alcohol, and salt preservation.

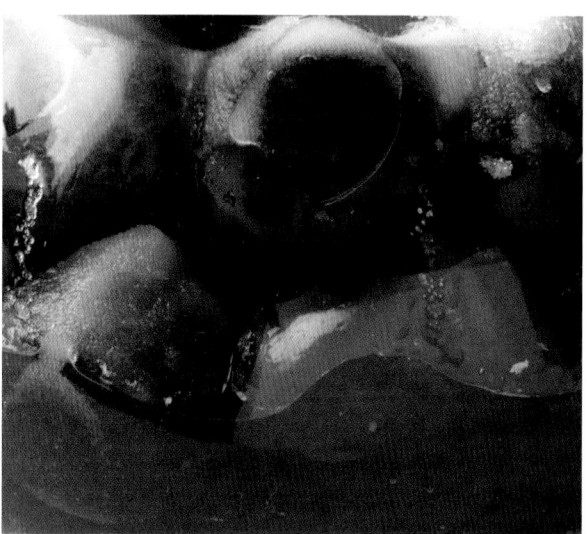

Cherries in brandy Pure alcohol preserves produce almost indefinitely.

Heating

The heat produced when food is cooked destroys both enzyme activity (which is why vegetables are blanched before being frozen) and virtually all micro-organisms. The more acidic the food, the more easily micro-organisms are destroyed by heat (when it comes to bottled produce, heat processing is suitable for acidic fruits and tomato-based sauces, but not for vegetables, which are less acidic. See section 3 for blanching, sections 4 and 5 for cooked preserves, and section 6 for bottling.

Raspberry jam Boiling jam kills most microbes and helps it to set.

Excluding air

A layer of oil or fat over food can provide a simple and effective short-term "seal" that prevents airborne micro-organisms from coming into contact with the produce, and starves any aerobic bacteria (which require oxygen to grow and survive) that are present in the food. Although this method has been used for centuries to preserve cooked meats and brined foods such as olives and cheeses, it has now largely been superseded by modern preserving methods. Nevertheless, it is still a useful technique to know about. Any food that is preserved in oil or fat must always be stored in the fridge (see box, p9). See section 7 for preserving in oil and section 8 for preserving in fat.

Vegetables in oil Produce must always be completely covered in oil.

Creating a vacuum

To prevent the re-contamination of bottled foods stored for the long term, air must be removed completely. This is achieved by creating a vacuum. Heat-processing and canning (both developed in the 19th century) are still the most common methods of creating a vacuum: the filled jars, bottles, and cans (with their lids in place) are heated, causing the air inside to expand and be released. (Vacuum packaging – wrapping foods tightly in thick plastic, then sucking out the air – is the modern equivalent, and is used to extend the shelf life of raw meat and fish, and cooked foods. Because the seal is so effective, vacuum-packed foods will also keep significantly longer in the freezer than using freezer bags.) See section 6 for bottling and page 19 for heat-processing.

Bottled fruit Heat-processing preserves produce for up to 12 months.

Fermentation

Not all micro-organisms are bad. Fermentation harnesses the benign bacteria, yeasts, and fungi present in the atmosphere to transform produce into food or drink with a long shelf life. Adding specially selected microbes, such as a brewer's yeast when making beer or a wine yeast when making wine, has the same effect. In this way hops can be fermented into beer, grapes into wine, and apples into cider, and – through the process of lactic-fermentation, where natural lactic bacteria in vegetables react with salt – cucumbers and cabbage into health-promoting pickles. See section 8 for vegetable lacto-fermentation and section 10 for brewing.

Fermenting beer Added yeast encourages beer to ferment properly.

Smoking

For centuries, food was smoked gently so that it would keep for longer and taste better. Salting the food first, which draws out the moisture, preserved it even longer. We now know that smoke contains minute quantities of over 200 complex compounds that help to preserve food. While traditional cold smoking is a specialized technique, hot smoking requires no special skills. Though smoked food tastes delicious, some smoke compounds (known as polycyclic aromatic hydrocarbons, or PAH) can also be hazardous to heath, so this short-term technique of preserving food should be enjoyed in moderation. See section 9 for smoking preservation.

Hot-smoked trout Meat or fish remains moist and succulent if smoked.

Natural preservatives

Traditionally, we have always made good culinary use of salt, sugar, vinegar, alcohol, and oil and fat. Home preserving using these natural preservatives produces superior results and more flavour than shop-bought items using modern preservatives.

Salt

Historically, salt (sodium chloride) is the most important preservative. It is a powerful preservative in concentrated solutions, as it draws out the moisture in food, which stops micro-organisms growing. The higher the concentration of salt, the greater its preserving powers and the longer the food keeps.

Use for

Salt is used to preserve vegetables, fish, meat, and occasionally fruit. Examples of salted preserves are Parma ham, morue (salt cod), gravadlax, sauerkraut, olives, and lemons.

Types of salt

• Sea salt and unrefined rock salt are ideal.
• Curing salt is specifically for curing meat. It is finer than sea salt, penetrates the meat effectively, and gives reliable and consistent results. It contains up to two and a half per cent added nitrite, which inhibits the growth of harmful bacteria and gives cured meat its pink colour. If you prefer, buy curing salt without these added preservatives, or use natural salts (which means the produce is greyer in colour and has a shorter shelf-life).
• Ordinary table salt has added anti-caking agents and so is not suitable for preserving.

Sugar

In sufficient concentrations (60 per cent or higher), sugar is as powerful a preservative as salt. Like salt, it draws out the moisture in foods, and the higher the concentration of sugar, the longer the preservative will keep.

Use for

Sugar is used mainly to preserve fruit, although, when combined with vinegar, it is used in fruit and vegetable mixtures such as chutneys. Examples of foods preserved in sugar are jams and jellies, fruit cheeses and butters, and crystallized fruits.

Types of sugar

• Cane, granulated cane, sugar beet, and golden unrefined sugars are all suitable.
• Dark brown and molasses sugars are too strong for sweet preserves, but fine for chutneys and some marmalades.
• Jam sugar contains added pectin and is used especially for low-pectin fruits (p89) that are difficult to set.
• Caster sugar is finer than granulated sugar and dissolves more readily, so it is useful for some preserves such as syrups and cordials.
• Preserving sugar produces less froth and scum, but is not essential for preserving.

Oils and fats

Both oils and animal fats provide a protective seal for foods, thus preventing contact with air. Neither are strictly preserving agents, so foods must be processed first. Meat, for example, is salted first until it loses its moisture, while vegetables are cooked in an acid, usually a vinegar, solution.

Use for

Examples of foods in oil include vegetables and feta cheese, and examples of food in fat include potted meats.

Types of oil and fat

• Olive oil, butter, duck and goose fat, and lard are ideal.
• Sunflower, grape, and rapeseed oil can also be used.
• The flavours of beef and lamb fat are too strong to be used for preserving.

Alcohol

Pure alcohol is the most powerful preserving agent of all: it kills all micro-organisms, and any food preserved in it will keep indefinitely. No other form of processing is required.

Use for

Alcohol is used to preserve fruits. Examples are sloe gin, cherries in brandy, and rumtopf.

Types of alcohol

• Brandy, Eau-de-vie, gin, rum, vodka, and whisky are all suitable to use.
• Wine, beer, and fortified wines are not strong enough to preserve foods effectively on their own.

Vinegar

Like salt, vinegar has traditionally been an important preserving agent. It is made by fermenting alcohol to produce acetic acid, and its acidity prevents or inhibits the growth of most of micro-organisms, including e-coli, that spoil food. To be effective, the vinegar must contain at least five per cent acetic acid.

Use for

Vinegar is used to preserve vegetables as pickles, relishes, and sauces, and also oily fish. Examples are pickled gherkins and rollmops.

Types of vinegar

• Malt (strong brown), distilled and spirit (colourless malt) vinegar, wine, and cider vinegars are all suitable for preserving.
• Pickling vinegar is a bought ready-spiced vinegar, although it's easy to make your own version.
• Balsamic vinegar is used as a flavouring only.

Vinegars
Savoury preserves rely primarily on the preserving power of vinegar. As long as the vinegar contains at least five per cent acetic acid, you can use any varitey. Malt vinegar has the strongest flavour and strength, while rice vinegar (right) has the mildest.

Equipment

Most equipment for preserving can be found in any kitchen (you can, for example, use a large, heavy-based stainless steel saucepan to make all sweet and savoury preserves). A few items are essential for a particular preserving method or specialist tasks.

Making

These pieces of equipment – some simple, others more specialist – will enable you to make successful preserves easily and professionally.

Wide-mouthed jam funnel
Buy non-reactive stainless steel funnels. Use to prevent the spillage of sweet and savoury preserves when potting them up.

Small ladle
Invaluable for potting up hot sweet and savoury preserves and bottled fruits.

Jam (sugar) thermometer
Useful for jams and marmalades, as it gives an accurate temperature for the setting point.

Slotted spoon
Useful for poaching fruit in syrup or vegetables in vinegar. Use a skimmer to skim scum off sweet preserves.

Wooden spoon
Large spoons with long handles are essential for jams and chutneys.

Long-spouted funnel
Choose non-reactive stainless steel or plastic funnels for bottling drinks, ketchups, and sauces.

Sturdy cheesecloth/calico straining bag
Use for filtering and straining produce for home brews. Hang it up by its handles.

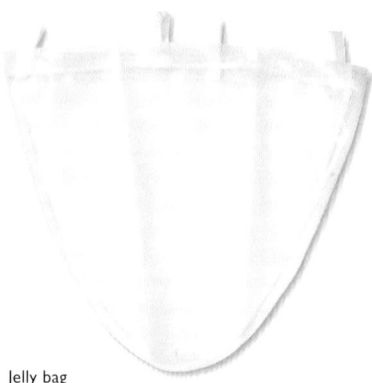

Jelly bag
Ideal for straining jellies and smaller quantities of liquids such as cordials. (To clean, turn inside out, soak in hot water, and then wash immediately.)

Muslin cloth
Use as a makeshift jelly bag (with a sieve), to wrap around hams and bacon, and to cover fermenting foods.

Stainless steel preserving pan
The thick, heavy base of this specialist pan ensures even heat distribution, while its wide sides allow for rapid boiling. It is ideal for making large quantities of jams, jellies, marmalades, chutneys, and other preserves.

Domestic stainless steel smoker
Purpose-built smoker with a drip tray and cover for hot smoking foods indoors and outside. Available in small and large sizes.

Wok
A wok with a rack and a glass lid makes an ideal instant hot smoker.

Siphon

Demijohn, airlock, and siphon
These three basic pieces of equipment are essential for brewing. Use a demijohn to store the fermenting brew and plug its narrow neck with an airlock, which controls the pressure in the demijohn. Use a siphon to transfer the brew into bottles. Also useful is a hydrometer to check the gravity, or density, of the liquid, and litmus papers to test its acidity or alkalinity.

Demijohn

Sausage-making kit
This kit has a mincer and nozzle for filling casings to make sausage-making easy. Electric versions are also available.

Airlock

Nozzles (in various sizes)

Mincer plate

Manual table-top mincer with handle

Nozzle attachment

Storing

Whether glass, earthenware, or freezer-grade plastic, the correct container for the right preserve is crucial for successful preserving. Collect functional and decorative containers in various sizes and shapes; reusing or buying secondhand containers saves money and is environmentally friendly. All must be in perfect condition and sterilized (p18) before use.

Jars

Use two types for preserving: jam jars, and specialist preserving jars. Both can be reused, but need a new rubber seal or lid each time (or use waxed paper discs, cellophane covers, and elastic bands instead of lids for jam jars).

Standard jam jars are classified by weight: small (225g/8oz), medium (350g/12oz), and large (450g/1lb). Standard preserving jars are classified by volume: small (500ml), medium (750ml), and large (1 litre). Imperial equivalents are not given for liquid measures.

Metal spring-clip preserving jar
Continental preserving jars (see box) have a hinged glass lid and a replaceable rubber band seal.

Kilner preserving jar
These glass jars have non-corrosive 1- or 2-piece lids with a screw band (see box).

SPECIALIST PRESERVING JARS

Metal spring-clip and kilner jars are all-purpose, toughened glass preserving jars with non-corrosive lids. As they can withstand high temperatures, they are essential for any preserves that require heat-processing in a water bath, or oven, but are also equally suitable for those that do not, such as jams, marmalades, chutneys, pickles, relishes, salsas, and preserved meats and fish. With correct use, they last a lifetime. Standard, wide-mouthed, and contemporary designs are available (which all look good enough to place straight on the table). Kilner jars are sold with 1-piece lids – where the screw band is incorporated into the lid – or 2-piece lids, which have an inner, replaceable, non-corrosive lid and a reusable screw band.

Two-piece lids
Non-corrosive lid with rubber seal and reusable screw band.

Jam jars
Use for jams, conserves, marmalades, and jellies, and use a new lid (or waxed disc and covers) each time. Collect pretty recycled jars, such as this hexagonal jar.

Ramekin dish
Useful to pot up fruit butters, cheeses, and jellies as gifts, and store potted meats and fish.

Freezer containers

Choose sturdy plastic containers that stack neatly in the freezer. Label each clearly with the name of the preserve and the date.

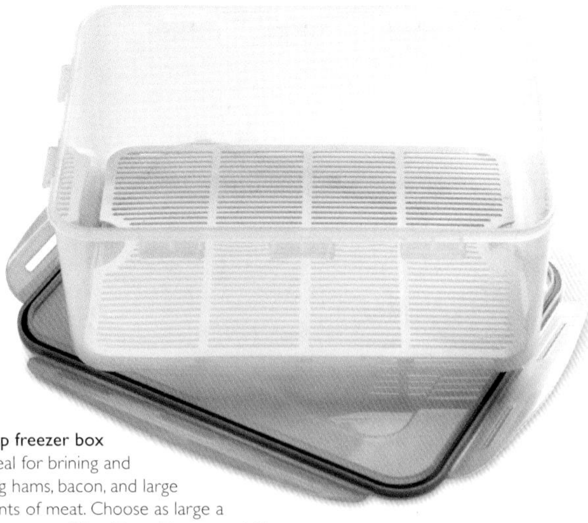

Deep freezer box
Ideal for brining and curing hams, bacon, and large joints of meat. Choose as large a box as possible with a drip tray and lid.

Plastic freezer boxes
Use for freezing freezer jams, fruit, vegetables, purées, and cooked sauces. Select various sizes with securely fitted lids.

Clear glass bottle
Use these larger bottles (750ml) for white wines, cider, and cordials. Ensure that the cork stoppers are always airtight.

Ice cube box
Use for freezing individual portions of herbs and edible flowers for decoration.

Brown beer bottle
These traditional brown bottles (500ml/16fl oz) are best for bottling beer. Seal with a metal cap using a capping machine.

Bottles

Glass bottles are environmentally friendly choices (the thicker the glass the better), and can be reused many times – or collect decorative bottles to use for gifts. Use for bottling cordials, syrups, and juices, ketchups and sauces, and home brews. Whether new, secondhand, or recycled, all bottles should be undamaged and must be sterilized (p18) before use.

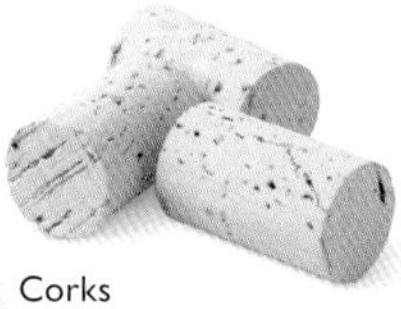

Corks
Made from the renewable outer bark of cork oak trees, corks are a natural, environmentally friendly choice for home brews.

Swing stopper bottles
These bottles are available in various sizes. Use to bottle cordials, syrups, juices, and elderflower champagne.

Good hygiene and food safety

Scrupulous hygiene and food safety are the keys to successful preservation. It's also vital to use good-quality produce in prime condition, keep it at the necessary temperatures during the preserving process, and adhere to recommended storage times.

Hygiene protocol

• All kitchen surfaces, tools, and equipment should be thoroughly clean. Use clean cloths and wash your hands frequently, especially when handling meat or fish.

• Check that your fridge is clean and is the correct temperature (4°C/40°F).

• Sterilize jars, bottles, and lids before use to remove microbes that cause spoilage (below).

• Ensure foods are sealed properly before storing. Check them regularly, use within their storage times, and discard any that smell odd or show signs of deterioration.

• Take extra precautions with raw or cooked meat or fish. Keep them cold at all times, and separate from other foods. Use clean equipment for each stage of processing.

Sterilizing methods

Oven Wash jars, bottles, and lids in hot water, drain upside down, and put in a cool oven (140°C/275°F/Gas 1) for 15 minutes.
Dishwasher Put jars, bottles, and lids through a hot wash timed to be ready when needed.
Microwave Suitable for screw-band jars, but not metal-clip jars. Put 4 tbsp of water in each clean jar and microwave for 2 minutes. Drain and dry upside down on kitchen paper.
Water bath Put clean jars, bottles, and lids in a pan of water to cover, bring slowly to the boil, turn off the heat, and leave until needed.

Immerse muslin, jelly bags, and rubber rings from jars in a bowl, pour over boiling water, and leave until needed.

Sterilized jars
It's best to sterilize jars and bottles just before you need them so they remain scrupulously clean.

Heat processing

For long-term storage, bottled fruits and sauces must be heated in an oven or a water bath. The air remaining in the filled jars and bottles expands and is released during heating, the seals are then tightened, and a vacuum forms on cooling. For processing times, see page 221.

1 Put the lids in place. For screw-band jars (1-piece or 2-piece, p16), fit with a new rubber band seal each time, screw on the screw band or lid, then release by a quarter turn. For jars with hinged metal spring-clip lids, fit the rubber band onto the lid and position the clip over the hinge to hold the lid in place (if using the oven), or clamp (if using a water bath). Some jars have plastic screw bands; if using the oven method, put the glass lid in place and fit the plastic screw band right after processing.

2 If using the **oven method**, place the jars or bottles on a baking tray lined with newspaper (to prevent any spills burning in the oven) about 5cm (2in) apart. Put the tray in the centre of a preheated oven (150°C/300°F/Gas 2) and heat for the required time. Remove the jars and tighten the clips or screw bands immediately (plastic screw bands should be fitted at this point).

If using the **water bath method**, put the jars on a folded tea towel or trivet in a preserving pan or large stainless steel pan. The jars should not touch each other. Fill the pan with enough warm water to cover the jars by 2.5cm (1in). Cover the pan, bring very slowly to a simmer, and heat for the required time (p221). Remove the jars with tongs and tighten the clips or screw bands immediately.

3 To test the seals to see if a vacuum has formed, wait for 24 hours after processing, then gently remove the screw band or undo the spring clips. Using your fingernail, see if you can prise off the lid. If it remains firmly in place, the seal is airtight and the jar can be re-fastened and stored for the recommended time. If the lid lifts easily, the heat processing was not successful; store the jar or bottle in the fridge and eat or drink within 2 weeks.

Flavourings

Salt, sugar, vinegar, and alcohol (pp12–13) give a preserve its main character, but adding a harmonious balance of flavourings to these salty, sweet, sharp, or alcoholic tastes is the key to sensationally good preserves. Use this chart to help you choose the right flavours.

BEDROCK – Foundation ingredients, to which others are often added to create a rounded flavour.		
FLAVOURING	**TYPES**	**HOW TO USE**
Chillies	Fresh, dried	Fresh and dried chillies give a preserve heat and a lively kick. Use in chutneys, pickles, relishes, ketchups, and sauces, and as a flavouring not only in smoked foods and preserved meats and fish but in jams, jellies, and bottled fruits. Add according to taste.
Citrus	Orange, lemon, lime	Citrus fruits add acidity and zing, and heighten the natural sweetness of most fruits. A squeeze of lemon can lift any preserve. Use finely grated rind sparingly in sweet and savoury preserves, bottled produce, and cured fish.
Ginger	Fresh, dried, crystallized	Ginger is a warm, invigorating spice. Use fresh and dried in savoury preserves, sauces, cordials, and home brews. Use crystallized for jams and bottled fruits.
Garlic	Fresh ("wet"), dried	The world's most popular flavouring, garlic has an unmistakable flavour. Use peeled and chopped in all savoury preserves, bottled ketchups and sauces, home-made sausages, and as a flavouring in smoked food marinades. Fresh garlic is much milder – use for a subtle garlic flavour. Choose dried garlic with care; reject any that smell stale or unpleasantly strong.
Bay leaves	Fresh, dried	Fresh bay leaves are best (or dry your own) for a rounded background flavour to all savoury preserves, sauces, ketchups, vegetables in oil, and cured food.

Fresh chillies

FRESH – Flavours that capture the essence of a season. They are best used on their own.		
FLAVOURING	**TYPES**	**HOW TO USE**
Herbs	Basil, coriander, dill, mint, parsley, oregano, rosemary, sage, tarragon, thyme	Use soft-textured herbs (basil, coriander, chervil, mint, parsley) in pestos, chutneys, and relishes. Use robust or strongly flavoured herbs (tarragon, thyme, mint, sage, rosemary) in sweet and savoury jellies, and to flavour vinegars. Use Mediterranean herbs (rosemary, thyme, oregano) for preserves in oil. Dill is essential in cucumber pickles and cured fish, and mint is ideal for some cordials.
Flowers	Bergamot, elderflowers, jasmine, lavender, pinks, roses	Richly scented flowers add unusual perfumed flavours. Use to infuse jams, conserves, jellies, fruit butters and cheeses, and bottled syrups and cordials. Pick the flowers fresh and use as soon as possible.

Dill

AROMATIC AND EXOTIC – These are subtle, complex, fragrant, or strong flavours. Use sparingly.		
FLAVOURING	**TYPES**	**HOW TO USE**
Whole spices	Allspice, anise seeds, caraway seeds, cardamom, celery seeds, cinnamon, cloves, coriander, cumin, dill seeds, fennel seeds, juniper berries, mace, mustard seeds, nutmeg, peppercorns, onion seeds (nigella seeds), star anise	Think of these spices as your painter's palette when flavouring sweet and savoury preserves, bottled foods, cordials (and mulled wines), cured meats and fish, or smoked foods, blending warm with peppery, and so on. Celery, caraway, dill, and juniper can be used to flavour sauerkraut and other salted vegetable pickles. For maximum flavour and fragrance use whole or freshly ground spices. They continue to flavour the preserve once made, so are often removed before the jars are sealed. Aniseed flavours are fennel, anise, and star anise, fragrant flavours are coriander and cardamom, peppery flavours are peppercorns, mustard seeds, and onions seeds (nigella seeds), and savoury flavours are celery seeds, caraway seeds, dill seeds, and mace. Nutmeg is a sweet flavour, while allspice, cinnamon, cloves, and star anise are warm flavours, and juniper and cumin are woody flavours.
Pickling spices	Allspice, bay leaves, cloves, coriander seeds, mace, peppercorns, white mustard seeds	These robust-flavoured spices blend well together. They are typically combined to make a pickling vinegar for chutneys, pickles, and relishes, or can be added in a muslin bag to a preserve to flavour it and then removed after cooking. Choose any combination you like and add fresh ginger and/or chillies as you wish.
Spice powders and blends	Cayenne, curry (blended Indian spices), five-spice (blended Chinese spices), mustard, smoked paprika, turmeric	Use these strong flavours to spice cooked chutneys and relishes, or add to marinades for smoked foods. Spice powder blends are also excellent for chutneys and relishes, and a wide range are now available to buy to experiment with. Spice powders lose their fragrance quite quickly, so buy in small quantities and use promptly. Chilli powder, ground turmeric, and cardamom pods.
Exotic leaves and pods	Kaffir lime leaves, lemongrass, lemon verbena, sweet geranium leaves, tamarind pods, vanilla pods	Exotic leaves have floral-citrus flavours; use instead of lemons and limes for bottled fruits and cordials or to flavour jellies and jams. Tamarind has a sour, fruity tang and texture similar to dried dates; use it in Indian-spiced chutneys. Sweet, fragrant vanilla pods are indispensible for jams, jellies, bottled fruits, cordials, and fruits in alcohol (for maximum flavour, split them, scrape out some of their seeds, and add the seeds to the preserve too).
Wood chips	Alder, apple, cherry, hickory, maple, mesquite, oak, pecan	Alder, apple, and maple wood chips produce a lighter smoked flavour, while hickory, mesquite, and pecan chips give a stronger smoked flavour and are commonly used for red meat. Oak chips give a sweet, rich flavour, and cherry wood is especially suited to game. Different woods can be mixed to create your own favourite smoke. Buy specially treated wood chippings specifically for smoking. You need very few chips (1 level teaspoon) to give smoked food a pronounced flavour.
Flavoured waters	Orange water, rosewater	These concentrated exotic orange and rose flower flavours are very powerful. Add just a few drops to jams, jellies, and fruit butters and cheeses.
Cracked kernels	Apricot, cherry, peach, plum, nectarine	The small creamy inner kernels of all stone fruits have a bitter almond flavour identical to amaretto. Add a few kernels of the relevant fruit to bottled stone fruits and jams (remove the skins first).

Good things to do with...

This chart lists the many varied ways to preserve fruits, vegetables, and herbs. Use it as a reference to inspire and help you choose how to preserve produce as it comes into season.

For more details on how to preserve these fruits and herbs, see "The best ingredients for..." at the beginning of each section.	NATURAL STORAGE	DRYING	FREEZING	JAMS	CONSERVES	JELLIES	FRUIT CHEESES, BUTTERS, & CURDS	MARMALADES	CRYSTALLIZED FRUITS	CHUTNEYS	PICKLES	RELISHES	BOTTLED PRODUCE	CORDIALS, SYRUPS, & JUICES	KETCHUPS & SAUCES	PRESERVING IN OIL	SALTING	BREWING AND WINE-MAKING
FRUITS																		
Apples	✓	✓	✓	✓		✓	✓			✓			✓	✓	✓			✓
Apricots		✓	✓	✓	✓		✓		✓	✓	✓	✓	✓	✓				
Blackberries			✓	✓	✓	✓	✓			✓	✓		✓	✓	✓			✓
Blackcurrants			✓	✓		✓	✓						✓	✓				
Blueberries			✓	✓	✓	✓							✓	✓				
Boysenberries			✓	✓	✓	✓	✓				✓		✓	✓				
Cherries		✓	✓	✓	✓				✓		✓	✓	✓	✓				✓
Citrus fruits		✓	✓				✓	✓	✓	✓	✓	✓	✓	✓			✓	
Crab apples	✓		✓			✓				✓								✓
Cranberries		✓	✓	✓		✓	✓			✓	✓	✓	✓	✓	✓			
Elderberries						✓								✓	✓			✓
Figs		✓	✓	✓	✓					✓	✓	✓	✓					✓
Gooseberries			✓	✓		✓	✓			✓	✓	✓	✓	✓	✓			✓
Grapes		✓		✓	✓	✓	✓		✓	✓				✓				✓
Loganberries			✓	✓	✓	✓	✓						✓	✓				
Medlars			✓			✓	✓											
Melons			✓	✓	✓				✓		✓		✓					
Nectarines		✓	✓	✓	✓				✓	✓	✓	✓	✓	✓				
Peaches		✓	✓	✓	✓				✓	✓	✓	✓	✓	✓				
Pears	✓	✓	✓	✓	✓		✓		✓	✓	✓		✓	✓				✓
Plums (all kinds)		✓	✓	✓	✓	✓	✓		✓	✓	✓		✓		✓			✓
Quinces	✓		✓	✓		✓	✓	✓		✓			✓	✓				
Raspberries			✓	✓	✓	✓	✓						✓	✓				
Red- and white currants			✓	✓		✓							✓	✓				
Rhubarb			✓	✓						✓	✓	✓	✓	✓				✓
Sloes			✓			✓							✓					
Strawberries			✓	✓	✓	✓							✓	✓				
Tayberries			✓	✓	✓	✓	✓						✓	✓				
Watermelon										✓			✓					
HERBS																		
Edible flowers		✓	✓	✓		✓			✓					✓				✓
Herbs		✓	✓			✓				✓		✓		✓		✓	✓	✓

For more details on how to preserve the vegetables listed here, see "The best ingredients for..." at the beginning of each section.

VEGETABLES

VEGETABLES	NATURAL STORAGE	DRYING	FREEZING	JAMS	JELLIES	CHUTNEYS	PICKLES	RELISHES	BOTTLED PRODUCE	CORDIALS, SYRUPS, & JUICES	KETCHUPS & SAUCES	PRESERVING IN OIL	SALTING	SMOKING	BREWING AND WINE-MAKING
Asparagus			✓									✓			
Aubergines			✓	✓		✓	✓	✓				✓			
Beans, broad		✓	✓												
Beans, French			✓			✓	✓	✓				✓	✓		
Beans, runner			✓			✓	✓	✓					✓		
Beetroots	✓					✓	✓	✓							✓
Broccoli			✓												
Brussels sprouts	✓		✓												
Cabbages (various)	✓		✓				✓	✓					✓		
Carrots	✓	✓	✓	✓		✓	✓	✓				✓			
Cauliflower	✓		✓				✓	✓				✓			
Celeriac	✓	✓	✓				✓					✓			
Celery						✓	✓	✓				✓			✓
Chillies	✓	✓		✓	✓	✓	✓	✓			✓	✓		✓	
Courgettes			✓			✓	✓	✓				✓			
Cucumber (various)							✓	✓					✓		
Fennel			✓				✓	✓				✓			
Garlic	✓	✓				✓	✓	✓			✓	✓		✓	
Globe artichokes (baby)			✓									✓			
Horseradish root							✓	✓			✓				
Jerusalem artichokes	✓		✓											✓	
Kohlrabi	✓						✓								
Leeks	✓		✓												
Mangetout and Sugarsnap peas			✓												✓
Marrows	✓			✓		✓	✓								✓
Mushrooms		✓	✓				✓	✓			✓	✓			
Onions and shallots	✓	✓				✓	✓	✓			✓	✓			
Parsnips	✓	✓	✓												✓
Peas		✓	✓												✓
Peppers	✓		✓	✓	✓	✓	✓	✓	✓			✓	✓		✓
Potatoes	✓													✓	
Radishes (various)							✓						✓		
Romanesco			✓				✓					✓			
Salsify and scorzonera	✓		✓									✓			
Spinach			✓												
Squashes and pumpkins	✓		✓	✓		✓	✓								
Swedes	✓		✓												
Sweet potatoes	✓		✓												
Sweetcorn		✓	✓					✓						✓	
Swiss chard and winter spinach	✓		✓												
Tomatoes	✓	✓	✓	✓	✓	✓			✓	✓	✓	✓	✓		
Turnips	✓		✓				✓						✓		

Natural storage – storing crops in their natural state in a cool, protected environment – is the next best thing to picking produce fresh from the garden. It's nature's way of lending a hand to extend an autumn harvest from the garden or allotment. Some crops are hardy enough to remain in situ or be clamped outside; for those that aren't, gentle, low-tech methods such as storing in boxes and hanging up mean that treasured home-grown fruit and vegetables can be savoured and enjoyed for months to come.

The best crops for...
Natural storage

Many crops that mature in autumn can be left in situ and picked fresh if hardy, or stored inside in cool conditions, to provide vegetables to eat all winter long. Choose maincrop varieties for storing.

Carrots
Harvest maincrop carrots when mature in early autumn. Stored in boxes (pp34–35), they will last throughout winter into spring.

Potatoes
In mild areas, maincrop potatoes are suitable for storing outside in a clamp (pp28–29). Harvest when fully mature in early autumn and store until after Christmas in frost-free areas.

Jerusalem artichokes
This hardy perennial tuber matures in autumn. Dig up as required, being careful not to damage the tubers, and use fresh.

Beetroots
Harvest maincrop beetroots well before the first frosts in autumn and store in boxes (pp34–35) through winter. Use the tops like spinach and the baby shoots for winter salads.

Leeks
Once matured in autumn, leave in the ground and dig up as required when the ground is not too hard or frosty. The hardiest varieties last until spring.

Brussels sprouts
Leave in the ground from autumn onwards and pick as needed from the base of the stem up. Late varieties last until spring.

GOLDEN RULES FOR SUCCESS

- For successful storing, harvest crops at their best and pick them at the right time. Grade the harvest and select the best produce only; damaged crops spread disease.
- Handle produce carefully. Any bruising leads to rot in storage.
- Correct storage temperatures and humidity levels are critical: avoid extreme temperatures and damp. If the conditions are less than ideal, use sooner rather than later.
- Check regularly and remove any fruit or vegetable showing signs of disease immediately.

Parsnips
A hardy winter vegetable with long deep roots. Leave in the ground and dig up carefully as needed. Keeps well until spring.

Tomatoes
Conveniently, tomatoes keep ripening once they're picked. Harvest unripened tomatoes on the vine in early autumn before the weather turns cold, and bring indoors to ripen (pp32–33).

Peppers
Like tomatoes, peppers ripen indoors once picked, and gradually turn yellow, orange, or red, depending on the variety. Store until Christmas.

Pears
Mid- to late-season pear varieties are suitable for cold storage (pp36–37). Pears are gloriously juicy when ripened naturally, but do not stay perfect for long, so check regularly.

Onions
Harvest onions in July and August and cure first (pp38–39) before storing. One of the easiest crops to hang up and store inside and, if kept cool, will last 6–9 months.

Garlic
Fresh "wet" garlic is a gourmet treat but, like onions, can be cured (pp38–39) and hung up inside to provide a supply of home-grown garlic until the New Year.

Apples
Mid- to late-season apple varieties continue to ripen once picked, and can be stored on shelves in autumn (pp36–37) to give a continuous supply of delicious fruits until early spring.

Winter squashes
Harvest squashes in autumn, but leave to ripen outside in the sun until their skins are fully hardened (p31), then store on shelves. They should keep until late spring.

OTHER CROPS

In situ	Harvest
Celeriac	Autumn–spring
Hamburg parsley	Autumn–December
Salsify	Autumn–spring
Scorzonera	Autumn–spring
Swiss chard	Autumn–spring
Winter cabbages e.g. savoy	Winter–spring
Winter cauliflower	Winter–spring
Winter spinach	Autumn–spring

Clamps	Store for
Swedes	3–4 months
Turnips	3–4 months
Winter radishes (hardy)	3–4 months

Store inside in compost or sand in boxes	Store for
Celeriac	1–2 months
Kohlrabi	1–2 months
Swedes	1–2 months
Turnips	1–2 months
Mooli radishes	1–2 months

Store inside on shelves	Store for
Dutch cabbage (white and red)	3–4 months
Marrows	1–2 months
Quinces	1–2 months
Sweet potatoes (after curing) in shallow trays	3–4 months

Hang indoors	Store for
Chillies	6 months
Shallots	6 months

Clamping

The technique of insulating potatoes and other root vegetables outside, known as clamping, often keeps them fresher for longer than storing in sacks or boxes. Clamping is unsuitable in areas where frosts are common or severe.

Clamping potatoes

1 Dig a shallow round trench 10cm (4in) deep, 1m (3ft) in diameter, in a sheltered, well-drained site. Pack it down and cover it with a layer of sand to deter slugs. Heap clean straw over the trench to make a thick circular nest about 20cm (8in) deep, and arrange the potatoes in the centre.

2 Pile the potatoes up in a cone or pyramid shape. The maximum height of the cone should be about 50cm (20in). Completely cover the potatoes with a protective layer of dry straw that is between 10–20cm (4–8in) thick.

Preparing potatoes
Dig up potatoes carefully on a dry day, shake off the excess soil, and leave to dry outside for 1–2 hours to "set" the skins. Only perfect specimens should be used for clamping.

STORING ROOT CROPS IN THE GROUND

Any crop with a tapering root – such as carrots, Hamburg parsley, salsify, scorzonera, and parsnips – can be stored in situ in the ground until needed. How well they keep there depends on the weather conditions, but expect slug damage and some deterioration over time. In severe winters, protect these crops as much as possible from frosts and snow with cloches or piles of straw heaped over them. Dig them up when the ground is suitable (not hard or frozen). Wash off the soil, leave to drain, and store in the salad drawer of the fridge.

3 When the potatoes are completely hidden by straw, use a spade to cover the straw with a 15cm (6in) layer of soil. Leave a 5cm (2in) "chimney hole" (or use a piece of pipe) at the top for ventilation and fill it loosely with straw.

4 Pack down the soil around the sides of the clamp with the back of the spade until it is firm, to allow the rain to run off more easily. As an extra precaution, dig a shallow trench around the base of the clamp to help with drainage. If clamped properly, the potatoes will keep for 4–5 months.

Storing squashes

Squashes are the only vegetable to become denser, sweeter, and more flavourful with age. The secret is in hardening the skin (called "curing"). Use only winter squashes (not softer-skinned varieties) for long storage.

On the plant Cure squashes by leaving them to ripen on the plant for as long as possible. Turn them over every so often so their skin hardens evenly. Avoid bruising the skin, as this may impair storing. Once the skin feels hard and the vegetable sounds hollow if tapped, cut off the squash, leaving 10–15cm (4–6in) of stem (to protect against rotting). Leave to dry outside on a bench, wall, or raised area, or in a well-ventilated cold greenhouse or conservatory, for 10 days. Turn regularly to expose all sides of the skin to the sun, and bring inside if it rains or turns really cold.

Indoors For long-term storage, squashes need good ventilation and a steady temperature of 10–15°C (50–60°F). A garage or shed will suffice as a storage room, as will a cool room indoors, or even a cool corner of the kitchen. Store the squashes singly on a raised shelf or hung up in a net bag where air can circulate. Check regularly for signs of deterioration.

Squashes curing
Nothing is more cheerful than the sight of winter squashes, such as 'Turk's Turban' (as shown here), basking in the autumn sun. Once cut, 'Acorn' squashes will store for 2 months, 'Butternut' for 2–3 months, 'Turk's Turban' for 3 months or more, and 'Hubbard' for up to 6 months.

Storing tomatoes, peppers, and chillies

Tomatoes, peppers, and chillies all continue to ripen once picked, which extends their season. So, as the weather cools at the end of summer, bring any unripened fruits inside.

Tomatoes Pick tomatoes on the vine and store in single layers on window ledges, trays, or decorative dishes indoors. They ripen gradually and, once red, keep for up to 1 month. Tomatoes dislike the cold, so don't store them in the fridge. Check regularly and remove any that turn mouldy or soft.

Peppers Cut undamaged peppers from the plant, leaving a little of the stalk. Store in the same way as tomatoes. They gradually turn from green to yellow or orange or red, depending on the variety. The deeper the colour, the better and richer the flavour. In the right conditions they will then gradually begin to dry, becoming more concentrated in flavour. Check regularly for any signs of mould: if you find any, cut away all the mould and use the rest of the pepper immediately.

Chillies As chillies will keep growing and ripening on the plant, bring the whole plant inside if you have room, and keep it in a warm, light spot. Otherwise, store in the same way as peppers and tomatoes.

Harvesting tomatoes
Rather than pick tomatoes individually, cut them off the plant in "bunches" so that they remain attached to a length of the vine as they ripen.

Storing root crops in boxes

Many root vegetables (pp26–27) can be left in situ through the winter months, but it's often more convenient and less risky to lift them and store them inside. Carrots, parsnips, beetroots, potatoes, among others, can be stored in this way.

Storing carrots in boxes

1 Dig up the carrots carefully on a dry day, shake off the excess soil, and twist off the tops. Don't scrub or wash the carrots, as this may damage the skin. Examine each carrot and set aside any that are damaged to use immediately.

2 Choose a shallow cardboard box, wooden box, crate, slatted tray, or polystyrene box (with holes for ventilation). Line the base with newspaper, sacking, or similar material, and put a thin layer of spent compost, moist sand, coir, untreated sawdust, vermiculite, or leaf mould in the bottom.

Parsnips
Crops of parsnips are usually left in the ground until the first frost, which sweetens them. They can then be dug up and stored.

STORING POTATOES IN BOXES

If you haven't got a large garden or don't own an allotment that can accommodate potato clamps (pp28–29), store crops of potatoes in tea chests or cardboard boxes with covers on top to exclude the light. These covers are essential, or the potatoes will turn green (the green parts are toxic, and must be cut away). Alternatively, store them in strong paper sacks that are folded or tied loosely at the top. Store the potatoes in a cool, dark place (5–10°C/41–50°F). As they age, they will develop sprouts, which must be cut away before eating.

3 Arrange the carrots side by side, without touching, on the covering material. Position the carrots so that they lie head to toe.

4 Hide the vegetables with more covering material and repeat until the container is full. Finish with a layer of covering material to exclude light. Store in a cool, preferably dark, place such as a garage, cellar, or spare room for 2 months or more. Use as required, ensuring the remaining vegetables are kept covered.

Storing apples and pears

Only apple and pear varieties that mature in autumn are suitable for long-term storing, as they need time to develop their flavour.

Harvest The way you harvest the fruit is crucial, as it bruises easily and cannot then be stored. Cradle each fruit in your hand (with pears, it helps to have your index finger close to the stalk), tilt it gently upwards, and give a slight twist: the fruit is ready to pick when the stalk comes away easily from the branch and the fruit drops into your hand. Lay each fruit carefully in a picking basket.

Pears ripen differently to apples: once fully ripe, their flesh quickly turns soft and woolly, so pick and store them while they are still unripe. To complete the ripening process, bring them into a warm room for a few days.

Store Arrange the fruit on greengrocer trays stacked on shelves in a cool, dark, not-too-dry place such as a garage, attic, or cellar (the ideal temperature is 2–4°C/35–40°F for apples, and slightly warmer for pears). Apples – but not pears – can also be wrapped in newspaper or tissue paper and put on trays or packed in layers in shallow boxes.

Alternatively, if you have the space, store the fruit in the fridge: put separate varieties in large freezer bags, pierce the bags with a few small holes, tie or fold over the tops loosely, refrigerate, and check regularly, as they ripen at different rates from November to March.

Late-cropping apples and pears
Pick fruits before the first frosts and store only the perfect ones separately on trays so they aren't crowded and have air circulating around them. Each variety ripens at a different pace.

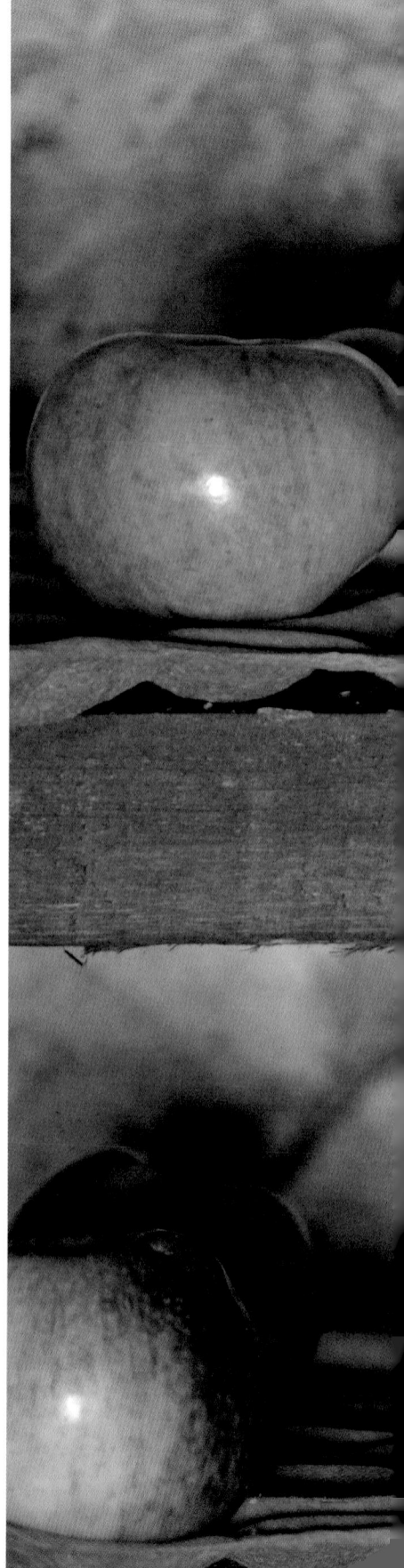

Storing onions and garlic

Onions and garlic store well indoors and take up hardly any storage space. They can be strung up in nets or old stockings, or you can add a touch of Mediterranean glamour by making traditional plaits.

Onion and garlic plaits

1 Choose only garlic (shown here) and onion bulbs that are in prime condition for long-term storing. Clean them by cutting off the roots at the base of each bulb. Remove the outer, dirty skins if necessary, but leave the stems attached to the bulb.

2 Take 3 onion or garlic bulbs, lay them on top of one another at angles so that the bulbs nestle as closely together as possible.

Shallots
Harvest and cure shallots in the same way as onions and garlic (see box, right). Store in nets or shallow boxes somewhere cool and airy. Once dried, store them in a basket or vegetable rack in the kitchen until needed.

**HARVESTING AND CURING
ONIONS AND GARLIC**

Onions and garlic are ready to harvest in July and August when the bulbs are swollen and the leaves have yellowed and collapsed. Pull them up when the weather is fine.

Leave to cure, or dry, for 2 weeks in a warm, dry place, or outside in suitable weather on a dry path or on pallets or upturned boxes, turning them to expose all sides to the sun. They are ready to plait and store when the skins are papery and the stems have shrivelled.

3 Take another 3 bulbs and place them directly on top of the first bulbs to form the same pattern. The 6 stems should make 3 separate strands. Take the strands on either side in each hand and cross them over the central strand.

4 Continue to plait the stems, adding 3 new bulbs every time, until you have a plait long enough to hang up. Make up more plaits in the same way and hang on separate hooks with string or rope. If kept cool, onions last 6 months and garlic 4 months.

Drying is useful for preserving seasonal or bumper crops of home-grown fruit such as apples and some vegetables. Dried foods such as mushrooms, sweetcorn, and tomatoes have a concentrated flavour and take up little storage room. Special drying trays and food dehydrators can be bought, but all you really need to dry some produce is the gentle **heat of the oven** to replace that of the sun. Other produce such as chillies and beans need even less attention: an even room temperature, a dry atmosphere, and good ventilation are all that you need for **air-drying**.

The best ingredients for...
Drying

If you choose top-quality produce, picked at its moment of perfection, and dry it correctly, it will taste superb. These vegetables and fruits are ideal to dry; store in a cool, dark, dry place.

Mushrooms
The soft texture and high water content of cultivated and wild mushrooms make them rewarding to dry and cook with. Dry in a very low oven or air-dry (pp44–45).

Chillies
Air-drying is an easy way to preserve chillies (p46–47). Choose firm, glossy, mature chillies that are just turning red. Use gloves when handling the hotter varieties.

Borlotti beans
Home-dried beans are extra creamy. Leave on the plant as long as possible, then pick and air-dry (pp46–47). They are ready when shrunk but still plump, not shrivelled.

DRYING HERBS
Generally, freezing is the best way to preserve herbs, but many dry well if hung upside down in small bunches in a warm, dark, dry, airy place until dry and crumbly. Use as culinary flavourings and to make herb teas. Oregano – one of the best herbs to dry – is an essential dried ingredient in authentic pizzas, and dried mint is ideal for Middle Eastern dishes. Collect the aromatic seeds from chervil, dill, coriander, cumin, and fennel to add to preserves.

Oregano

Tomatoes
Nothing beats a home-dried tomato for flavour. Dry meaty, ripe home-grown or good-quality tomatoes in the oven, or air-dry in a very hot, dry climate (pp50–51).

Hops
For beer, pick the aromatic mature female flower clusters in early autumn when they are slightly papery and remain flat when squeezed. Hops air-dry easily.

Sweetcorn
Oven-drying is a traditional way to preserve sweetcorn. The nutty, brittle cobs are great for making popcorn, or add the kernels (p210) to winter soups and chowders.

TIPS FOR SUCCESS

Effectively dried vegetables contain no more than 10 per cent moisture and fruits 20 per cent moisture (weigh before and after drying to check). Store correctly (in a warm place, reduce storage times up to 50 per cent) and check regularly.

Pears

To oven-dry pears, cut into quarters or eighths and treat like apples (pp48–49). Dried pears retain their grainy texture and perfumed flavour, and are delightful as a snack or added to game and pork braises.

Figs

Halve large, ripe figs, leave small ones whole (if they are hard to peel, dip in boiling water first for 30 seconds to crack the skins), and oven-dry for 36–48 hours.

Peaches

Choose ripe, perfumed fruit, cut in half, remove stones, and oven-dry for 36–48 hours, or slice and oven-dry for 12–16 hours (dip halves or slices in lemon juice first).

Apples

Choose well-ripened, sweet dessert varieties. They can be air-dried on necklaces of string above a warm heat source such as an Aga, but are usually dried in a low oven (pp48–49).

OTHER INGREDIENTS

FRUITS

Cherries oven-dry
Cranberries oven-dry
Grapes oven-dry
Nectarines oven-dry
Plums (all types) oven-dry

VEGETABLES

Black-eyed beans air-dry
Broad beans air-dry
Cannellini beans air-dry
Carrots oven-dry
Celeriac oven-dry
Mexican black beans air-dry
Navy (haricot) beans air-dry
Parsnips oven-dry
Pea beans air-dry
Pinto beans air-dry
Soya beans air-dry

HERBS

Bay leaves air-dry
Lavender air-dry
Lemon verbena air-dry
Mint air-dry
Oregano air-dry
Rosemary air-dry

TROPICAL PRODUCE

Mangoes, pineapples, and bananas make a great snack if dried in the oven. Choose organic or fairtrade if buying tropical fruits (fairtrade fruit ensures fair wages and working conditions for employees).

Apricots

Cut apricots in half, remove skins and stones, and oven-dry, cut side up, for 36–48 hours until leathery. Use as a snack or in sweet and savoury dishes.

Citrus peel

The peel of citrus fruits is easy to air-dry. Scrub and shave the peel thinly into strips, removing all the pith, and air-dry for 8–12 hours. Use to flavour Moroccan dishes and cakes.

Drying mushrooms

With their sweet earthy flavour, mushrooms are deservedly popular. When dried, that flavour intensifies and makes them an essential storecupboard ingredient. All types of mushrooms can be air-dried or oven-dried, as shown here.

Dried mushrooms

MAKES APPROX 60G (2OZ)

TAKES 15 MINUTES, PLUS DRYING TIME

KEEPS 9–12 MONTHS

INGREDIENTS

450g (1lb) brown chestnut, shitaki, and buna-shimeji mushrooms, or freshly picked wild mushrooms

FORAGING FOR MUSHROOMS

Edible wild mushrooms are a forager's delight. The best-known varieties to dry are ceps (*Boletus edulis*), morels (*Morchella vulgaris*), field mushrooms (*Agaricus campestris*), and chanterelles (*Cantharellus cibarius*). Never eat or preserve a wild mushroom unless you can identify it without doubt, or it has been identified by an expert. Pick mushrooms on a dry day; don't preserve any that are wet. Brush off dirt with a soft mushroom brush and discard any imperfect or older specimens. Dry or eat within 24 hours of picking.

1 Leave small mushrooms whole and slice large ones into 5mm–1cm (¼–½in) thick slices. Arrange on trays lined with kitchen paper or wire racks, making sure they don't overlap. Place in the oven on the lowest setting (50–60°C/120–140°F/Gas ¼) for 4–6 hours. Leave the door of an electric oven slightly ajar using a skewer.

2 The mushrooms are ready when they have shrunk to at least half their original size, but are still pliable. Remove from the oven and leave on the trays until they are completely cold. To air-dry the mushrooms, leave the racks or trays 5–10cm (2–4in) above a wood-burning stove radiator, boiler, Aga, night storage heater, or warm airing cupboard overnight.

3 Put in glass containers. Add a few grains of rice, if you wish, as an extra precaution to help keep the mushrooms dry. Store in a cool, dark place. If properly dried, they will keep for 9–12 months. Alternatively, freeze on open trays, then pack into small freezer bags or pots, and freeze for 12 months.

Air-drying beans and chillies

Beans that you can shell, such as borlotti and climbing French beans (kidney beans), are grown primarily for their plump seeds. These can be dried and stored at home and are much creamier than those you can buy. Ripe red chillies are traditionally air-dried by being strung up in garlands.

Beans Leave the pods on the plants for as long as the weather is warm enough to dry them outdoors. The beans inside swell as the pods fade in colour and become parchment-like. Harvest the pods on a fine day by pulling up the vines.

Leave the pods on wire racks or newspaper until dry and crisp. Shell the beans and arrange on trays on a window sill to complete the drying process, shaking the trays regularly until the beans are dry and plump, but not wrinkled. Keep in storage jars, out of direct sunlight, for up to 1 year. To use, soak overnight and cook in the usual way.

Chillies Harvest red chillies (green chillies are generally too immature) from the plant and hang to air-dry: wrap strong thread around the cut stem of each chilli where it meets the fruit, tie a knot, and repeat at 2.5cm (1in) lengths to make a garland. Hang in a warm, dry, airy place for 2 weeks or until shrivelled. Use crumbled in recipes.

Borlotti beans on a rack
Arrange the pods to dry in a single or shallow layer on wire racks or newspaper somewhere warm and airy.

Oven-drying fruit

Dried fruits make healthy, additive-free snacks, and are an excellent addition to muesli, baked pies, and lamb, pork, or vegetarian dishes. Apples are ideal fruits to oven-dry (all fresh fruits are dried in the same way).

Dried apples

MAKES APPROX 115–225G (4–8OZ)

TAKES 15–20 MINUTES, PLUS DRYING AND COOLING TIME

KEEPS 6 MONTHS IF DRIED PROPERLY (12 MONTHS FROZEN)

INGREDIENTS

1kg (2¼lb) ripe apples

2 tbsp lemon juice or ½tsp citric acid in 600ml (1 pint) of water

---

TIPS FOR DRYING FRUIT

Keep the door of an electric oven slightly ajar with a skewer to create an airflow so the slices dry rather than cook.

Keep the oven on its lowest setting; if it is too warm, the fruits form a skin that stops moisture escaping and they turn mouldy.

Remove the stones first from fruits such as apricots; if you cut them in half, dry them cut side up.

For fruits with rind or thick skin such as melons and bananas, remove the rind or peel first and take out any seeds.

For fruits with skins left on, such as grapes and cherries, dip into boiling water for 30 seconds to split the skins, then drain and pat them dry before oven-drying.

Cut slightly larger fruits such as peaches and large figs in half and dry them cut side up.

---

1 Briefly wash the apples in cold water, then core and slice them into 3–5mm (⅛–¼in) rings. If using windfalls, cut away any bruised, damaged, or soft parts first. Discard the outer rings that have the most skin on them.

2 Drop the slices into the bowl of acidulated water, drain on a tea towel, and place separately in a single layer on wire racks over baking trays. Dry in the oven on the lowest setting (50–60°C/120–140°F/Gas ¼) for 8–24 hours, depending on the temperature (this can be done in stages).

3 Turn the slices occasionally as they dry. They are ready when they look and feel like soft, pliable, chamois leather. (For a crunchier version, dry the slices until they are crisp.) Remove from the oven, cover with kitchen paper, leave for 12–24 hours, and turn occasionally to ensure they contain as little moisture as possible. This reduces the risk of mould later on.

4 Pack into airtight jars and store in a cool, dry, dark place. Check regularly for any signs of deterioration. Alternatively, pack into small freezer bags and freeze.

Oven-drying tomatoes

Dried ripe tomatoes, with their rich flavour and chewy texture, are now a fixture of modern cooking. Using a very low oven heat to semi-dry tomatoes gives a result similar to that of sun-dried tomatoes. Do a trial batch first with half the quantities.

Oven-dried tomatoes

MAKES APPROX 900G (2LB)

TAKES 10 MINUTES, PLUS DRYING AND COOLING TIME

KEEPS 2 WEEKS (12 MONTHS FROZEN)

INGREDIENTS

3kg (6½lb) ripe, but firm, medium-sized tomatoes

2–3 tsp sea salt

SUN-DRIED TOMATOES

In Mediterranean countries, it's normal to preserve tomatoes by drying them outside in the sun instead of putting them in the oven. The high sugar and acid content of tomatoes makes them safe to dry out in this way. Very hot (32°C/90°F), dry, breezy days are best. Prepare in the same way, but cover the fruit with muslin to keep off insects. Keep the trays off the ground (the higher the better), make sure the air can circulate easily around them, and bring the trays inside at night. Sun-drying takes between 2 and 4 days, depending on how hot the weather is each day.

1 Cut each tomato in half, round ones horizontally, plum ones vertically. Score the middle of each tomato with a cross shape and push the centres up from below with your fingertips to expose more of the flesh.

2 Arrange the tomato halves side by side, cut side up, on wire racks positioned over baking trays. Sprinkle each lightly with salt. Leave for a few minutes to allow the salt to start to draw out the moisture, then place cut side down without touching each other.

3 Put the trays in the oven on a low setting (60–80°C/150–175°F/Gas ¼–½) and dry for 8–12 hours. (Keep the door of an electric oven slightly ajar with a skewer to create an airflow.) The tomatoes are ready when they have shrivelled to half their size, but are still soft and pliable. Remove from the oven and leave to cool on the racks.

4 When the tomatoes are completely cold, pack into sterilized jars and store in the fridge. For longer-term keeping, freeze on open trays, pack into small bags, and freeze. Once thawed, cover with olive oil, refrigerate, and use within 1 week.

Freezing is often the most convenient way to store some cherished home-made preserves. Freezing foods below -18°C (0°F) slows life processes down to a minimum, keeping vegetables, fruits, and herbs almost as fresh as when they were picked and prepared. To minimize any deterioration and loss of flavour over time, most produce is best blanched, cooked, or packed in sugar or made into tasty freezer jams or pickles before being frozen. Prepare and pack all produce in the correct way, and used within the recommended storage times.

The best...
Vegetables to freeze

These vegetables are the best for freezing. The firmer (or less watery) the texture, the better they freeze. Also included are vegetables that freeze well if cooked first – always a bonus if time is short.

Asparagus
Locally produced or home-grown asparagus is far superior to imported all-year round varieties. Cook it first on a griddle before freezing it to retain its delicate texture and flavour.

Runner beans
Tender beans can be sliced, blanched, and open-frozen, but also make crunchy, fresh-tasting freezer pickles (cook older beans in a tomato sauce, then freeze).

Peas
Nothing is sweeter, or freezes better, than freshly podded home-grown peas. Choose tender peas, but wait until the pods have fully swollen. Blanch the peas briefly before freezing.

French beans
Many delicious varieties of French bean are easy to grow and crop all summer. Blanch and open-freeze tender beans (pp58–59). (Older beans are best cooked in a tomato sauce, and then frozen.)

Spinach
Spinach has a creamy texture and freezes well, taking up little space. Blanch briefly, then gently squeeze out the moisture. Freeze spinach beet and chopped Swiss chard leaves in the same way.

FREEZING HERBS AND FLOWERS

Summer herbs – basil, coriander, dill, chervil, fennel, lemon verbena, mint, oregano, parsley, and tarragon – all freeze well. Chop and freeze in water in ice cube trays (pp84–85). Pop individual violets, rose petals, and jasmine and borage flowers in water in ice cube trays to garnish drinks and iced soups.

Borage flowers

Tarragon

Carrots

All varieties of carrot can be sliced, blanched, and frozen, or cooked and frozen as a vegetable purée with other root or starchy vegetables.

OTHER VEGETABLES

Aubergines griddled
Broccoli blanched
Brussels sprouts blanched
Cabbages freezer pickles
Cauliflower freezer pickles
Celeriac griddled
Courgettes griddled
Cucumbers freezer pickles
Fennel cooked
Globe artichokes (bottoms) cooked
Jerusalem artichokes cooked purées
Leeks cooked
Mangetout blanched
Mushrooms cooked
Parsnips cooked purées
Peppers griddled, freezer pickles
Squashes cooked
Sugarsnap peas blanched
Swedes cooked purées
Sweet potatoes griddled
Swiss chard blanched
Turnips cooked purées

Broad beans

This gourmet bean is in season from May to July. It freezes supremely well, retaining all its texture. Blanch and open-freeze tender beans, and freeze older beans as a cooked purée or in a tomato sauce.

Romanesco

This delicious vegetable combines the virtues of cauliflower and broccoli (it tastes like a mixture of both); look out for it from late summer to early autumn. Blanch and freeze in in small florets like broccoli and cauliflower.

Tomatoes

Raw tomatoes are not suited to freezing (their texture goes mushy) but if cooked into rich tomato sauces and soups, they are a godsend to have in the freezer.

Sweetcorn

Corn freezes extremely well, whether blanched and frozen whole or as kernels (strip from the cob, then blanch). It is in season from late to end of summer; select cobs with silky brown tassles and sweet, milky kernels.

The best...
Fruits to freeze

A freezer is the best place for surplus seasonal fruits. Sloes (for sloe gin), quinces (for fruit cheese), and Seville oranges (for marmalade) can be stored whole; other fruits are best prepared first, then frozen (p60).

Blackberries
Cultivated and wild blackberries (brambles) are autumn fruits. Open-freeze, or make freezer jam. Avoid brambles that grow on the roadside. Wash first to remove any dust.

Cranberries
This unique native American wetland fruit is available fresh from October to December. Open-freezing is best. Use straight from the freezer without thawing.

Apricots
Choose ripe fruits, as they have a perfumed flavour and creamy, dense texture. One of the best fruits for freezing poached in syrup, or cooked and puréed.

Rhubarb
Choose tender stalks (either garden or early spring pink forced rhubarb) to freeze. Best frozen poached in syrup, or cooked and puréed. It can be sliced and open-frozen, but its texture suffers.

Blackcurrants

These are one of the most delicious high-summer fruits, and are very high in vitamin C and antioxidants. They open-freeze exceptionally well (strip the berries from their stalks first).

Raspberries

These soft, fragile summer fruits need handling with care. Pick and open-freeze without delay (discard any blemished fruits). They are also excellent for freezer jams and uncooked purées.

Blueberries

A soft-skinned summer fruit that is packed with goodness. These berries will open-freeze (pp62–63), and are good for freezer jams. Look for the bloom on the skins – a sign of ripeness.

OTHER FRUITS

Boysenberries open-freeze, freezer jam
Cherries freezer jam, cooked in syrup
Citrus fruits whole
Damsons cooked purées
Figs freezer jam, cooked in syrup
Gooseberries cooked purées, cooked in syrup
Greengages cooked purées, cooked in syrup
Melons freezer jam
Nectarines freezer jam, uncooked purées, cooked in syrup
Pears freezer jam, cooked in syrup
Quinces cooked in syrup
Red- and white currants uncooked purées
Sloes open-freeze
Strawberries freezer jam, uncooked purées
Tayberries open-freeze, freezer jam

Loganberries

This modern blackberry/ raspberry hybrid is less fragile than a raspberry, but just as juicy. Choose perfect fruits (remove the cores first) and open-freeze, poach in syrup, or make freezer jam.

Plums

All types of plum freeze well – just cut in half and open-freeze. If using for jams or chutneys, freeze whole. They can also be poached in syrup and frozen.

Apples

Apples must first be peeled, sliced, and dipped into lemon juice to prevent discolouration. Poach in syrup, open-freeze, or cook and purée, and then freeze.

Peaches

Choose ripe, juicy, fragrant peaches (in season from July to September). They are too fragile to freeze well uncooked, but are ideal poached in syrup, then frozen, or made into freezer jams.

Freezing blanched vegetables

Blanching vegetables before freezing them destroys the enzymes that cause their colour, texture, and flavour to deteriorate in the freezer. For blanching and freezing vegetables other than beans, see the chart on pp60–61.

Blanched French beans

MAKES APPROX 450G (1LB)

TAKES 10–15 MINUTES

KEEPS 6–12 MONTHS

INGREDIENTS

Approx 450g (1lb) French beans, trimmed

1 Bring a large saucepan of lightly salted water to the boil. Keeping the heat high, add a small handful of beans and bring back to the boil. Cook small batches of beans at a time so the water boils sooner. Blanch each batch for 2–3 minutes.

2 Transfer each batch of beans immediately to a large bowl of iced water to halt the cooking process and set the colour. The beans will cool very quickly.

3 Remove the beans, drain, and pat them dry on kitchen paper. Leave to one side until all the batches have been blanched, drained, and dried.

4 Pack in convenient portions in freezer bags or containers. Alternatively, freeze on open trays (pp62–63), then store in larger freezer bags.

Freezing times

Only freeze fresh, top-quality food. The freezing times listed in these charts are the maximum storage times to ensure quality.

Fruit

All fruits are best frozen with sugar in some form to help retain their texture when thawed. Remove any stones and cut larger fruits (apart from citrus fruits) in half or into slices first before freezing and dating. Pale fruits discolour, so dip them in lemon juice first if freezing raw.

FREEZER TIMES FOR FRUITS					
FRUITS	**RAW**			**COOKED**	
	Sprinkle with sugar and open-freeze on trays (pp62–63) (Months)	Pack in freezer pots, cover in syrup or sugar, and freeze (Months)	Purée (p62), pack in freezer pots, and freeze (Months)	Blanch or poach in syrup, pack in freezer pots, cover in syrup, and freeze (Months)	Purée (p62), pack in freezer pots, and freeze (Months)
Apples	9	9		9	9
Apricots (ripe)	9	9	6	9	9
Blackberries	12	12	6	9	9
Blackcurrants	12	12	6	9	9
Blueberries	12	12	6	9	9
Cherries	6	6	6	9	9
Citrus fruits	6				
Cranberries	12	12	6	9	9
Figs	9	9	6	9	9
Gooseberries	12	12	6	9	9
Loganberries	12	12	6	9	9
Melons	9	9	6	9	9
Nectarines	9	9	6	9	9
Peaches	9	9	6	9	9
Pears				9	9
Plums (all kinds)	9	9	6	9	9
Raspberries	12	12	6	9	9
Rhubarb	12	12		9	9
Strawberries	9	9	6	9	9
Fruit juices and syrups	Pot up in freezer pots and freeze for 9 months				

Vegetables

Prepare the vegetables, then either blanch, cool, and pack them in conveniently sized clean freezer pots and freeze, or freeze on open trays, pack in freezer bags, label, and date. Blanching times apply after the water returns to the boil. Vegetables with a high water content, such as aubergines, courgettes, mushrooms, and tomatoes, are better cooked first (pp64–67), then frozen. Frozen cooked and raw vegetables (except sweetcorn cobs) can be cooked from frozen, but cooked purées should be thawed first.

GOLDEN RULES FOR FREEZING

Foods suitable for freezing will freeze well if you follow these rules:

The faster you freeze food, the better and safer the result.

When freezing produce in anything other than small quantities, always use the fast freezer facility.

Freezing times are for maximum storage times at -18°C (0°F). Adhere to these storage times and aim to use the dated, labelled produce well before these time limits.

Thaw frozen produce in the fridge. Never refreeze food that has already been thawed – it's not safe.

FREEZER TIMES FOR VEGETABLES				
VEGETABLES	HOW TO PREPARE	COOKED	PRE-BLANCHED	
		Freeze (Months)	Blanch (Minutes)	Freeze (Months)
Asparagus	Trim	9	2–4	9
Aubergines	Slice, griddle	9		
Beans, broad	Pod	9	2–3	12
Beans, French	Leave whole	6	2–3	9
Beans, Runner (tender)	Slice	6	2	9
Broccoli florets	Separate	6	2	9
Brussels sprouts	Leave whole	6	3	9
Cabbages	Slice	4	2	6
Carrots (small)	Leave whole	9	5	9
Carrots	Slice	9	2–3	9
Cauliflower florets	Separate	4	3	6
Celeriac	Slice, griddle	9		
Courgettes	Slice, griddle	9		
Fennel	Slice	4	2	6
Globe artichokes (bottoms)	Leave whole	9	4	9
Globe artichokes (baby)	Leave whole	6	3	9
Mangetout	Leave whole		1	9
Mushrooms	Chop	9		
Peas	Pod	9	1–2	12
Peppers	Slice, griddle	9		
Romanesco florets	Separate	6	2	9
Salsify/scorzonera	Peel, chop	9	2–3	9
Sugarsnap peas	Leave whole		2	9
Spinach	Wash		1	9
Sweet potatoes	Slice, griddle	9		
Sweetcorn (whole cob)		9	6	12
Sweetcorn (kernels)		9	2	12
Swiss chard (leaves/stalks)	Wash, chop		1–2	9
Tomatoes	Chop	9		
Root vegetable purées	Pot up in freezer pots and freeze for 9 months			

Freezing uncooked fruit

A perfect way to preserve the flavour and nutritional content of fresh fruit is to freeze it. Freezing breaks down the cell walls of fruit, so whole fruit will be squashy when thawed – but the flavour will be just as delicious as fresh.

Frozen blueberries

MAKES 450G (1LB)

TAKES 5 MINUTES

KEEPS 6–12 MONTHS

INGREDIENTS

450g (1lb) soft,
   whole blueberries

Caster sugar, to sprinkle

1 Discard any blueberries that are over-ripe or blemished. Lay them in a single layer on baking trays. Sprinkle liberally with caster sugar and put the trays in the freezer.

FREEZING PURÉES

Very juicy fruits such as peaches, raspberries, and strawberries can be puréed uncooked in a mouli or food processor with a little sugar and lemon juice and frozen in freezer pots (leave 2cm/¾in of space at the top to allow for expansion). Serve over ice cream, as fruit coulis, or mixed with yoghurt and cream for instant fruit fools. Uncooked purées keep frozen for 6 months.

Over-ripe fruit, or fruit not perfect enough to freeze uncooked, can be stewed lightly, baked, or poached in a sugar syrup (p222) with added flavourings or a wine-based syrup (p241). Freeze cooked fruit (leave 2cm/¾in of space at the top of each pot to allow for expansion) for up to 9 months.

2 As soon as the fruit is frozen (after 1 hour or so), scrape it from the trays and put it into portion-sized freezer bags.

3 Label and date the freezer bags and return the berries to the freezer until they are needed.

Freezing cooked foods

Freezing cooked vegetables and fruits is a convenient way to preserve them, and suits produce that doesn't freeze well in its natural state, such as aubergines. Gluts of tomatoes are ideal frozen as a sauce for pizzas and other savoury dishes.

Concentrated tomato sauce

MAKES APPROX 1 LITRE (1¾ PINTS)

TAKES 1–1¼ HOURS

KEEPS 12 MONTHS

INGREDIENTS

2.5–3kg (5½–6½lb) very ripe tomatoes, roughly chopped

1 large onion, sliced

1 large sprig of parsley, basil, and/or celery leaves

1 bay leaf

1 large garlic clove, peeled

1 Put all the ingredients into a preserving pan or a large heavy-based saucepan and bring to the boil.

2 Simmer over a very low heat for about 1 hour or until the mixture becomes thick and concentrated. Stir frequently. The sauce is ready when there is no discernible liquid left.

3 Remove the bay leaf and garlic and sieve the sauce through a mouli or metal sieve into a bowl, pressing hard to extract as much of the sauce as possible. Leave the sauce to cool.

4 Pour the concentrated tomato sauce into small, clean freezer pots, then seal, label, and freeze. Thaw before using as required.

These frozen vegetables are a great accompaniment to grilled fish, chicken, or steak, or mixed with flageolet, haricot beans, or chickpeas and dressed with pesto. Otherwise, use them chopped and tossed with extra olive oil and pasta, or layered in lasagnes.

Griddled Mediterranean vegetables

MAKES APPROX 1.35KG (3LB)

TAKES 30–40 MINUTES

KEEPS 6 MONTHS

INGREDIENTS

2 smallish aubergines, trimmed and cut into strips lengthways, about 5mm (¼in) thick

4 courgettes, trimmed and cut into strips lengthways, about 5mm (¼in) thick

A little olive oil

4 red peppers (or orange and yellow peppers, if you prefer), halved, cored, deseeded, and cut into 6–8 strips

1 Preheat a griddle pan or electric griddle. Prepare 3–4 baking sheets with a layer of greaseproof paper or baking parchment on top. Brush the aubergines and courgettes with oil on both sides. Put the peppers in a shallow dish, drizzle with a little oil, and toss with your hands to coat them completely in the oil.

2 When the griddle is very hot, but not smoking, add a single layer of vegetables (don't overcrowd them). Press them down firmly with a fish slice until the undersides are nicely striped. Turn the vegetables over and cook for a further 2–3 minutes until just cooked and striped. Don't overcook them, or they will become too soft. If using an electric griddle, close the lid, and cook for about 3 minutes.

3 Once the vegetables are cooked until striped and just tender, transfer to the prepared baking sheets to cool. Reheat the griddle between each batch.

4 When cold, open-freeze the vegetables on the baking sheets until firm, then pack together in a plastic bag or sealable freezer box and store in the freezer. Finish cooking from frozen in a preheated moderate oven on a lightly oiled baking sheet, covered with oiled foil, for 30 minutes – or in a shallow, covered, dish in the microwave, turning once – until piping hot.

This combination of vegetables makes a lovely winter alternative to the Griddled Mediterranean vegetables, and is a delicious accompaniment to casseroles and roast meats instead of the more traditional roasted or baked vegetables.

Griddled sweet potato and celeriac

MAKES APPROX 1KG (2¼LB)

TAKES 40–45 MINUTES

KEEPS 6 MONTHS

INGREDIENTS

2 small or 1 large celeriac, cut in half if small, quarters if large, and then in slices, and brushed all over with sunflower oil to prevent browning

2–3 medium sweet potatoes, peeled and cut into 5mm (¼in) thick slices

Freshly ground black pepper

A little sweet or smoked paprika (optional)

1 Season the celeriac and sweet potato on both sides with black pepper and dust lightly with paprika, if using. Preheat a griddle pan or electric griddle. Prepare 2–3 baking sheets with a layer of greaseproof paper or baking parchment on top. Brush the vegetables with oil on both sides.

2 When the griddle is very hot, but not smoking, add a single layer of vegetables (don't overcrowd them). Press them down firmly with a fish slice until the undersides are nicely striped. Turn the vegetables over and cook for a further 2–3 minutes until just cooked and striped. Don't overcook them, or they will become too soft. If using an electric griddle, close the lid, and cook for about 3 minutes.

3 Once the vegetables are cooked until striped and just tender, transfer to the prepared baking sheets to cool. Reheat the griddle between each batch.

4 When cold, open-freeze the vegetables on the baking sheets until firm, then pack together in a plastic bag or sealable freezer box and store in the freezer. Finish cooking from frozen in a preheated moderate oven on a lightly oiled baking sheet, covered with oiled foil, for 30 minutes – or in a shallow, covered, dish in the microwave, turning once – until piping hot.

This purée is great for topping minced meat pies, such as cottage pie or bobotie, a South African baked curried meat dish. It also makes a delicious accompaniment to meat or poultry, or just add stock and a pinch of mixed herbs or ground cumin for a quick soup.

Mixed vegetable purée

MAKES APPROX 1.8KG (4LB)

TAKES 1 HOUR 20 MINUTES

KEEPS 6 MONTHS

INGREDIENTS

1 swede

450g (1lb) carrots

2 sweet potatoes

2 large turnips or 1 celeriac

Large pinch of salt

60g (2oz) unsalted butter

Freshly ground black pepper

1 Peel and chop all the vegetables into evenly sized chunks or thick slices.

2 Place in a large saucepan of cold water with a good pinch of salt added. Bring to the boil, reduce the heat slightly, part-cover, and simmer for 20–25 minutes or until all the vegetables are really tender. Drain well.

3 Put the vegetables through a potato ricer, purée with a hand blender, process in a food processor, or mash thoroughly with a potato masher.

4 Return the purée to the pan and add the butter and a good grinding of pepper. Heat gently, beating well until the butter is absorbed. Leave to cool, then pack in small portion-sized freezer containers with lids, or plastic freezer bags. Seal, label, and freeze. Thaw before reheating or using to top a pie before baking.

Making a purée is one of the best ways to store Jerusalem artichokes. This purée tastes sublime with roasted meat and game, baked with eggs and cream, or thinned as a soup and topped with crisp crumbled bacon.

Jerusalem artichoke purée

MAKES APPROX 1KG (2¼LB)

TAKES 40–55 MINUTES

KEEPS 6 MONTHS

INGREDIENTS

1 tbsp lemon juice

1kg (2¼lb) Jerusalem artichokes

5 tbsp double cream

50g (1¾oz) butter

A splash of milk

Salt and freshly ground black pepper

Freshly grated nutmeg

1 Stir the lemon juice into a large bowl of cold water. Peel the artichokes as thinly as possible (or leave the skins on and just scrub the vegetables if you don't mind a discoloured purée). Cut into neat pieces and put immediately into the acidulated water.

2 Drain, place in a large saucepan, and cover with fresh water. Bring to the boil, reduce the heat slightly, and simmer for about 25 minutes or until really tender. Drain and return to the pan. Heat gently to dry out.

3 Put the vegetables through a potato ricer, purée with a hand blender, process in a food processor, or mash thoroughly with a potato masher. Beat in the cream, butter, and milk, and season to taste with salt, black pepper, and a good grating of fresh nutmeg.

4 Leave to cool, then pack in small portion-sized freezer containers with lids, or plastic freezer bags. Seal, label, and freeze. Thaw before reheating.

This freezer purée has just the right level of sweetness with a hint of vanilla. If you want a more pronounced vanilla flavour, split the pod before you add it to the saucepan so that the seeds can also flavour the rhubarb. Thaw overnight in the fridge before using.

Rhubarb and vanilla freezer purée

MAKES APPROX 400G (14OZ)

TAKES 30 MINUTES

KEEPS 6 MONTHS

INGREDIENTS

400g (14oz) rhubarb

100g (3½oz) granulated or light soft
   brown sugar

1 vanilla pod

1 Chop the rhubarb into chunks and put them in a saucepan. Add the sugar, 100ml (3½fl oz) of water, and the vanilla pod.

2 Bring the ingredients to the boil, then simmer for 25–30 minutes or until the rhubarb reduces down. Stir occasionally to prevent the mixture sticking to the base of the pan.

3 When the rhubarb is the consistency of purée, take out the vanilla pod and put the purée into clean freezer pots, leaving 1cm (½in) of space at the top. Leave to cool, then seal and freeze.

Rhubarb
If you use forced rhubarb (as shown here), which is a vivid pink colour, the purée will have a lovely pink hue. If you use normal rhubarb, which is green or dark red, the purée will be a duller colour.

Soft fruits such as berries won't keep for long after they've been picked, so one of the best ways to preserve their juicy freshness is to turn them into ice lollies. This recipe uses less sugar than is normal, so the lollies are not overly sweet.

Fruit lollies

MAKES APPROX 500G (1LB 2OZ) (4–6 SMALL LOLLIES)

TAKES 20 MINUTES

KEEPS 6 MONTHS

INGREDIENTS

115g (4oz) granulated sugar

500g (1lb 2oz) ripe, fresh berries such as raspberries, strawberries, or blackberries, washed

Juice of 1 lemon

1 Make a sugar syrup first (p222): put the sugar and 120ml (4fl oz) of water in a heavy-based saucepan. Place the pan over a low heat and stir the mixture with a wooden spoon until the sugar has dissolved.

2 Cook the syrup on a medium to high heat to achieve a steady boil for 1–2 minutes. Then turn off the heat and allow the syrup to cool.

3 Purée the berries by passing them through a sieve (which will also remove all the seeds) and collect the purée in a clean bowl beneath. If the fruit is too hard to go through the sieve easily, blitz it with a hand blender or in a processor to make a purée first, then sieve.

4 Add the lemon juice and sugar syrup to the bowl and mix them into the berry purée.

5 Pour the mixture into ice lolly moulds, slot an ice lolly stick into each mould (if needed), and freeze.

Making freezer pickles

Freezer pickles are a quick, modern way to achieve wonderfully fresh-flavoured condiments with bite. This pickle, which is so popular in sandwiches, can also be served with salads, cold meats, cheese, or barbecued fish.

Bread and butter pickle

MAKES 350–450G (12OZ–1LB)

TAKES 15 MINUTES, PLUS STANDING TIME

KEEPS 6 MONTHS

INGREDIENTS

2 large cucumbers

2 shallots

½ green pepper (optional)

1–2 tsp sea salt

120ml (4 fl oz) cider or wine vinegar

30–60g (1–2oz) caster sugar

A good pinch of ground turmeric and celery or dill seeds, or ½–1 tsp wholegrain mustard seeds

1 Scrub and slice the cucumbers thinly. Slice the shallot into wafer thin slices, and finely chop the green pepper, if using.

2 Put the vegetables into a large bowl, sprinkle the salt over them, mix well, and leave for 2 hours to draw out the moisture.

3 Tip the vegetables into a colander, rinse in cold water, and drain well, pressing them down lightly to squeeze out the moisture. Then put them into a clean, dry bowl.

4 Mix the vinegar and sugar to taste. Stir the liquid to dissolve the sugar, then add the spices. Pour the mix over the vegetables, cover, and leave in the fridge overnight.

5 Transfer to clean portion-sized freezer pots, leaving 1cm (½in) of space at the top, seal, label, and freeze. To use, thaw overnight in the fridge, then keep refrigerated and use within 1 week.

If you don't have runner beans, use flat helda beans and prepare them in the same way, although there is no need to string them before slicing. To use, thaw overnight in the fridge, then keep refrigerated and use within one week.

Sweet and sour runner bean freezer pickle

MAKES APPROX 600G (1LB 5OZ)

TAKES 10–20 MINUTES, PLUS STANDING TIME

KEEPS 6 MONTHS

INGREDIENTS

450g (1lb) runner beans

1 tbsp sea salt

6 tbsp rice vinegar

2 tbsp light soft brown sugar

2 tsp light soy sauce

½ tsp ground allspice

2.5cm (1in) piece fresh root ginger, grated

1 shallot, finely chopped

A good handful of raisins (approx 55g/2oz)

1 String the beans and cut them into thin diagonal slices. Place them in a colander over a bowl and sprinkle over the salt. Toss the beans well in the salt and leave to stand for 3 hours.

2 Rinse the beans well under cold water, turning them to remove the salt. Drain thoroughly and press down well with your hand to remove all excess moisture.

3 Mix the vinegar, sugar, soy sauce, allspice, and ginger together in a bowl. Stir until the sugar has dissolved. Add the beans, chopped shallot, and raisins, and mix thoroughly. Cover and leave in the fridge overnight.

4 The next day, stir the mixture well and pack it into clean freezer pots, leaving 1cm (½in) of space at the top. Seal and freeze for at least 3 weeks or more to help the flavours mature.

Runner beans
Pick or buy runner beans that are young and tender rather than large, stringy, and tough.

This lovely crunchy pickle is delicious served with cheese, anchovies, smoked mackerel, continental sausages, and even hard-boiled eggs. To use, thaw overnight in the fridge, then keep refrigerated and use within one week.

Cauliflower, pepper, and spring onion freezer pickle

MAKES APPROX 750G (1LB 10OZ)

TAKES 15–20 MINUTES, PLUS STANDING TIME

KEEPS 6 MONTHS

INGREDIENTS

¼ cucumber, diced

1 small red pepper, diced

4 spring onions, trimmed and cut into 1cm (½in) lengths

½ small cauliflower, cut into tiny florets

1 tbsp sea salt

1 red chilli, deseeded and sliced

6 tbsp white wine vinegar

2 tbsp clear honey

½ tsp ground turmeric

1 tsp cumin seeds

1 bay leaf

1 Put the cucumber, pepper, spring onions, and cauliflower in a colander. Sprinkle over the salt, toss the vegetables well, and leave to stand for 3 hours.

2 Rinse the vegetables well under cold water, turning them to remove the salt. Drain them thoroughly, press down well with your hand to remove all excess moisture, and tip into a bowl.

3 Mix the remaining ingredients together and pour them over the vegetables. Mix everything thoroughly, cover the bowl, and leave in the fridge overnight.

4 The next day, stir the ingredients well, remove the bay leaf, and pack into clean freezer pots. Seal and freeze for at least 3 weeks to help the flavours mature.

Making freezer jam

Uncooked freezer jams are a great solution for anyone who wants fresh-tasting, low-sugar spreads. Very ripe, juicy fruits, especially those low in acid that are difficult to set properly (pp88–89), are ideal as thickened purées.

Strawberry freezer jam

MAKES APPROX 600G (1LB 5OZ)

TAKES 15 MINUTES, PLUS STANDING TIME

KEEPS 6 MONTHS

INGREDIENTS

500g (1lb 2oz) ripe strawberries at room temperature

1 tbsp lemon juice

1 tbsp agar flakes or 1 tsp agar powder

60–115g (2–4oz) caster sugar

1 Wash the strawberries briefly if necessary, put into a large bowl with the lemon juice, and crush all the berries with the back of a fork (you want a rough, rather than smooth, purée, keeping some of the texture of the fruit intact).

2 Put 250ml (8fl oz) of water in a small saucepan and add the agar. Leave for 2–3 minutes to soften, give the pan a swirl, and slowly bring to the boil over a low heat without stirring. Simmer gently for 3–5 minutes, stirring occasionally to ensure all the agar has dissolved.

3 Once the agar flakes have dissolved, keep the pan on the heat and add the sugar. Stir the mixture occasionally until all the sugar has dissolved – about 2–3 minutes.

GELLING AGENTS

This method uses agar, a healthy, tasteless, Japanese gelling agent, made from seaweed, which is available in supermarkets and organic and health shops. The agar gives these quick jams a jelly-like set; they can be used, thawed on toast, desserts, or yoghurt.

4 Pour the hot agar syrup onto the fruit, stirring constantly until it is well mixed (use a rubber spatula to scrape all the syrup out of the pan).

5 Pour the jam into clean freezer pots, leaving 1cm (½in) space at the top to allow for expansion. Allow the jam to cool, then seal, label, leave in the fridge overnight to thicken fully, and then freeze.

6 To use a pot of freezer jam, thaw overnight in the fridge, then refrigerate and use within 2 weeks.

The addition of a little spice brings out the flavour of this delicious autumn jam. Try it on scones, toasted buttered crumpets, or muffins with clotted cream or crème fraîche. To use, thaw overnight in the fridge, then keep refrigerated and use within two weeks.

Pear and blackberry freezer jam

MAKES APPROX 750G (1LB 10OZ)

TAKES 15–20 MINUTES, PLUS STANDING TIME

KEEPS 6 MONTHS

INGREDIENTS

2 ripe pears, peeled, cored, and roughly chopped

225g (8oz) cultivated ripe blackberries

2 tbsp lemon juice

1 tsp mixed spice

1 tbsp agar flakes or 1 tsp agar powder

140g (5oz) caster sugar

1 Make sure the fruit is at room temperature. Put the pears and blackberries in a bowl with the lemon juice and spice. Roughly crush the fruit with a potato masher or fork; you want to keep some texture, not reduce them to a smooth pulp.

2 Put 200ml (7fl oz) of water in a small saucepan, sprinkle the agar flakes or powder over it, and leave to soften for 2–3 minutes. Give the pan a gentle swirl, then bring the water slowly to the boil over a low heat without stirring it. Simmer gently for 3–5 minutes, stirring occasionally to make sure all the agar has dissolved.

3 Add the sugar and stir until it has dissolved – about 2–3 minutes – over a low heat. Then remove the pan from the heat.

4 Pour the hot agar syrup over the fruit in the bowl, stirring the fruit gently and constantly until the ingredients are well mixed.

5 Pour into clean freezer pots, leaving 1cm (½in) of space at the top. Leave to cool, then seal and label. Leave overnight in the fridge to thicken fully, then freeze.

This recipe makes quite a firm jam. If you prefer a softer texture, add an extra 60ml (2fl oz) of water. Try it as a filling for a chocolate cake to make a black forest gateau. To use, thaw overnight in the fridge, then keep refrigerated and use within two weeks.

Cherry freezer jam

MAKES APPROX 700G (1½LB)

TAKES 20 MINUTES, PLUS STANDING TIME

KEEPS 6 MONTHS

INGREDIENTS

450g (1lb) cherries

1 tbsp lemon juice

1 tbsp agar flakes or 1 tsp agar powder

115g (4oz) caster sugar

A few drops natural almond extract

1 Make sure the fruit is at room temperature. Halve and stone the cherries and put them in a bowl with the lemon juice. Roughly crush them with a potato masher or fork; you want to keep some texture, not reduce them to a smooth pulp.

2 Put 200ml (7fl oz) of water in a small saucepan, sprinkle the agar flakes or powder over it, and leave to soften for 2–3 minutes. Give the pan a gentle swirl, then bring the water slowly to the boil over a low heat without stirring. Simmer gently for 3–5 minutes, stirring occasionally to make sure all the agar has dissolved.

3 Add the sugar and stir until it has dissolved – about 2–3 minutes – over a low heat. Then remove the pan from the heat and stir in the almond extract.

4 Pour the hot agar syrup over the cherries in the bowl, stirring the fruit gently and constantly until everything is well mixed.

5 Pour into clean freezer pots, leaving 1cm (½in) of space at the top. Leave to cool, then seal and label. Leave overnight in the fridge to thicken fully, then freeze.

Cherries
Any flavoursome dessert cherry is suitable for this recipe. Try 'Stella', 'Merton Glory', and 'Sunburst' varieties.

This deliciously tangy combination of berries makes a healthy instant dessert served with natural yoghurt and granola or on top of sliced, perfectly ripe peaches. To use, thaw overnight in the fridge, then keep refrigerated and use within two weeks.

Blueberry and raspberry freezer jam

MAKES APPROX 500G (1LB 2OZ)

TAKES 15 MINUTES, PLUS STANDING TIME

KEEPS 6 MONTHS

INGREDIENTS

225g (8oz) blueberries

225g (8oz) raspberries

2 tsp lemon juice

1 tbsp agar flakes or 1 tsp agar powder

115g (4oz) caster sugar

1 Make sure the fruit is at room temperature. Put it in a bowl with the lemon juice and roughly crush with a potato masher or fork; you want to leave some texture, not reduce the berries to a smooth pulp.

2 Put 200ml (7fl oz) of water in a small saucepan, sprinkle the agar flakes or powder over it, and leave to soften for 2–3 minutes. Give the pan a gentle swirl, then bring the water slowly to the boil over a low heat without stirring it. Simmer gently for 3–5 minutes, stirring occasionally to make sure all the agar has dissolved.

3 Add the sugar and stir until it has dissolved – about 2–3 minutes – over a low heat. Then remove the pan from the heat.

4 Pour the hot agar syrup over the fruit in the bowl, stirring the fruit gently and constantly until the ingredients are well mixed.

5 Pour into clean freezer pots, leaving 1cm (½in) of space at the top. Leave to cool, then seal and label. Leave overnight in the fridge to thicken fully, then freeze.

This jam is equally good made with nectarines instead of peaches, or raspberries instead of strawberries. As the fruit is juicy, this recipe will make quite a lot of jam. To use, thaw overnight in the fridge, then keep refrigerated and use within two weeks.

Peach and strawberry freezer jam

MAKES APPROX 700G (1½LB)

TAKES 30–40 MINUTES, PLUS STANDING TIME

KEEPS 6 MONTHS

INGREDIENTS

2 ripe peaches

225g (8oz) strawberries, hulled

1 tbsp lemon juice

Finely grated zest of ½ organic orange

1 tbsp agar flakes or 1 tsp agar powder

140g (5oz) caster sugar

1 Make nicks in the peach skins and put the peaches in a bowl, cover with boiling water so that they are submerged, and leave for 30 seconds. Drain off the water, pour in cold water, then lift out the peaches and peel their skins. Halve the fruits, remove the stones, roughly chop the flesh, and put the pieces in a bowl.

2 Add the strawberries and lemon juice and roughly crush the fruits with a potato masher or fork.

3 Put 200ml (7fl oz) of water in a small saucepan, sprinkle the agar flakes or powder over it, and leave to soften for 2–3 minutes. Give the pan a gentle swirl, then bring the water slowly to the boil over a low heat without stirring. Simmer gently for 3–5 minutes, stirring occasionally until the agar has dissolved. Add the sugar and stir until dissolved – about 2–3 minutes – over a low heat. Then remove the pan from the heat.

4 Pour the hot agar syrup over the fruit, stirring the ingredients gently and constantly until well mixed.

5 Pour into clean freezer pots, leaving 1cm (½in) of head space. Allow to cool, then seal and label. Leave overnight in the fridge to thicken fully, then freeze.

Unlike most freezer jams, you have to cook the carrot first in this recipe, but as you use the liquid it is cooked in, the "marmalade" retains maximum goodness. To use, thaw overnight in the fridge, then keep refrigerated and use within two weeks.

Carrot and orange freezer "marmalade"

MAKES APPROX 400G (14OZ)

TAKES 35–45 MINUTES, PLUS STANDING TIME

KEEPS 6 MONTHS

INGREDIENTS

2 medium carrots (approx 225g/8oz in total)

1 large organic orange

200ml (7fl oz) fresh orange juice

1 tbsp agar flakes or 1 tsp agar powder

85g (3oz) caster sugar

Finely grated zest and juice of 1 small organic lemon

1 Peel and coarsely grate the carrot into a heavy-based saucepan. Zest the orange and add the zest to the pan. Add the fresh orange juice, bring to the boil, reduce the heat, cover, and cook gently, stirring occasionally for 20 minutes until the grated carrot is really soft.

2 Meanwhile, holding the orange over a bowl to catch all the juice, cut away all the pith from the orange. Segment the fruit, cutting either side of each membrane. Squeeze any remaining juice from the membranes into the bowl. Then finely chop the flesh and add it to the juice.

3 Put 2 tbsp of water in a small bowl, sprinkle the agar flakes or powder over it, and leave to soften for 2–3 minutes. Add the sugar and softened agar to the cooked carrots and stir over a very gentle heat for about 3 minutes until the sugar is completely dissolved. Remove the pan from the heat and add the orange flesh, reserved orange juice, lemon zest, and its juice.

4 Pour into clean freezer pots, leaving 1cm (½in) of head space. Leave to cool, then seal and label. Leave in the fridge overnight to thicken fully, then freeze.

Freezing herbs

Freezing culinary herbs is an ideal way to preserve them. Their colour, flavour, and essential oils are all retained and though their texture suffers a little, they are almost as good as using fresh herbs in cooking.

Basil ice cubes

MAKES APPROX 20 ICE CUBES

TAKES 5 MINUTES

KEEPS 6 MONTHS

INGREDIENTS

Approx 3 bunches of basil

FRAGRANT HERB AND OIL PURÉES

This is an excellent way to freeze herbs such as basil, parsley, and coriander, as the oil locks up all their flavour and fragrance. Use to make pesto, or add to sauces, soups, and cooked savoury dishes.

Strip the leaves from their stalks, put in a food processor and pulse until finely chopped. Add enough good extra-virgin olive oil to make a thick paste, pulse for a few seconds more, then divide into small freezer bags, label, and freeze. Stores well for up to 3 months.

1 Separate the leaves from their stalks, put them in a food processor, and chop them finely using the pulse button. Alternatively, chop the leaves finely by hand using a small knife or a mezzaluna.

2 Fill an ice cube tray with the chopped herbs and add approximately 1 tsp of water (to reach the rim of each cube). Freeze, then pack into plastic freezer bags, label, and return to the freezer.

Sweet preserves are irresistible. Whether made from fruit from your own garden, a local pick-your-own farm, or a farmers' market, the pleasure that these preserves bring can last all year round. Jams, conserves, and curds can be used in many delicious and varied ways as spreads, with desserts, and in baking. Fruit cheeses and butters are ideal as a rich flavouring in meat dishes and savoury sauces, or served with soft cheeses. Marmalades and jellies are also versatile preserves that are full of seasonal flavours. Making all these preserves is a straightforward skill that's easy to learn.

Making sweet preserves

All sweet preserves are made in the same way: fruit is simmered to release a gum-like substance, pectin (a natural setting agent), then boiled vigorously with sugar to reach the setting point. For a good set, the balance of sugar, pectin, and acid must be correct.

Pectin

It is the pectin in fruit that causes sweet preserves to set when mixed with sugar. Fruits fall into three categories according to the amount of pectin they contain:

High-pectin fruits set easily to give a solid set. Water is sometimes added to dilute their pectin levels. They also absorb more sugar.

Medium-pectin fruits often set satisfactorily, but because their pectin levels can vary, they may not, and usually give a softer set. Testing pectin levels (p90) can determine whether or not extra pectin is needed for a set.

Low-pectin fruits need extra pectin and acid to achieve a set. Combining high- and low-pectin fruits usually gives a satisfactory set, as can using a small amount of pectin stock (pp90–91). Otherwise, use jam sugar.

The amount of pectin (and acid) also varies with each batch of fruit according to the variety, season, and how dry, ripe, or juicy it is. Use firm, dry, just-ripe, undamaged, very fresh fruit with no blemishes; damaged or wet fruit causes preserves to go mouldy, and over-ripe fruit lacks sufficient pectin and acid. Lemon juice (an acid) can be added to simmering fruit to help release its pectin. Water is added to firm fruits, hard-skinned fruits, and those with high pectin levels.

Acid

Fruits also contain acid, which helps to release pectin. The tarter a fruit tastes, the higher it is in acid. Acid levels usually correspond to pectin levels.

Where acid levels are low, extra acid helps to achieve a set. Use lemon juice or citric or tartaric acid (available from most chemists). As a guide, add the juice of 1 lemon (2 tbsp) – or ½ tsp of citric or tartaric acid dissolved in 4 tbsp of water – for every 1 kg (2¼lb) of fruit used. Acid also improves the colour and flavour of a preserve and prevents sugar crystallization.

Sugar

Sugar plays a critical part in enabling pectin to gel: the more pectin there is, the more sugar it will absorb and set. It also helps to protect pectin from breaking down during the boiling stage. However, it inhibits the release of pectin and toughens the skins of fruits, so it is added after the fruit has been softened. Sugar also keeps fruit firm, so fruits for conserves are first steeped in sugar. An equal quantity of sugar to fruit (or more, if the fruit is tart or high in pectin) gives a long-lasting, sweet preserve; reduce the amount of sugar by a quarter for a fresher, fruitier jam. Half sugar to fruit gives a semi-sweet, fruit-filled jam that must be refrigerated.

TESTING FOR A SET

As a general guide, jams and conserves usually take 5–20 minutes, jellies 5–15 minutes, and marmalades 10–30 minutes to set.

Rolling boil Recipe setting times (which are not precise and can vary) indicate the time from which a sweet preserve such as jam starts to boil. Start testing for a set (below) as jam reaches 105°C (220°F), thickens around the sides of the pan, boils sluggishly, and the bubbles "plop" rather than froth.

Flake test Put some jam in a bowl. Scoop up some of the jam with a wooden spoon, allow to cool for a moment, then tilt the spoon. If the last part of the jam falls in a flake rather than a stream, it is set. Always remove the pan from the heat when testing for a set.

Wrinkle test Put a few saucers in the fridge before you make the jam. Put 1 tsp of boiling jam on a chilled saucer, allow to cool, then push it from one side with your finger. If your finger leaves a trail on the plate and the jam wrinkles slightly, it is set. Always remove the pan from the heat when testing for a set.

PECTIN AND ACID CONTENT OF KEY FRUITS

This chart refers only to fruit; most vegetables have no or negligible pectin and acid levels.

FRUITS	PECTIN CONTENT	ACIDITY
Blackcurrants	High	High
Crab apples	High	High
Cranberries (unripe)	High	Medium
Gooseberries	High	High
Plums (unripe), damsons	High	High
Quinces	High	High-medium
Red- and white currants	High	High
Citrus fruits (pectin is found in the skins, peel, and pith)	High-medium	High-medium
Cooking apples	High-medium	High-medium
Apricots	Medium	Medium
Cranberries (ripe)	Medium	Medium
Grapes (unripe) (variable pectin content)	Medium	Medium
Loganberries	Medium	Medium
Medlars	Medium	Low
Morello (cooking) cherries	Medium	Medium
All plums (ripe)	Medium	Medium
Raspberries	Medium	Medium
Blackberries	Low-medium	Low
Blueberries (variable pectin content)	Low-medium	Low
Wild blackberries (brambles)	Low	Low
Cherries (dessert)	Low	Low
Figs	Low	Low
Grapes (ripe) (variable pectin content)	Low	Low
Melons	Low	Low
Nectarines	Low	Low
Peaches	Low	Low
Pears	Low	Low
Rhubarb	Low	High
Strawberries	Low	Low

Making pectin stock

Pectin stock is simple to make and takes the guesswork out of making preserves from medium- or low-pectin fruits (pp88–89). Cooking apples make an excellent pectin stock, as they have a naturally high pectin and acid content.

Apple pectin stock

MAKES APPROX 450ML (15FL OZ)

TAKES 45–55 MINUTES

KEEPS 1–2 WEEKS, REFRIGERATED (2 MONTHS FROZEN)

INGREDIENTS

1kg (2¼lb) sour cooking apples (windfalls are good, but cut out bruised or damaged parts), chopped

SIMPLE PECTIN TEST

This test enables you to judge if your stock (or fruit) contains enough pectin to achieve a set: Put 1 tsp of stock (or simmered fruit) in a small container. When cold, add 1 tbsp of methylated spirit, swirl together, leave for 1 minute, then check for a set:
High pectin: The mixture forms a jelly-like clot.
Medium pectin: 2–3 soft clots form. The stock (or fruit) may or may not set satisfactorily. Return to the heat to reduce a little further and test again.
Low pectin: Numerous small globules form. Return to the heat, reduce the volume of the stock, and test again.
NB Discard the tested stock – methylated spirit is poisonous.

1 Put the apples in a preserving pan and pour in enough water to just cover the fruit. Cover, bring to the boil, and then simmer for 20 minutes or until soft.

2 Strain the pulp through a large sieve lined with muslin, or a jelly bag set over a bowl, and allow the juice to drip through into a bowl positioned below.

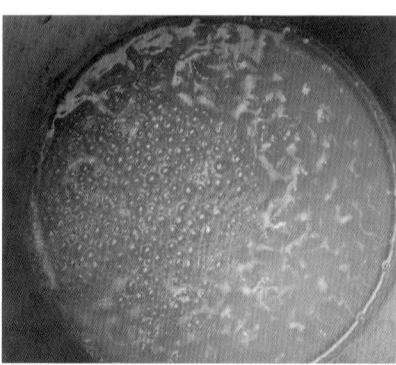

3 Pour the strained juice into a clean pan and simmer gently until thick and reduced by half its volume. Then test its pectin strength (see box, left).

4 Pour into small freezer pots (generally, 150ml/5fl oz of strong pectin stock will be sufficient to set 2kg (4½lb) of medium- or low-pectin fruit as jam).

5 Leave to cool, then seal, label, and refrigerate or freeze until required.

The best...
Fruits for jam
Berries and soft fruits

These fruits are classic ingredients for jam-making, as they mostly have thin skins, are juicy, and soften quickly with just a little added water. They make stunningly fruity jams.

Boysenberries
These large, succulent, piquant hybrid berries are excellent used either on their own or in mixed berry jams. They crop from late July to the end of August; pick and use promptly.

Tayberries
A hybrid that is similar to the loganberry, but has larger, sweeter fruits. The plant crops from July to early August. Pick the berries on a dry day and use immediately.

Raspberries
This berry makes a splendid jam (pp96–97). Both red and yellow varieties have a medium pectin content and usually set easily (in a wet season they are likely to have less pectin). Use the berries as soon as possible after picking.

STORING TIMES FOR JAMS
The amount of sugar you use to make jam is not only a question of taste, it determines how long you can keep the jam. A very sweet, traditional-tasting jam (made with equal quantities of sugar and fruit) can be stored for 12 months. A fruitier jam (containing a quarter less sugar), more suited to modern tastes, can be stored for 6 months. A semi-sweet jam (half quantities of sugar to fruit) should be refrigerated and used within 1 month.

Loganberries
A sweetly-sharp-flavoured fruit that is available from July to September. It generally sets reliably well and can be combined with other summer fruits. Remove the white inner core before using.

Strawberries

A quintessential summer jam fruit, strawberries have a low (and variable) pectin content and need extra pectin and acid to achieve a set (pp88–89). Pick in dry weather and make into jam without delay.

Blackberries

Cultivated blackberries are low-medium pectin fruits (wild brambles are low in pectin). Combine with apples for a classic autumn jam, or with other berries for a mixed berry jam.

Redcurrants

A high-pectin fruit with a pure fruit flavour that is invaluable for adding to mixed berry jams and low- and medium-pectin fruits to achieve a good set.

Blueberries

The pectin content of blueberries varies more than most fruits, ranging from medium to low. They are often combined with other summer fruits for jam.

Cranberries

The pectin content of cranberries can vary according to their ripeness. Fresh berries are likely to have more pectin than frozen ones. They taste lovely combined with apples or oranges for jam.

Blackcurrants

Summer would be unthinkable without blackcurrants, which are easy to grow and make one of the best and fruitiest jams, even with very ripe fruit.

Tree fruits

These fruits make jams that have a wealth of flavours and textures, be they everyday favourites such as plum jam or luxurious peach jams. Being firmer than soft fruits, they need more water to soften them first.

Apricots

Medium-pectin apricots make sensational jams, though their pectin and acid content can vary: some fruits will produce a softer set than others.

Greengages

These ambrosial plums are in season briefly in August and make the most luxurious of plum jams. They have a medium pectin content; unripe (green) fruits contain the most pectin.

Figs

These are low-pectin, low-acid fruits, but their satisfying texture makes thick, honeyed, exotic jams that taste glorious if served with soft cheeses.

Plums

Unripe plums and cooking plums, such as 'Czar' and 'Marjorie's Seedling', have a high-pectin content. Treat ripe and dessert plums as medium-pectin fruits.

Damsons

If you like jams that pack a punch, damsons, with their mouth-puckering astringency and uniquely rich flavour, are ideal. The fruits are high in pectin, so will set easily as a jam.

Pears

For a pear jam that sets well, combine this low-pectin, low-acid fruit with apples to increase the pectin content, or team with lemon or lime for added acid and flavour.

OTHER FRUITS

Apples
Gooseberries
Grapes
Melons
Mulberries
Quinces
Rhubarb

Nectarines

This low-pectin, low-acid fruit has a fabulous melt-in-the-mouth, silken texture. Nectarines, like peaches, make luxurious jams and, if combined with redcurrants, give a jam with a good set.

Peaches

High-pectin red- or white currants are a good natural partner for peaches, which are low in pectin and acid. Choose perfumed, just-ripe fruit to make memorable summer jams.

VEGETABLE JAMS

Though not generally well-known as ingredients for jam, certain vegetables make unusual sweet preserves that are guaranteed to delight. As they contain little or no pectin, vegetables don't produce a traditional firm set, but their bulky texture gives them a spreadable consistency when cooked that helps to make up for this. Depending on the vegetable, they can also be combined with apples, or made with added pectin stock or jam sugar. Vegetables suitable for making jam are carrots, aubergines, marrows, red peppers, squashes, and tomatoes.

Cherries

Both dessert cherries (low in pectin and acid) and cooking cherries such as 'Morello' cherries (medium pectin and acid content) make superlative jams. Dessert cherries need added pectin.

Carrots

Containing more pectin than most vegetables, carrots also have a natural sweetness, bright colour, and spreadable consistency when cooked that make them ideal for turning into jam.

Making simple fruit jam

Jams are the simplest of preserves: fruit cooked with sugar over a high heat until set. This method, suitable for all soft-skinned berries, produces a soft-set jam. Once opened, refrigerate and use within three to four weeks.

Raspberry jam

MAKES APPROX 450G (1LB) (2 SMALL JARS)

TAKES 25–30 MINUTES

KEEPS 6 MONTHS

INGREDIENTS

650g (1½lb) raspberries

Juice of ½ lemon

500g (1lb 2oz) granulated sugar

TIPS ON MAKING JAM

Technically, jam sets when sugar reaches 105°C (220°F) using a sugar thermometer. With a little experience, you can judge this by observing how jam boils. When it begins to boil rapidly, the mixture soon rises in the pan and becomes frothy, with masses of small bubbles. As the bubbles become large and "plop", that's the time to start testing (p89).

Jam that won't set is usually under-boiled or has low pectin (pp88–89); boil again briefly with extra pectin stock. Flavourless, dull, hard jam is over-boiled; next time start testing sooner. If jam has mould, next time sterilize jars properly, put on jam covers while the jam is hot, and don't store in a damp place. If your jam ferments, the fruit was over-ripe, the jam wasn't boiled long enough, has too little sugar, isn't well sealed, or has been stored in a warm place.

1 Put a small saucer in the fridge to cool. Wash the fruit only if needed and put in a preserving or large saucepan. Add the lemon juice and pour in 150ml (5fl oz) of water.

2 Simmer gently for 3–5 minutes to soften and release the juices from the fruit. Add the sugar, stir it in over a gentle heat until it has dissolved, then turn up the heat.

3 Bring the jam to a rolling boil. Boil for 5–10 minutes or until a setting point is reached. Take the pan off the heat to test for a set using the cold saucer (p89).

4 Ladle the jam into warm sterilized jars (p18) using a sterilized jam funnel, filling the jars almost to the brim.

5 Cover with discs of waxed paper, seal with cellophane covers and elastic bands, or metal lids, label, and store in a cool, dark place.

Sometimes called jumbleberry jam, this can be made with any assortment of juicy summer fruits, so choose what is plentiful and in season. Try blackberries, blackcurrants, redcurrants, or cherries in the mix, but keep the total weight the same.

Mixed berry jam

MAKES APPROX 350G (12OZ)
(1 MEDIUM JAR)

TAKES 20 MINUTES

KEEPS 6–9 MONTHS

INGREDIENTS

450g (1lb) mix of strawberries, raspberries, and blueberries, hulled if needed

450g (1lb) granulated sugar

Juice of 2 lemons

1 Put the fruit in a preserving pan or a large heavy-based saucepan and lightly crush it with the back of a wooden spoon.

2 Add the sugar and heat gently, stirring until the sugar has all dissolved. Turn up the heat and bring to the boil. When the jam reaches a rolling boil, cook for 5–10 minutes or until it reaches the setting point. Remove the pan from the heat while you test for a set (p89).

3 Use a skimmer to skim off any surface scum. Leave the jam to cool slightly so that a thin skin forms and the berries are evenly distributed throughout the jam. Ladle into a warm sterilized jar, cover with a waxed paper disc, seal, and label. Store in a cool, dark place, and refrigerate after opening.

Although they have a gentle flavour, blueberries are rich in antioxidants. Their low pectin and acid content makes for softer-set jams and conserves. Spread this glossy, dark jam on pancakes and waffles, spoon it over yoghurt, or try a little with soft cheeses.

Blueberry jam

MAKES APPROX 450G (1LB)
(2 SMALL JARS)

TAKES 40 MINUTES

KEEPS 6–9 MONTHS

INGREDIENTS

900g (2lb) blueberries

Juice of 2 lemons

675g (1½lb) granulated sugar

1 Put the blueberries, 150ml (5fl oz) of water, and the lemon juice into a preserving pan or a large heavy-based saucepan and bring to the boil, then simmer for 10–15 minutes to extract the pectin and soften the fruit.

2 Add the sugar, stir until it dissolves, then increase the heat and bring the mixture to the boil. Boil rapidly for 10–12 minutes, or until it reaches the setting point. Take the pan off the heat while you test for a set (p89).

3 With the pan still off the heat, use a large skimmer to skim any surface scum off the jam. Leave the jam to cool slightly, then ladle into warm sterilized jars, cover with discs of waxed paper, seal, and label. Store in a cool, dark place. Refrigerate after opening.

Blueberries
The skins of these juicy little berries are thin, so you don't need to add much water when you first heat the fruits to soften them.

It's important to simmer blackcurrants first in water to soften their skins, which are tougher than most fruits. These currants are rich in pectin and acid, so blackcurrant jam is one of the easiest jams to make, and reigns supreme with its intense fruity flavour.

Blackcurrant jam

MAKES APPROX 450G (1LB) (2 SMALL JARS)

TAKES 45 MINUTES

KEEPS 6–9 MONTHS

INGREDIENTS

500g (1lb 2oz) blackcurrants, washed

675g (1½lb) granulated sugar

Juice of 1 lemon

1 Put the fruit and 450ml (15fl oz) of water in a preserving pan or a heavy-based saucepan. Simmer the fruit gently for 15–20 minutes.

2 Add the sugar and lemon juice and and stir until dissolved. Then increase the heat and boil the jam rapidly for 10 minutes or until it reaches the setting point. Take the pan off the heat while you test for a set (p89).

3 Ladle the jam into warm sterilized jars, cover with discs of waxed paper, seal, and label. Store the jars in a cool, dark place. Refrigerate after opening.

Blackcurrants
These berries are so high in pectin that you only need to add lemon juice towards the end of cooking to cut through their richness and bring out their fabulous flavour.

A combination of flavours and textures makes this jam a little bit more special than most. The soft stem ginger enhances the jam, which tastes lovely in a pastry tart or spread as a filling in a sponge cake.

Rhubarb, pear, and ginger jam

MAKES APPROX 1KG (2¼LB) (3 MEDIUM JARS)

TAKES 45 MINUTES

KEEPS 9 MONTHS

INGREDIENTS

675g (1½lb) fresh rhubarb, rinsed and chopped into 2.5cm (1in) pieces

2 pears, peeled, cored, and chopped

800g (1¾lb) granulated sugar

Juice of 1 lemon

Juice of ½ orange

2 small balls of stem ginger, finely chopped

1 Put the rhubarb and pears in a preserving pan or a large heavy-based saucepan then tip in the sugar. Using a wooden spoon, stir all together.

2 Add the lemon juice, orange juice, and stem ginger and cook on a low heat, stirring continuously, until the sugar has all dissolved.

3 Raise the heat, bring to the boil, and cook at a rolling boil for 15–20 minutes or until the mixture reaches the setting point. Remove the pan from the heat while you test for a set (p89).

4 Ladle into warm sterilized jars, cover with discs of waxed paper, seal, and label. Store in a cool, dark place, and refrigerate after opening.

Enjoy this chunky, pear-packed, soft-set jam on buttered slices of crusty artisan bread or toast. Pears are low in pectin, so to ensure a good set use home-made pectin stock or jam sugar when you make it.

Pear jam

MAKES APPROX 1KG (2¼LB) (2 LARGE JARS)

TAKES 1 HOUR

KEEPS 9 MONTHS

INGREDIENTS

1kg (2¼lb) just-ripe pears, peeled and chopped into 2.5cm (1in) pieces

Juice of 2 lemons

Juice of 1 orange

600g (1lb 5oz) granulated sugar and 5–6 tbsp strong pectin stock (pp90–91), or use 600g (1lb 5oz) jam sugar (which has a quicker setting point)

1 Put the pears in a preserving pan or a large heavy-based saucepan with the lemon and orange juice and cook gently for 10 minutes.

2 Add the sugar (and pectin stock, if using) and heat gently, stirring until the sugar has all dissolved. Turn up the heat, bring to the boil, and boil rapidly for about 20 minutes or until the setting point is reached. Remove the pan from the heat while you test for a set (p89).

3 The pears will still be chunky, so carefully ladle the hot jam into warm sterilized jars, cover with discs of waxed paper, seal, and label. Store in a cool, dark place, and refrigerate after opening.

This recipe is designed to use a mixture of ripe and not-so-ripe fruit, which is often how you end up picking it! If you prefer to substitute greengages for plums, use just 200ml (7fl oz) of water, or use a lemon instead of a lime if you wish.

Plum and lime jam

MAKES APPROX 1.5KG (3LB 3OZ) (4 MEDIUM JARS)

TAKES 45 MINUTES

KEEPS 9 MONTHS

INGREDIENTS

900g (2lb) whole plums, washed

Grated zest and juice of 1 organic lime, washed

900g (2lb) granulated sugar

A knob of butter

1 Put the plums in a preserving pan or a large heavy-based saucepan and add 300ml (10fl oz) of water. Bring slowly to the boil, reduce the heat, and simmer gently for 20–30 minutes, depending on the ripeness of the fruit, until it is really pulpy.

2 Add the lime zest and juice and the sugar. Heat gently, stirring until all the sugar has dissolved. Stir in the knob of butter. Bring to the boil and boil rapidly for about 10 minutes or until the setting point is reached. Remove the pan from the heat while you test for a set (p89).

3 Use a slotted spoon to lift out the plum stones and skim off any surface scum, then ladle into warm sterilized jars, cover with discs of waxed paper, seal, and label. Store in a cool, dark place, and refrigerate after opening.

The addition of some port and cinnamon turns this into a rather special plum jam with more than a hint of festive flavours. This is a jam to enjoy in winter, dolloped onto hot steamed puddings, spread onto dark fruit tea breads, or given as a gift.

Spiced port and plum jam

MAKES APPROX 2KG (4½LB)
(6 MEDIUM JARS)

TAKES 45 MINUTES

KEEPS 9 MONTHS

INGREDIENTS

1.8kg (4lb) dark plums, halved and stoned

1 cinnamon stick, snapped in half

Juice of 1 lime

1.35kg (3lb) granulated sugar

2–3 tbsp port (depending on
   your taste preference)

1 Put the plums, cinnamon stick, and lime juice into a preserving pan or a large heavy-based saucepan, then pour over 600ml (1 pint) of water.

2 Simmer gently on a low heat for 15–20 minutes or until the plums begin to break down and soften.

3 Add the sugar, stir until it has all dissolved, then bring to the boil and keep at a rolling boil for 5–8 minutes or until the jam begins to thicken and reaches the setting point. Remove the pan from the heat while you test for a set (p89).

4 Discard the cinnamon stick, stir in the port, then ladle into warm sterilized jars, cover with waxed paper discs, seal, and label. Store in a cool, dark place, and refrigerate after opening.

Plums
Grown widely in the USA and Europe, plums crop prolifically. Any dark red, purple, or blue variety, such as 'Czar' (shown here), works well. Select just-ripe fruit.

Rum enhances the flavour of plums superbly. Although most of the fruit will disintegrate as you cook this jam, the occasional piece of succulent plum may remain, adding welcome texture. Try this on dark, wholegrain pumpernickel or rye breads.

Plum and rum jam

MAKES APPROX 1.5KG (3LB 3OZ) (4 MEDIUM JARS PLUS 1 SMALL JAR)

TAKES 1½ HOURS

KEEPS 9 MONTHS

INGREDIENTS

1kg (2¼lb) plums, washed, halved, and stoned

1kg (2¼lb) granulated sugar

3 tbsp dark rum

1 Place the plums in a preserving pan or a large heavy-based saucepan with 250ml (9fl oz) of water and bring to the boil.

2 Simmer for 30 minutes until the plums have softened, then add the sugar and heat gently, stirring until the sugar has all dissolved.

3 Bring to the boil. When the jam reaches a rolling boil, cook for 5–10 minutes or until the setting point is reached. Remove the pan from the heat while you test for a set (p89).

4 Add the rum and mix well, then ladle into warm sterilized jars, cover with discs of waxed paper, seal, and label. Store in a cool, dark place, and refrigerate after opening.

The flavour of both gooseberries and raspberries comes through distinctly in this jam, making it delectable not only as a spread on good bread or scones but also warmed with a little water as a sauce to spoon over sponge pudding or ice cream.

Gooseberry and raspberry jam

MAKES APPROX 1.1KG (2½LB)
(3 MEDIUM JARS PLUS 1 SMALL JAR)

TAKES 1 HOUR

KEEPS 9 MONTHS

INGREDIENTS

450g (1lb) gooseberries, topped and tailed

Grated zest of ½ organic lemon, washed

225g (8oz) raspberries

675g (1½lb) granulated sugar

Small knob of butter

1 Wash the gooseberries and put them in a preserving pan or a large heavy-based saucepan with 150ml (5fl oz) of water and the lemon zest. Bring to the boil, reduce the heat, cover, and cook gently until the gooseberries are soft and pulpy, about 30 minutes. Add the raspberries and cook just until their juices run.

2 Add the sugar and stir over a gentle heat until the sugar has dissolved. Bring to the boil and boil rapidly for about 15 minutes or until the setting point is reached. Remove the pan from the heat while you test for a set (p89).

3 Use a skimmer to skim off the surface scum, then stir in the butter to disperse any residual scum. Ladle into warm sterilized jars, cover with discs of waxed paper, seal, and label. Store in a cool, dark place, and refrigerate after opening.

Raspberries
A perennial soft fruit, raspberries are in season in mid- to late summer and again in autumn. They are prolific croppers, but also fragile – always pick on a dry day when using for jam. Tried and tested varieties are 'Malling Jewel', 'Malling Admiral', and 'Autumn Bliss'.

This fruit jam has just a hint of brandy to help cut through the sweetness of the cherries. Unless you own a cherry pitter, it's probably easiest to halve the fresh cherries first before removing their stones. Serve as a topping on scones or soft cheeses.

Cherry jam

MAKES APPROX 1KG (2¼LB)
(3 MEDIUM JARS)

TAKES 45 MINUTES

KEEPS 9 MONTHS

INGREDIENTS

500g (1lb 2oz) dark cherries, stoned, with the stones reserved

Juice of 2 lemons

500g (1lb 2oz) granulated sugar and 6 tbsp strong pectin stock (pp90–91), or use 500g (1lb 2oz) jam sugar (which has a quicker setting point)

2 tbsp brandy or cherry brandy

1 Place the cherry stones in a small square of muslin, gather into a small bag, and tie with string. Put the cherries in a preserving pan or a large heavy-based saucepan and pour in 300ml (10fl oz) of water. Bring to the boil, then reduce to a simmer and cook for 10–15 minutes or until the cherries are tender and begin to soften. If you want some of the cherries to remain chunky in the jam, don't cook them for too long.

2 Pour in the lemon juice and add the sugar (and pectin stock, if using). Heat gently, stirring until the sugar has all dissolved. Bring to the boil and keep at a steady rolling boil, stirring occasionally, for about 10 minutes or until it reaches the setting point. Remove the pan from the heat while you test for a set (p89).

3 Stir in the brandy, then ladle into warm sterilized jars, cover with discs of waxed paper, seal, and label. Store in a cool, dark place, and refrigerate after opening.

Redcurrants add flavour and pectin and are a natural partner for ripe strawberries when you want an extra fruity red jam. This soft-set jam is ideal as a filling in cakes and desserts, or serve with soft cheese or hot or cold rice pudding.

Strawberry and redcurrant jam

MAKES APPROX 1.5KG (3LB 3OZ) (4 MEDIUM JARS)

TAKES 55 MINUTES

KEEPS 6 MONTHS

INGREDIENTS

1.1kg (2½lb) strawberries, hulled and roughly chopped

Zest and juice of 2 organic lemons, washed

175g (6oz) redcurrants

800g (1¾lb) granulated sugar and 5 tbsp strong pectin stock (pp90–91), or use 800g (1¾lb) jam sugar (which has a quicker setting point)

1 Put the strawberries, lemon zest and juice, and redcurrants in a preserving pan or a large heavy-based saucepan and cook for a few minutes until the berries begin to soften, but some still retain their shape.

2 Add the sugar (and pectin stock, if using) and heat gently, stirring until the sugar has all dissolved. Turn up the heat and bring to the boil. When the jam reaches a rolling boil, cook for 10–20 minutes or until it reaches the setting point. Remove the pan from the heat while you test for a set (p89).

3 Ladle into warm sterilized jars, cover with discs of waxed paper, seal, and label. Store in a cool, dark place, and refrigerate after opening.

This classic soft-set jam is divine with thick cream and scones. In hot dry weather, freshly picked organic or outdoor-grown strawberries should have sufficient pectin to set well; if using bought strawberries, or the season is wet, use jam sugar.

Strawberry jam

MAKES APPROX 1KG (2¼LB) (3 MEDIUM JARS)

TAKES 1 HOUR

KEEPS 9 MONTHS

INGREDIENTS

1kg (2¼lb) strawberries, hulled and halved

6 tbsp lemon juice

900g (2lb) granulated sugar and 5–6 tbsp strong pectin stock (pp90–91), or use 900g (2lb) jam sugar (which has a quicker setting point)

1 Put the berries and lemon juice in a preserving pan or a large heavy-based saucepan and cook gently for 5–10 minutes or until the berries are soft.

2 Add the sugar (and pectin stock, if using) and heat gently, stirring until the sugar has all dissolved. Turn up the heat and bring to the boil. When the jam reaches a rolling boil, cook for 15 minutes or until it reaches the setting point. Remove the pan from the heat while you test for a set (p89).

3 Use a skimmer to skim off any surface scum. Leave the jam to cool slightly so that a thin skin forms and the berries are evenly distributed throughout the jam. Ladle into warm sterilized jars, cover with discs of waxed paper, seal, and label. Store in a cool, dark place, and refrigerate after opening.

Strawberries
Pick strawberries when they become darker in colour, but are still just ripe and not too soft. Use the strawberries as soon as you can after picking, as they do not keep well.

A rich, densely fruity jam such as this can be served with sweet or savoury food – it's delicious with some cold ham or cheese. Add two teaspoons of chopped crystallized ginger to the figs as they cook, or add a splash of ginger wine at the end, if you wish.

Fig and vanilla jam

MAKES APPROX 1.1KG (2½LB)
(3 MEDIUM JARS PLUS 1 SMALL JAR)

TAKES 50–55 MINUTES

KEEPS 6 MONTHS

INGREDIENTS

675g (1½lb) ripe figs with soft skins, topped and tailed and cut into quarters

Zest and juice of 1 organic lemon, washed

1 small cooking apple, peeled, cored, and roughly chopped

1 vanilla pod, sliced lengthways

675g (1½lb) granulated sugar

1 Put the figs in a preserving pan or a large heavy-based saucepan with the lemon zest and juice, chopped apple, and vanilla pod. Cook on a low heat for about 20 minutes or so, stirring occasionally, until the figs have softened and broken down.

2 Add the sugar and cook on a low heat, stirring continuously, until the sugar has all dissolved. Then bring to the boil and cook at a rolling boil, stirring occasionally, for about 15–20 minutes or until it reaches the setting point. Skim away any scum as it cooks. Remove the pan from the heat while you test for a set (p89).

3 Carefully remove the vanilla pod, then ladle into warm sterilized jars, cover with discs of waxed paper, seal, and label. Store in a cool, dark place, and refrigerate after opening.

Apricots make luscious, richly flavoured jams; cooking them with sugar enriches their flavour and texture. These fruits have a medium pectin and acid content, so adding lemon juice helps to achieve a good set. Spread on fresh bread or toast.

Apricot jam

MAKES APPROX 1KG (2¼LB) (3 MEDIUM JARS)

TAKES 40 MINUTES

KEEPS 6–9 MONTHS

INGREDIENTS

675g (1½lb) apricots, stoned and roughly chopped

1 tbsp lemon juice

675g (1½lb) granulated sugar and 5–6 tbsp strong pectin stock (pp90–91), or use 675g (1½lb) jam sugar (which has a quicker setting point)

1 Put the apricots, lemon juice, and 150ml (5fl oz) of water in a preserving pan or a large heavy-based saucepan. Gently bring to the boil and simmer, stirring occasionally, for 15 minutes or until the apricot skins are soft and the fruit is tender.

2 Add the sugar (and pectin stock, if using) to the pan and stir until completely dissolved. Increase the heat and bring the mixture to the boil, then boil without stirring for 10 minutes or until it reaches the setting point. Remove the pan from the heat while you test for a set (p89).

3 With the pan still off the heat, use a skimmer to remove any scum from the surface. Ladle into warm sterilized jars, cover with discs of waxed paper, seal, and label. Store in a cool, dark place, and refrigerate after opening.

Apricots
Look for larger apricots when making this jam, and ensure that they are just ripe rather than very soft.

This classic jam has been enlivened with a little dessert wine and fruit juice: it tastes lovely and fresh, and the orange and lemon juice give it an appealing sharpness. It is equally delicious on toast, used in sweet tarts and pastries, or spooned on yoghurt.

Apricot, orange, and Sauternes jam

MAKES APPROX 1.5KG (3LB 3OZ) (4 MEDIUM JARS PLUS 1 SMALL JAR)

TAKES 1 HOUR

KEEPS 6–9 MONTHS

INGREDIENTS

900g (2lb) apricots, stoned and roughly chopped

Juice and zest of 1 organic lemon, washed

Juice of 3 large oranges

900g (2lb) granulated sugar and 5–6 tbsp strong pectin stock (pp90–91), or use 900g (2lb) jam sugar (which has a quicker setting point)

1–2 tbsp Sauternes, depending on how much alcohol you like

1 Put the apricots in a preserving pan or a large heavy-based saucepan and add the lemon juice and zest, and the orange juice. Put the pan on a medium heat, bring the ingredients to simmering point, and simmer for 15–20 minutes or until the apricots are soft.

2 Add the sugar (and pectin stock, if using) and stir over a gentle heat until it has all dissolved. Then bring to the boil and cook at a rolling boil for 20 minutes or until it reaches the setting point. Remove the pan from the heat while you test for a set (p89).

3 Stir in the Sauternes and ladle into warm sterilized jars, cover with discs of waxed paper, seal, and label. Store in a cool, dark place, and refrigerate after opening.

This orange-scented jam has a great colour and subtle, spiced flavour. It is as tasty served with savoury foods, such as tangy blue cheese, as it is spread on toast. Choose smaller pumpkins with smooth flesh and a good flavour.

Pumpkin and orange spiced jam

MAKES APPROX 2KG (4½LB)
(4 LARGE JARS)

TAKES 50 MINUTES

KEEPS 6 MONTHS

INGREDIENTS

1.4kg (3lb) pumpkin, peeled, deseeded, and cut into small pieces

2 cooking apples, peeled, and chopped into small pieces

1.35kg (3lb) granulated sugar

Juice of 1 lemon

Juice of 1 orange

Pinch of cinnamon

Pinch of freshly grated nutmeg

1 Put the pumpkin and apple in a preserving pan or a large heavy-based saucepan. Pour in 50ml (2fl oz) of water (just enough to stop the pumpkin from catching and burning). Bring to the boil, then reduce to a simmer and cook for 10–20 minutes or until the pumpkin is soft. Mash roughly with a potato masher or fork, keeping a few chunks of pumpkin whole.

2 Add the sugar, lemon and orange juice, cinnamon, and nutmeg. Stir until all the sugar has dissolved. Then turn the heat up and bring to the boil. Cook at a rolling boil for 15–20 minutes or until the jam thickens and reaches the setting point. Remove the pan from the heat while you test for a set (p89).

3 Ladle into warm sterilized jars, cover with waxed paper discs, seal, and label. Store in a cool, dark place, and refrigerate after opening.

Pumpkins
There are a huge variety of pumpkins and squashes in all shapes and sizes. For sweet preserves, use those with a sweet, smooth, denser flesh, such as 'Jack Be Little' shown here, rather than fibrous varieties.

This traditional preserve uses young fresh marrows when they are in season. The orange lends a distinct sweetness and depth to the marrow, giving it a lovely fresh flavour. Use as a spread, or put a dollop on top of yoghurt for a refreshing dessert.

Marrow and orange jam

MAKES 1.5KG (3LB 3OZ)
(4 MEDIUM JARS PLUS 1 SMALL JAR)

TAKES 40–45 MINUTES

KEEPS 9 MONTHS

INGREDIENTS

1 large marrow (approx 900g/2lb), peeled and cut into 1cm (½in) pieces

Juice of 2 lemons

Juice of 1 orange and zest of 2 large organic oranges, washed

900g (2lb) granulated sugar and 5–6 tbsp strong pectin stock (pp90–91), or use 900g (2lb) jam sugar (which has a quicker setting point)

1 Put the marrow pieces and lemon juice in a preserving pan or a large heavy-based saucepan. Bring to the boil and simmer gently for about 15 minutes or until the marrow starts to soften. Add a little water if it starts to dry out too much and be careful it doesn't burn. This will all depend on the water content of your marrow.

2 Add the sugar (and pectin stock, if using) and orange juice and zest and heat gently, stirring until the sugar has all dissolved. Turn up the heat and bring to the boil. When the jam reaches a rolling boil, cook for about 20 minutes or until it reaches the setting point. Remove the pan from the heat while you test for a set (p89).

3 Leave the jam for 5–10 minutes so that the marrow peices are evenly distributed throughout the jam, then ladle into warm sterilized jars, cover with discs of waxed paper, seal, and label. Store in a cool, dark place, and refrigerate after opening. The flavours will improve with keeping.

Tomato jam is traditionally a sweet jam, but here it has been adapted slightly to give it a savoury note. You can make a simple sweet tomato jam by omitting the chilli and herbs, if you prefer. Serve with cheese, on burgers, or with sausages.

Tomato and chilli jam

MAKES 350G (12OZ)
(1 MEDIUM JAR)

TAKES 40–45 MINUTES

KEEPS 6 MONTHS

INGREDIENTS

500g (1lb 2oz) tomatoes, plunged into boiling water for 1 minute and then peeled and roughly chopped

1 tsp chilli flakes

1 tsp dried mixed herbs

Juice of 1 lemon

Pinch of salt

250g (9oz) granulated sugar

1 Put all the ingredients except the sugar into a preserving pan or a large heavy-based saucepan. Bring to the boil and simmer gently for about 8 minutes or until the tomatoes break down and soften.

2 Add the sugar and heat gently, stirring until the sugar has all dissolved. Turn up the heat and bring to the boil. When the jam reaches a rolling boil, cook for 10–15 minutes or until it starts to thicken and become glossy and reaches the setting point (stir occasionally to prevent the jam sticking or burning in the pan). Remove the pan from the heat while you test for a set (p89).

3 Ladle into a warm sterilized jar, cover with a disc of waxed paper, seal, and label. Store in a cool, dark place, and refrigerate after opening.

The best ingredients for...
Conserves

Use the finest, juiciest, and most fragile fruits for conserves, which represent the zenith of jam-making. Other thin-skinned succulent fruits are also well-suited, and make handsome conserves.

Blackberries
These berries need time to reach perfection and become plump, sweet, and ebony blue-black. Choose only the best berries for conserves, and remove the inner core first.

Greengages
This exquisite variety of plum, with its honeyed sweetness, needs no other flavourings. Choose scented fruit showing a golden blush.

Dessert pears
Pears make gentle tea-time conserves. Choose dessert pears with a buttery flesh and copious juice, and flavour with lemon, lime, ginger, pear liqueur, or scented geranium leaves.

Apricots

Conserves made with fragrant apricots are unrivalled for flavour (pp124–25). Add a few cracked kernels or Amaretto for a finishing touch.

OTHER INGREDIENTS

Boysenberries
Grapes
Melons
Mulberries
Peaches
Raspberries
Tayberries

Loganberries

A hybrid berry with a richer flavour than raspberries, and equally as juicy. Pick perfect, just-ripe fruit for conserves in dry, warm weather.

Blueberries

This mild-flavoured berry is ideal for conserves used either on its own, jazzed up with citrus fruit, or as part of a mixed berry conserve.

Figs

These luscious fruits make classy conserves. Choose fine-flavoured, thin-skinned varieties that just yield when gently pressed. Snip off the stalks first.

Strawberries

Small whole fruits (even tiny wild strawberries) are best for conserves. Pick just-ripe fruit with care in warm, dry weather without squashing the berries.

Cherries

Black 'Morello' cherry is the classic sour cherry for making conserves, but any seasonal freshly picked black, red, or yellow-skinned cherries make delectable conserves.

Nectarines

The soft, juicy flesh of nectarines is perfect for conserves, and is heavenly if combined with strawberries (their paper-thin skin should peel easily when ripe).

Making fruit conserve

Conserves differ from jams in that they contain large pieces of fruit or whole fruits, the fruits are steeped in sugar before cooking to firm them up, and they are boiled more gently than jam. Serve on toast or bread, muffins, or scones.

Apricot conserve

MAKES 700G (1½LB) (2 MEDIUM JARS)

TAKES 25–30 MINUTES, PLUS STANDING TIME

KEEPS 6 MONTHS

INGREDIENTS

500g (1lb 2oz) ripe apricots

350g (12oz) granulated sugar

Juice of 1 lemon

ABOUT CONSERVES

The term "conserve" is a European term to describe jams. They can be used in different ways, such as glazes for fruit tarts and flans, as cake fillings, or on yoghurt. Potting them into pretty jars shows them at their best.

Conserves can be made with a standard amount of sugar, or less for a fresher flavour. They can be made more luxurious by adding a small glass of wine when the sugar is added, or a splash of liqueur or spirit just before potting. To keep juicy fruit such as melons or pears intact, set the fruit aside in step 3 and boil the sugar and juices until reduced in volume. Then add the fruit and complete the boiling process.

1 Put a small saucer in the fridge to cool. Wash the apricots briefly only if they need it. Cut the fruits in half and stone them.

2 Layer the apricots and sugar in a large bowl, cover, and leave for several hours or overnight at room temperature.

3 Put the fruit and sugar in a preserving pan with the lemon juice. Heat gently, stirring to dissolve the sugar, but being careful not to break up the fruit.

4 Raise the heat and bring to a steady – rather than a fast – boil for 7–10 minutes until a setting point is achieved. Try not to stir the ingredients unless necessary.

5 Take the pan off the heat, test for a set with the cold saucer (p89), then leave to cool a little until it has formed a wrinkle on the surface – this helps the fruit to distribute evenly, rather than rise to the top of the jar, when potted.

6 Ladle into clean, hot, sterilized jars, ensuring an even amount of juice and fruit per jar.

7 Cover with discs of waxed paper, seal with cellophane covers and elastic bands, or metal lids, label, and store in a cool, dark place.

The addition of a little champagne or sparkling wine transforms this classic conserve into a premium preserve for special occasions, or to give away as a present. Its golden-orange colour and fresh, fruity tang should make it an instant favourite.

Apricot and champagne conserve

MAKES APPROX 675G (1½LB) (3 SMALL JARS)

TAKES 40–50 MINUTES, PLUS STANDING TIME

KEEPS 6 MONTHS

INGREDIENTS

500g (1lb 2oz) ripe apricots, stoned and chopped

300g (10oz) granulated sugar and 3 tbsp strong pectin stock (pp90–91), or use 300g (10oz) jam sugar (which has a quicker setting point)

Juice of 1 lemon

200ml (7fl oz) champagne or dry sparkling wine

1 Layer the fruit and sugar in a large bowl, cover, and leave for several hours or overnight at room temperature.

2 Put the fruit, sugar (and pectin stock, if using), lemon juice, and champagne in a preserving pan or a large heavy-based saucepan and simmer gently for 10–12 minutes or until the apricots become quite soft.

3 Turn up the heat and bring to the boil. When the jam reaches a rolling boil, cook for about 10 minutes or until it reaches the setting point. It will begin to set very quickly, so test frequently. Remove the pan from the heat while you test for a set (p89).

4 Ladle into warm sterilized jars, cover with discs of waxed paper, seal, and label. Store in a cool, dark place, and refrigerate after opening.

Ripe summer fruits are combined here to produce a beautifully red-orange-coloured, soft-set conserve. The relatively low sugar content gives it a freshness, while the chunks of peach and the raspberry seeds add texture. Use in desserts or as a spread.

Peach and raspberry conserve

MAKES APPROX 900G (2LB)
(3 MEDIUM JARS)

TAKES 45 MINUTES–1 HOUR,
PLUS STANDING TIME

KEEPS 6 MONTHS

INGREDIENTS

700g (1½lb) just-ripe peaches,
  stoned and diced

175g (6oz) fresh raspberries

400g (14oz) granulated sugar and
  3–4 tbsp strong pectin stock (pp90–91),
  or use 400g (14oz) jam sugar (which
  has a quicker setting point)

Juice of 1 lemon

1 Layer the fruit and sugar in a large bowl, cover, and leave for several hours or overnight at room temperature.

2 Put the fruit, sugar (and pectin stock, if using), and lemon juice in a preserving pan or a large heavy-based saucepan and cook at a gentle simmer for 15 minutes until the fruit softens.

3 Turn up the heat and bring to the boil. When the jam reaches a rolling boil, cook for about 10 minutes or until it reaches the setting point. Remove the pan from the heat while you test for a set (p89).

4 Ladle into warm sterilized jars, cover with discs of waxed paper, seal, and label. Store in a cool, dark place, and refrigerate after opening.

This rich, chunky conserve is just as delicious spooned onto ice cream as it is on freshly baked bread. Use really ripe peaches for this recipe – they will be full of flavour and wonderfully scented. You could use ripe nectarines instead, if you prefer.

Peach and walnut conserve

MAKES APPROX 1KG (2¼LB)
(3 MEDIUM JARS)

TAKES 45 MINUTES,
PLUS STANDING TIME

KEEPS 6 MONTHS

INGREDIENTS

1.25kg (2¾lb) ripe peaches

1 orange, peeled (but with pith still attached), and finely sliced

900g (2lb) granulated sugar

Juice of 1 lemon

50g (2oz) walnuts, roughly chopped

1–2 tbsp brandy (optional)

1 Cut a cross in the skin of the peaches and plunge them in a bowl of boiling water for 30 seconds. Then plunge in cold water, remove, and peel away the skins. Cut the peaches in half, remove the stones and reserve them, and roughly chop the flesh. Layer the peaches and orange slices in a large bowl with the sugar, cover, and leave for at least 4 hours or overnight.

2 Tip the fruit and sugar into a preserving pan or a large heavy-based saucepan. Place the peach stones in a small square of muslin, gather into a small bag, tie with string, and add it to the pan. Cook over a gentle heat, stirring until the sugar dissolves. Then bring to the boil and cook at a gentle rolling boil for 15–20 minutes or until the setting point is reached. Remove the pan from the heat while you test for a set (p89).

3 Remove the muslin bag of peach stones, then stir in the lemon juice, walnuts, and brandy (if using). Ladle into warm sterilized jars, cover with discs of waxed paper, seal, and label. Store in a cool, dark place, and refrigerate after opening.

The addition of a little mint adds a subtle hint of flavour to this deep-red sweet conserve. If you like a little alcohol in your preserves, or prefer a slightly richer flavour, stir a tablespoon of kirshe into the jam before you pot it up.

Raspberry and mint conserve

MAKES APPROX 900G (2LB) (3 MEDIUM JARS)

TAKES 45 MINUTES, PLUS STANDING TIME

KEEPS 9 MONTHS

INGREDIENTS

675g (1½lb) raspberries

500g (1lb 2oz) granulated sugar

A handful of fresh mint, very finely chopped

Juice of 1 lemon

1 Layer the fruit and sugar in a large bowl, cover, and leave for several hours or overnight at room temperature.

2 Put the fruit and sugar, mint, and lemon juice in a preserving pan or a large heavy-based saucepan and cook gently for 5–8 minutes until the raspberries are just beginning to break down and release their juices.

3 Increase the heat until the jam reaches a rolling boil and cook for 5–10 minutes or until it reaches the setting point. Keep a close eye on it, as it will set very quickly. Remove the pan from the heat while you test for a set (p89).

4 Ladle into warm sterilized jars, cover with discs of waxed paper, seal, and label. Store in a cool, dark place, and refrigerate after opening.

This fabulous soft-set breakfast conserve will awaken your taste buds in the morning with its pleasant zing. If you want to increase the balance of berries to citrus flavours, a tablespoon of cassis will taste delicious if added before potting the conserve.

Blueberry, lemon, and lime conserve

MAKES APPROX 900G (2LB) (3 MEDIUM JARS)

TAKES 45 MINUTES, PLUS STANDING TIME

KEEPS 6 MONTHS

INGREDIENTS

600g (1lb 5oz) blueberries

600g (1lb 5oz) granulated sugar and 3–4 tbsp strong pectin stock (pp90–91), or use 600g (1lb 5oz) jam sugar (which has a quicker setting point)

Zest and segments of 2 organic lemons, washed (keep the segment membranes on unless you don't like pieces of white membrane in the jam)

Zest and segments of 2 organic limes, washed (keep the segment mebranes on unless you don't like pieces of white membrane in the jam)

1 Layer the fruit and sugar in a large bowl, cover, and leave for several hours or overnight at room temperature.

2 Put the blueberries, sugar (and pectin stock, if using), and lemon and lime zest and segments in a preserving pan or a large heavy-based saucepan. Cook on a low heat for about 6–8 minutes.

3 Increase the heat until the jam reaches a rolling boil and cook for 10–15 minutes or until it reaches the setting point. Remove the pan from the heat while you test for a set (p89).

4 Ladle into warm sterilized jars, cover with discs of waxed paper, seal, and label. Store in a cool, dark place, and refrigerate after opening.

Limes
Organic limes receive no post-harvest chemicals, are not waxed, and are a good choice whenever the zest is required. Choose limes that feel heavy, and store in the fridge.

It's worth preparing a rich cherry conserve such as this to make the most of the short cherry season. It should be a soft-set texture, so don't overcook it or it will turn sticky. The cassis added at the end of the cooking time gives a lovely depth to the flavour.

Cherry and cassis conserve

MAKES APPROX 1.1KG (2½LB)
(3 MEDIUM JARS PLUS 1 SMALL JAR)

TAKES 50 MINUTES,
PLUS STANDING TIME

KEEPS 9 MONTHS

INGREDIENTS

600g (1lb 5oz) whole cherries, stoned

300g (10oz) granulated sugar and
 3–4 tbsp strong pectin stock (pp90–91),
 or use 300g (10oz) jam sugar (which
 has a quicker setting point)

1 tsp vanilla extract

Juice of 2 lemons

4 tbsp cassis

1 Layer the fruit and sugar in a large bowl, cover, and leave for several hours or overnight at room temperature.

2 Put the fruit, sugar (and pectin stock, if using), vanilla, and lemon juice in a preserving pan or a large heavy-based saucepan and cook gently for 15 minutes or until the cherries are soft.

3 Turn up the heat until the conserve reaches a rolling boil and cook for 5–8 minutes or until it reaches the setting point. Remove the pan from the heat while you test for a set (p89).

4 Stir in the cassis, then ladle into warm sterilized jars, cover with discs of waxed paper, seal, and label. Store in a cool, dark place, and refrigerate after opening.

This conserve delivers a real taste of late summer. If you like the idea of adding some finely grated lemon or orange zest to give a subtle tang, include it with the ingredients you add to the pan in step 2. It's best eaten spread on toast or added to a sweet pie.

Blackberry and apple conserve

MAKES APPROX 900G (2LB) (2 LARGE JARS)

TAKES 50 MINUTES, PLUS STANDING TIME

KEEPS 6 MONTHS

INGREDIENTS

300g (10oz) blackberries

300g (10oz) cooking apples, peeled and roughly chopped

500g (1lb 2oz) granulated sugar

Juice of 1 lemon

1 Layer the fruit and sugar in a large bowl, cover, and leave for several hours or overnight at room temperature.

2 Put the fruit and sugar, and lemon juice in a preserving pan or a large heavy-based saucepan and cook on a gentle heat until all the fruit is soft.

3 Turn up the heat until the conserve reaches a rolling boil and cook for 10–15 minutes or until it reaches the setting point. Don't overcook it, or it will become too jammy. Remove the pan from the heat while you test for a set (p89).

4 Ladle into warm sterilized jars, cover with discs of waxed paper, seal, and label. Store in a cool, dark place, and refrigerate after opening.

This classic soft-set conserve requires juicy whole strawberries bought in season. Steeping the strawberries in sugar helps draw out some of their juices and stops them breaking up too much while cooking. It tastes divine served with thick cream and scones.

Strawberry conserve

MAKES APPROX 1KG (2¼LB) (3 MEDIUM JARS)

TAKES 45 MINUTES, PLUS STANDING TIME

KEEPS 6 MONTHS

INGREDIENTS

900g (2lb) juicy strawberries, hulled

900g (2lb) granulated sugar

Juice of 1 lemon

Juice of 1 lime

1 Layer the strawberries and sugar in a large bowl, cover, and leave for several hours or overnight.

2 Tip the fruit and sugar into a preserving pan or a large heavy-based saucepan, cook over a low heat, stirring continuously, until the sugar has all dissolved. Then boil gently for about 5 minutes, just enough for the fruit to soften but not to break up too much. Remove the pan from the heat, cover it loosely with some muslin, and leave the cooked fruit overnight.

3 Remove the muslin, put the pan back on the heat, stir in the lemon and lime juice and bring to the boil. Boil gently for 5–10 minutes or until thickened and the setting point is reached, skimming any scum off the surface as needed. Remove the pan from the heat while you test for a set (p89).

4 Ladle into warm sterilized jars, cover with discs of waxed paper, seal, and label. Store in a cool, dark place, and refrigerate after opening.

The best ingredients for...
Jellies

The queen of preserves, jellies require fruits that are juicy or high in pectin, and preferably both. All the fruits illustrated here fit the bill admirably, and will make a range of stunning jellies to be proud of.

Grapes
These fruits produce delicate, sweet jellies (pectin levels vary so include a chopped organic lemon when making them). Flavour with perfumed spices such as cloves and cardamom, or lime instead of lemon.

Strawberries
These berries make delicate, fruity jellies (add a chopped organic lemon or lime to provide extra pectin). Choose ripe juicy fruits and flavour with basil.

Blackberries
Make a classic autumn jelly with blackberries and apple (to provide necessary pectin). Choose plump, deep-purple cultivated or wild bramble fruits, and flavour with cinnamon, cloves, or allspice.

Crab apples
High in pectin, crab apples can be used instead of apples for all sweet or savoury jellies. They taste excellent if combined with other hedgerow fruits.

Medlars
An ancient autumn fruit, traditionally used for jelly. Use when the flesh has turned soft and brown (known as "bletting"). They produce a mellow, subtle wine-flavoured jelly.

Redcurrants

Arguably, these currants make the best jelly of all: a pure, perfectly textured, and intensely fruity jelly. Use also with delicate low-pectin fruits such as strawberries.

Blackcurrants

For superb, richly flavoured jellies that set easily, use blackcurrants (you don't need the best quality, and they can be very ripe). For an extra indulgence, add cassis.

Chillies

A modern ingredient for savoury jellies, chillies add a fiery note to jellies made from apples and other fruit. Experiment with different kinds of dried chillies.

OTHER INGREDIENTS

FRUITS
Boysenberries
Damsons
Gooseberries
Loganberries
Mulberries
Nectarines (ripe)
Peaches (ripe)
Plums (all kinds)
Tayberries
White currants
WILD FRUITS
Rosehips
Rowanberries
Sloes
VEGETABLES
Red peppers
Tomatoes

Cranberries

For one of the best winter jellies, use cranberries. They also make good partners with apples, oranges, and cinnamon.

Apples

Ideal for all herb jellies, including unusual mixes such as lavender, lemongrass, and lemon verbena. Choose sour apples or windfalls (high in pectin) and include the core.

Raspberries

These berries produce clear, fruity jellies. For a scented version, flavour with rose petals or rosewater. For added pectin, combine with apples, lemon, or redcurrants.

Quinces

Another fruit traditionally used for jellies, quinces have their own unique apple-pear flavour (apples and pears are natural partners). Wait until the skins have turned yellow and are perfumed before using.

Making jellies

These beautiful jewel-like preserves are made from the strained juice of fruit. Red grapes produce a delicate garnet-coloured jelly that is delicious with roast poultry or cheeses. Halve the quantities if you wish.

Grape, lemon, and clove jelly

MAKES APPROX 1KG (2¼LB) (3 MEDIUM JARS)

TAKES 50 MINUTES–1 HOUR, PLUS STRAINING TIME

KEEPS 12 MONTHS

INGREDIENTS

1.5kg (3lb 3oz) under-ripe red grapes (with pips)

1 organic lemon, washed

Approx 750g (1lb 10oz) granulated sugar (see method)

½ tsp cloves

TIPS ON JELLY-MAKING

Use perfect fruit, slightly under-ripe, and for the freshest flavour boil for the minimum time to achieve a set. Prolonged boiling is detrimental and may mean the jelly will not set.

The quantity of strained juice always varies so calculate the sugar after measuring the juice.

The pectin content will also vary. To ensure there is sufficient pectin to achieve a set, simmer the fruit with a chopped organic lemon or test the strained juice for pectin first (p90). If there's not quite enough, either simmer the strained juice further and test again or, if low, use jam sugar.

---

1 Wash the grapes and chop them roughly. Put all the grapes in a preserving pan or a large heavy-based saucepan. Chop the lemon and add it to the pan together with 300ml (10fl oz) of water.

2 Bring to the boil, cover, and cook gently for 35–40 minutes, squashing the grapes with the back of a wooden spoon to a pulp as soon as they are soft enough to release their juice.

3 Strain the pulp through a jelly bag or clean nylon sieve set over a clean bowl. Leave to strain naturally until no more juice drips through. You can press the pulp if you wish to extract more juice, but this will result in a cloudy, rather than crystal-clear, jelly.

4 Measure the strained juice and calculate the quantity of sugar: allow 450g (1lb) of sugar for every 600ml (1 pint) of juice.

5 Put the juice, sugar, and cloves back into the pan, bring gently to the boil, stirring to dissolve the sugar, then boil rapidly for 5–10 minutes to reach the setting point.

6 Take the pan off the heat to test for a set (p89). Remove the cloves with a ladle if you wish, then skim off any surface scum with a skimmer.

7 Pot into warm sterilized jars, cover with waxed paper discs, seal, and label. Store in a cool, dark place and keep refrigerated once opened.

This beautiful deep red, clear jelly sets well, as cranberries are rich in pectin. It's not too sweet, and has a pure, tart, fruity flavour that is perfect with poultry, pork, sausages, and any cold meats. Once opened, it will keep well in the fridge for up to three weeks.

Cranberry jelly

MAKES APPROX 400G (14OZ) (2 SMALL JARS)

TAKES 1 HOUR 10 MINUTES, PLUS STRAINING TIME

KEEPS 6–9 MONTHS

INGREDIENTS

500g (1lb 2oz) fresh or frozen cranberries (discard any that have brown spots or are shrivelled)

1 tbsp lemon juice

Approx 500g (1lb 2oz) granulated sugar (see method)

1 Put the berries, 600ml (1 pint) of water, and lemon juice in a preserving pan or a large heavy-based saucepan and bring to the boil over a medium heat.

2 Turn the heat down, cover, and simmer for 25–30 minutes or until the cranberries are tender (frozen cranberries will soften sooner). Mash the berries to a pulp with a potato masher or fork.

3 Tip the pulp into a fine sieve or a clean jelly bag set over a large clean bowl and leave to strain for several hours or overnight until all the juice has dripped through.

4 Measure the strained juice and calculate the quantity of sugar (allow 450g/1lb of sugar per 600ml/1 pint of cranberry juice). Pour this juice into a clean preserving pan or a large heavy-based saucepan, add the sugar, and stir gently until all the sugar has dissolved.

5 Bring to the boil and boil steadily for 10–15 minutes, then remove the pan from the heat and test for the setting point (p89). Remove any surface scum from the jelly with a skimmer, then pot up immediately in warm sterilized jars (before it sets), cover with discs of waxed paper, seal, label, and store in a cool, dark place. Refrigerate after opening.

Just two ingredients are needed to make this wonderfully coloured jelly. Redcurrants are high in pectin so the jelly will set well, but only leave it a minute or so in between testing, as it can become too thick in an instant. It is delicious served with roast lamb.

Redcurrant jelly

MAKES APPROX 1KG (2¼LB) (3 MEDIUM JARS)

TAKES 30–45 MINUTES, PLUS STRAINING TIME

KEEPS 6–9 MONTHS

INGREDIENTS

900g (2lb) redcurrants

Approx 900g (2lb) granulated sugar (see method)

1 Add the redcurrants and their stalks and 600ml (1 pint) of water to a preserving pan or a large heavy-based saucepan and bring to the boil over a medium heat.

2 Turn the heat down and cook for about 10 minutes or until the currants are soft. Mash the currants to a pulp with a potato masher or a fork.

3 Tip the pulp into a fine sieve or a clean jelly bag set over a large clean bowl and leave to strain for several hours or overnight until all the juice has dripped through.

4 Measure the strained juice (you should have about 900ml–1.2 litres/1½–2 pints) and calculate the quantity of sugar (allow 450g/1lb of sugar per 600ml/1 pint of juice). Pour the juice into a clean preserving pan or a large heavy-based saucepan, add the sugar, and stir gently until all the sugar has dissolved.

5 Bring to the boil and cook on a rolling boil for 10–20 minutes or until the setting point is reached (start testing after 10 minutes). Remove the pan from the heat while you test for a set (p89). Pot up in warm sterilized jars, cover with discs of waxed paper, seal, label, and store in a cool, dark place. Refrigerate after opening.

This red-flecked, jewel-like jelly can be served with almost any savoury dish from cheese to lamb to give it a fiery kick. Use sour cooking apples (which have the most pectin), and your favourite type of chilli flakes or finely chopped dried chillies.

Chilli jelly

SPECIAL EQUIPMENT
JELLY BAG OR MUSLIN

MAKES APPROX 450G (1LB)
(2 SMALL JARS)

TAKES 1½ HOURS,
PLUS STRAINING TIME

KEEPS 9 MONTHS

INGREDIENTS

675g (1½lb) sour cooking apples with skin
   on, roughly chopped

Approx 675g (1½lb) granulated sugar
   (see method)

Juice of 1 lemon

1–2 tsp chilli flakes (depending on how
   hot you like it)

1 Put the chopped apples, including the cores and pips, in a preserving pan or a large heavy-based saucepan. Pour in 1.7 litres (3 pints) of cold water, bring to the boil, and simmer for 30–40 minutes or until the apples are mushy and completely stewed down. Mash them a little with a potato masher or a fork.

2 Spoon the pulpy mixture into a jelly bag or muslin-lined sieve set over a large clean bowl. Leave the juice to drip through naturally overnight. Don't be tempted to squeeze the pulp mixture if you want a crystal-clear jelly.

3 Measure the strained juice and calculate 450g (1lb) of sugar for every 600ml (1 pint) of juice (you should have about 1.7 litres/3 pints of juice). Pour the juice into a clean pan, bring to the boil, then add the sugar and lemon juice. Stir until the sugar has dissolved, then bring to a rolling boil and remove any scum that comes to the surface. Continue to boil, stirring occasionally, for 20–30 minutes or until the jelly reaches the setting point. Remove the pan from the heat while you test for a set (p89).

4 Leave to cool for 10 minutes, then stir in the chilli flakes. Ladle into warm sterilized jars, cover with discs of waxed paper, seal, and label. Store in a cool, dark place, and refrigerate after opening.

Make this jelly in autumn when crab apples are in abundance. You can add various aromatic flavours, such as rosemary or star anise, in step 1 or mix with rowan berries or rosehips. The jelly tastes delicious with roast poultry or pork.

Crab apple jelly

MAKES APPROX 1.35KG (3LB) (4 MEDIUM JARS)

TAKES 1 HOUR, PLUS STRAINING TIME

KEEPS 9 MONTHS

INGREDIENTS

1.1kg (2½lb) crab apples, washed and roughly chopped with pips and stalks left intact

Zest of 1 organic lemon, washed and thinly pared

Approx 900g–1.1kg (2–2½lb) granulated sugar (see method)

1 Put the crab apples (with pips and stalks) in a preserving pan or a large heavy-based saucepan, pour over 1.4 litres (2½ pints) of water, and add the lemon zest. Cook gently for 30 minutes or so, until the apples soften and become pulpy.

2 Tip the pulp into a nylon sieve set over a large clean bowl, or a jelly bag suspended over the bowl, and leave to strain. You can press the pulp gently to extract the juice, but if you want a crystal-clear jelly, let the juices drip naturally overnight without squeezing the bag.

3 Measure the juice and calculate 450g (1lb) of sugar for every 600ml (1 pint) of juice. Pour the juice back into a clean preserving pan or large, heavy-based saucepan and bring to a simmer over a moderate heat. Add the sugar and stir until it has all dissolved. Then bring to the boil and cook at a rolling boil for about 10 minutes or until the setting point is reached. Remove the pan from the heat while you test for a set (p89).

4 Skim off any surface scum with a skimmer. Then ladle into warm sterilized jars, cover with waxed paper discs, seal, and label. Store in a cool, dark place, and refrigerate after opening.

Slightly caramelized apples combine harmoniously with cider and sage to create this jelly of distinction, which is bound to become a favourite. Use good-quality strong cider (choose organic, if you prefer). The jelly is ideal served with roast pork or sausages.

Apple, cider, and sage jelly

MAKES APPROX 1.25KG (2¾LB)
(4 MEDIUM JARS)

TAKES 1½ HOURS,
PLUS STRAINING TIME

KEEPS 9 MONTHS

INGREDIENTS

450g (1lb) cooking apples,
   roughly chopped

1 organic lemon, washed and chopped

900g (2lb) granulated sugar

600ml (1 pint) dry cider

25g (scant 1oz) sage leaves,
   finely chopped

1 Put the apples and lemon in a preserving pan or a large heavy-based saucepan, and pour over 600ml (1 pint) of water. Bring to the boil, half cover, and simmer until the apples are reduced to a pulp, about 20–30 minutes. Then mash gently with a potato masher or fork.

2 Tip the pulp into a nylon sieve set over a large clean bowl, or a jelly bag suspended over the bowl, and leave to strain. You can press the pulp gently to extract the juice, but if you want a crystal-clear jelly, let the juices drip naturally overnight without squeezing the bag.

3 Measure the juice and calculate 450g (1lb) of sugar for every 600ml (1 pint) of juice. Pour the juice into a clean preserving pan with the cider and sage and bring to a simmer. Add the sugar and stir until it has all dissolved. Bring to the boil, then reduce the heat to a simmer and cook gently for about 20 minutes or until it reaches the setting point. Remove the pan from the heat while you test for a set (p89).

4 Leave to cool for 10 minutes (to ensure the chopped sage is distributed evenly), then ladle into warm sterilized jars, cover with waxed paper discs, seal, and label. Store in a cool, dark place, and refrigerate after opening.

Sage
An evergreen herb with grey-green, purple, or variegated leaves, sage has a distinctive taste that lifts the flavour of a jelly.

Herb jellies capture all the essence of the fresh herb used: tarragon jelly complements roast chicken perfectly, sage jelly marries well with roast pork, and this aromatic, robust rosemary jelly is best served with lamb. Make half quantities, if you wish.

Rosemary jelly

SPECIAL EQUIPMENT
JELLY BAG OR MUSLIN

MAKES APPROX 2KG (4½LB)
(6 MEDIUM JARS)

TAKES 1½ HOURS,
PLUS STRAINING TIME

KEEPS 9 MONTHS

INGREDIENTS

A large handful of rosemary sprigs

900g (2lb) sour cooking apples,
   roughly chopped

Approx 900g (2lb) granulated sugar
   (see method)

Juice of 1 lemon

Rosemary
This herb is a Mediterranean classic. Pick new shoots in summer when the essential oils (which contain the flavour) are at their highest.

1 Preheat the oven to 150°C (300°F/Gas 2). Strip the rosemary leaves from their stalks. Reserve the stalks and scatter the leaves onto a baking sheet and put in the oven for 30–40 minutes to dry out. Remove the dried leaves and put to one side.

2 Put the chopped apples, together with their cores and pips, into a preserving pan or a large heavy-based saucepan. Pour in 1.2 litres (2 pints) of water and add the reserved rosemary stalks. Bring to the boil, then simmer gently for 30–40 minutes or until the apples have turned to mush. Then mash them with a potato masher or fork.

3 Put the pulp into a jelly bag or a muslin-lined sieve and leave to strain overnight. Measure the strained juice and calculate the sugar: for every 600ml (1 pint) of juice use 450g (1lb) of sugar (you should have about 1.2 litres/2 pints of juice).

4 Put the strained juice, sugar, lemon juice, and dried rosemary leaves into a saucepan and heat over a moderate heat, stirring until the sugar has all dissolved. Bring to the boil and cook at a rolling boil for 20 minutes or until the jelly reaches the setting point. Remove the pan from the heat while you test for a set (p89).

5 Leave to cool for 10 minutes (to ensure the rosemary is distributed evenly). Ladle into warm sterilized jars, cover with waxed paper discs, seal, and label. Store in a cool, dark place, and refrigerate after opening.

The best ingredients for...
Fruit cheeses, butters, and curds

The main requirement for these versatile preserves is that the various fruits from which they are made are delicious and in plentiful supply. Enhance their taste by adding unusual flavourings or aromatic liqueurs.

Lemons
The original, and still the most popular, fruit for making fruit curds. Use ripe organic lemons to produce a refreshing, tangy fruit curd.

Plums
Use cooking plums or unripe dual-purpose plums such as 'Victoria' plums to make autumnal fruit butters or cheeses enlivened with spices or oranges.

Quinces
This fruit has a slightly grainy texture. Quince cheese, or membrillo (pp150–51), is the ultimate fruit cheese (and butter) and tastes utterly delicious.

Pears
Combine pears with quinces, apples, or cranberries to make spiced fruit butters and cheeses. Use fairly firm dessert pears, and flavour with cinnamon, cloves, or ground ginger.

Apples
These fruits are best for soft butters, but are often combined with quinces or damsons to make fruity cheeses. Use windfalls or cooking apples.

Oranges

All oranges, including blood oranges and tangerines, are good flavourings for fruit cheeses, butters, and curds. Seville oranges make a splendid sweet-sour winter fruit curd that is perfect for Christmas. Use organic oranges.

OTHER INGREDIENTS

Apricots fruit curds
Blackcurrants fruit curds
Boysenberries fruit butters and cheeses
Gooseberries fruit curds
Grapefruit fruit curds
Grapes fruit butters and cheeses
Greengages fruit butters and cheeses
Loganberries fruit butters and cheeses
Medlars fruit butters and cheeses
Mulberries fruit butters and cheeses
Tayberries fruit butters and cheeses

Limes

The uniquely tropical flavour of limes blends superbly well with butter and eggs to produce a fruit curd of distinction. Use ripe organic limes.

Blackberries

A surplus of ripe blackberries combined with apples is ideal for fruit butters and cheeses or a buttery autumn fruit curd.

Cranberries

Their sweet-sharp flavour and garnet colour make cranberries perfect for fruit butters and cheeses. Combine with apples or firm pears for added body.

Raspberries

Fruit curds are usually made with citrus fruits, but raspberries make a pleasant change and produce fresh-tasting curd.

Damsons

Like quinces, damsons make a superlative fruit cheese. They give consistent results, and have a magnificent concentrated flavour.

Making fruit cheeses

Fruit butters and cheeses are intensely flavoured fruit purées cooked until they are very concentrated. Butters have a spreadable texture, while cheeses are solid enough to slice. Serve membrillo, made from quinces, with a cheeseboard.

Membrillo

MAKES APPROX 750G–1KG
(1LB 10OZ–2¼LB)
(APPROX 6 X 150G/5½OZ
RAMEKIN DISHES)

TAKES 1½ HOURS

KEEPS 12 MONTHS
OR LONGER

INGREDIENTS

1kg (2¼lb) quinces, scrubbed

Juice ½ lemon

Approx 450g (1lb) granulated
sugar (see method)

FRUIT BUTTERS
AND CHEESES

To make fruit butter, simply stop the cooking halfway through the process of reducing the purée (step 4) so that it is a thick, but not yet stiff, paste. The butter is ready when a spoon pressed down on it leaves a clear indent.

Both butters and cheeses are long-keepers and can be used in innumerable ways: slice cheeses thinly and serve with cold meats and cheeses, or use as an after-dinner sweetmeat; or use butters and cheeses to enrich winter braises of meat and game and sweet or savoury wine sauces, to sweeten fruit compotes, or to give added flavour to fruit pies and crumbles. Since they are so concentrated, use them sparingly.

1 Roughly chop the whole quinces and put them in a preserving pan or a large heavy-based saucepan with 600ml (1 pint) of water. Add the lemon juice, bring to the boil, and simmer the ingredients for 30 minutes.

2 Once the fruit is soft enough, crush it with a potato masher or fork until it has become a soft, syrupy pulp. Leave the cooked pulp to one side to cool.

3 Sieve the pulp in batches over a large, clean bowl, pressing the pulp hard against the sieve with a wooden spoon to extract as much of the purée as possible (or use a mouli food mill). Measure the purée: for every 450ml (15fl oz), add 450g (1lb) of sugar.

4 Put the purée and sugar back in the pan and stir over a low heat to dissolve the sugar. Bring to the boil. Simmer gently for 45–60 minutes or longer. Near the end of cooking, watch and stir it so it doesn't burn.

5 The purée will reduce down to a dark, very thick, glossy paste. It is ready when it makes a "plopping" noise, sticks to the wooden spoon, and leaves a trail if the spoon is scraped across the bottom of the pan.

6 Lightly grease some warm sterilized ramekin dishes or moulds with a little oil. Spoon in the paste and level the top. Seal with waxed paper discs and cellophane if leaving in the ramekin dishes, otherwise leave to cool.

7 Loosen with a palette knife, turn out, and wrap in waxed paper. Leave to mature in a cool, dark place for 4–6 weeks.

If you can't find fresh cranberries for this recipe, use frozen berries instead, although they won't pop like the fresh fruits as they are heated and they soften much more quickly. Use as a sweet spread, a savoury accompaniment, or with freshly shelled nuts.

Cranberry and orange butter

MAKES APPROX 800G (1¾LB) (4 SMALL JARS)

TAKES 50 MINUTES

KEEPS 6 MONTHS

INGREDIENTS

450g (1lb) fresh or frozen cranberries

Approx 350–450g (12oz–1lb) granulated sugar (see method)

Approx 15g (½oz) butter (see method)

Juice and 1 tsp grated zest of 1 large sweet organic orange, washed

1 Put the cranberries and 300ml (10fl oz) of water into a preserving pan or a large heavy-based saucepan, cover, and bring to the boil, keeping the lid on until all the cranberries have popped.

2 Remove the lid and simmer the berries for 10 minutes or until they are soft. Then mash the berries to a pulp with a potato masher or fork.

3 Sieve the fruit in batches and collect the juice and purée in a clean bowl. Measure the purée (for every 600ml (1 pint) of purée, allow 350g (12oz) of sugar and 15g (½oz) butter; if the pulp seems very tart, allow 450g (1lb) of sugar). Put the purée, sugar, butter, orange juice, and zest in a preserving pan or a large heavy-based saucepan over a moderate heat. Stir gently until the sugar has dissolved.

4 Bring the ingredients to the boil, then simmer gently, stirring often, for about 40 minutes or until the mixture has reduced to a soft, moist, spreadable paste: a wooden spoon drawn across the bottom of the pan should leave a clear trail.

5 Ladle into warm sterilized jars. Cover with discs of waxed paper, seal, label, and store in a cool, dark place. Refrigerate after opening.

Cranberries
Look for berries that are dry and bright red, and discard any that are shrivelled or have brown spots. Cranberries can taste quite sharp, but when mixed with sugar they give a pleasant tang.

Apples make classic fruit butters and cheeses, and their subtle, sweet flavour combines well with warm spices and citrus fruit. This mild, sweet, soft spread is best enjoyed on good, fresh bread or in desserts.

Apple butter

MAKES APPROX 1KG (2¼LB)
(3 MEDIUM JARS)

TAKES 2 HOURS 25 MINUTES

KEEPS 6 MONTHS

INGREDIENTS

900g (2lb) cooking apples,
   roughly chopped

Juice of 1 orange

Pinch of ground allspice

Pinch of ground cinnamon

675g (1½lb) granulated sugar

1 Put the apples in a preserving pan or a large heavy-based saucepan and pour in 250ml (8fl oz) of water. Bring to the boil and simmer the apples for about 10 minutes or until they are soft.

2 Sieve the fruit in batches and collect the juice and purée in a clean bowl. Put this mixture back into the pan and add the orange juice, spices, and sugar. Cook on a low heat, stirring until the sugar has all dissolved.

3 Bring the mixture back up to boil and simmer gently for about 2 hours, or longer if needed, until the mixture thickens. Stir every so often so that it doesn't catch on the bottom of the pan.

4 The butter is ready when it is thick enough to rest on the back of a spoon without running off, or a wooden spoon drawn across the bottom of the pan leaves a clear trail. It should now be a soft, moist, spreadable paste.

5 Ladle into warm sterilized jars. Cover with discs of waxed paper, seal, label, and store in a cool, dark place. Refrigerate after opening.

This classic rich, glossy fruit cheese is packed with flavour and improves with keeping. For an added subtle flavour, stir in one or two teaspoons of rosewater. Serve sliced with cold meats and cheeses or as an after-dinner sweetmeat.

Damson cheese

MAKES APPROX 400G (14 OZ)
(2 SMALL JARS OR
3 X 150G/5½OZ RAMEKIN DISHES)

TAKES 2–2½ HOURS

KEEPS 2 YEARS

INGREDIENTS

1kg (2¼lb) damsons, stoned and chopped

Granulated sugar – for quantity,
   see method

15–30g (½–1oz) butter (optional)

1 Put the fruit in a preserving pan or a large heavy-based saucepan with 300ml (10fl oz) of water, bring to the boil, and simmer for 30–40 minutes until the fruit is reduced to a thick, syrupy pulp. Crush the fruit occasionally with a potato masher or fork as it cooks.

2 Sieve the fruit in batches and collect the juice and purée in a clean bowl. Measure the purée and add the sugar (for every 600ml/1pint of damson purée, allow 450g/1lb of sugar. If the purée seems tart, use 600g/1lb 5oz of sugar).

3 Put the purée back in the pan, and add the butter if you wish (this softens and mellows the sharpness of the damsons). Stir over a low heat to dissolve the sugar and bring to a gentle boil.

4 Simmer very gently for 35–45 minutes or longer, stirring often, until the pulp reduces to a black-purple glossy paste that "plops" and sticks to the wooden spoon, or will leave a clear trail if the spoon is drawn across the bottom of the pan.

5 Lightly oil some warm sterilized pots, ramekins, or moulds. Spoon in the cheese and level the top. Cover with discs of waxed paper and seal with cellophane covers if leaving in their pots. Otherwise leave to cool, turn out using a palette knife, and wrap in waxed paper or cling film. Label and store in a cool, dark place for at least 6–8 weeks before eating.

Damsons
As these fruits will be cooked, they can be picked once they develop their characteristic bloom on their skins and while they are still slightly under-ripe.

Why not try this buttery spread as a filling for a sponge cake? When adding the beaten eggs to the butter, sugar, and lemon juice, it's much better to whisk them in to avoid them scrambling. Once opened, the refrigerated curd will last three to four weeks.

Lemon curd

MAKES APPROX 750G (1LB 10OZ)
(3 SMALL JARS)

TAKES 15 MINUTES

KEEPS 6–9 MONTHS

INGREDIENTS

150g (5½oz) butter

450g (1lb) granulated sugar

Juice and zest of 4 organic lemons
(about 350ml/12fl oz in total)

4 very fresh small or medium eggs,
lightly beaten

1 Put the butter in a saucepan, let it melt over a medium heat, then add the sugar, lemon juice, and zest and stir until the sugar dissolves and no gritty bits remain in the mixture.

2 Turn the heat down low and add the beaten eggs to the pan with a hand whisk. Then stir the mixture for about 5–8 minutes until it starts to thicken.

3 Pour into warm sterilized jars, cover with discs of waxed paper, seal, and label. Store in a cool, dark place and refrigerate once opened.

Making easy candied peel

Home-made candied peel has much more flavour than bought varieties, is preservative-free, and a delicious addition to cakes or desserts or as a sweetmeat with coffee. This method is for citrus fruits, though wax-free peel from any fruit can be used.

Candied citrus peel

MAKES APPROX 225G (8OZ) (1 SMALL JAR)

TAKES 2 HOURS 5 MINUTES, PLUS STANDING TIME

KEEPS 6 MONTHS

INGREDIENTS

1 large or 2 small organic grapefruit, plus a pink organic grapefruit, or an organic pomelo (or a mixture of all three), washed

Granulated sugar – for quantity, see method

Caster sugar for coating

1 Score the surface of each piece of fruit into quarters with a sharp knife, then carefully remove the peel. Weigh the pieces of peel altogether. Put the peel in a saucepan, cover with water, and cook gently for up to 1 hour until soft, changing the water 2 or 3 times.

2 Drain the peel and scrape out any ragged or inner pulp from the inside of the shells. Either leave the peel in quarters, or cut into thick strips.

3 Use the same weight of sugar to peel. Put the prepared peel and sugar into a snug-fitting pan, barely cover with water, set over a low heat, and stir to dissolve the sugar. Bring to the boil and simmer very gently for 45 minutes or until the peel is translucent and has absorbed nearly all the syrup.

4 Remove the peel from the pan and spread it out on trays lined with baking parchment. Leave at room temperature for 24 hours or longer to dry out.

5 Dip each piece of dried peel in a bowl of caster sugar so it is thoroughly coated.

6 Place the sugared candied peel in a sterilized jar and seal. Store in a cool, dry place.

Crystallizing fruit

Nothing looks more impressive than a dish of home-made crystallized fruit. Choose firm fruits, such as apricots, cherries, peaches, pears, and figs, that are in perfect condition and just ripe (soft berries are not suitable).

Make a sugar syrup For every 450g (1lb) of fruit, use 175g (6oz) of granulated sugar and 300ml (10fl oz) of water (use the water the fruit was poached in, if applicable – see below). Put the sugar and water into a saucepan, heat gently, stir to dissolve the sugar, and bring to the boil.

Poach the fruit in syrup Peel the fruit, cut any large fruit in half, and remove any stones. If firm, poach apricots, cherries, plums, greengages, pineapple, kumquats, and figs in water first until just soft. Lay the fruit in a single layer in a shallow heatproof dish and pour over enough boiling syrup to cover it (make more syrup if needed). Leave for 24 hours. Then drain the syrup into a pan, add 60g (2oz) of granulated sugar, bring to the boil, pour over the fruit and leave for another 24 hours. Repeat every 24 hours for the next 3 days. On the 6th and 7th days, add 85g (3oz) of sugar to the drained syrup and repeat the process.

Dry the fruit After 8 days of poaching in syrup, lay the fruit on a wire rack with a tray beneath to catch drips. Dry in a very low oven (50–60°C/120–140°F/Gas ¼), turning once, for 1–2 hours or until the fruit no longer feels sticky.

Sugar-dipped crystallized figs

For a luxurious finish, dip the fruit briefly in boiling water, then dip or roll in caster sugar. Store in individual paper cases in a box or tin and separate each layer with waxed paper. They will last for 6 months.

Making marmalade

Marmalade is a classic seasonal breakfast preserve. It's made in the same way as jam, but with citrus fruit that gives marmalade its glorious tang. Citrus fruits require a long preliminary cooking period first to soften the peel.

Orange marmalade

MAKES APPROX 450G (1LB) (2 SMALL JARS)

TAKES 1¾–2 HOURS

KEEPS 12 MONTHS

INGREDIENTS

1kg (2¼lb) large sweet organic oranges, scrubbed, with stalks removed

2 organic lemons

1kg (2¼lb) granulated sugar

MARMALADE TIPS

Although marmalade is made with high-pectin citrus fruits, the pectin content can vary between batches, as some fruits are higher in acid and pectin than others.

The setting point of marmalade is also easy to miss; prolonged boiling will affect both flavour and set, so start testing early.

Sugar hardens the peel, so it's essential that you cook the fruit long enough to soften the peel before adding the sugar. To overcome this, adding a lemon is always a good idea.

The basic method of making marmalade is the same, though there are many different recipes. Differing amounts of sugar are also used, depending on whether the fruit is sweet or tangy.

1 Halve the oranges and lemons, squeeze the fresh juice into a jug, and reserve it in the fridge. Put the pith and pips in the centre of a muslin square and tie into a bundle with a length of string.

2 Put the citrus shells and 1.2 litres (2 pints) of water in a preserving pan. Tie the bag of pith and pips to the pan and add to the water. Bring to the boil, half cover, and simmer for 1 hour or until soft.

3 Tip the ingredients into a large colander over a bowl to collect the liquid: press lightly to extract maximum liquor and scoop out the mush from the shells with a spoon.

4 Using a sharp knife, slice the peel into evenly sliced thick or thin strands according to how you like it. Use as much or as little lemon peel as you wish.

7 Cover with discs of waxed paper, seal with cellophane covers and elastic bands, or metal lids, label, and store in a cool, dark place.

5 Add the liquor, sliced peel, reserved fruit juice, and sugar to a preserving pan. Heat gently, stirring until the sugar has dissolved. Turn the heat to high and boil rapidly, from 5–20 minutes, until a set is achieved (left).

6 Skim off any scum, leave for 10–15 minutes until the surface forms a skin and the peel stops floating to the top. Stir to redistribute the peel and pot the marmalade into warm sterilized jars.

Seville oranges, which are available from December to February, have a fine flavour, and always produce authentic, bitter-sweet marmalade. This is a sensationally fruity breakfast marmalade, with a clear jelly and lots of peel, to be enjoyed on toast.

Seville marmalade

MAKES APPROX 1KG (2¼LB) (2 LARGE JARS)

TAKES 2¼ HOURS

KEEPS 12 MONTHS

INGREDIENTS

1kg (2¼lb) Seville oranges, scrubbed in hot water, with stalk ends removed

1 large organic lemon, washed

1.1kg (2½lb) granulated sugar

1 Cut the oranges and lemon in half, squeeze out the juice into a jug and reserve in the fridge. Gather the pith and pips in muslin (or a clean new disposable kitchen cloth) to make a bag, and tie with string.

2 Put the citrus shells, muslin bag of pith and pips, and 1.7 litres (3 pints) of water into a preserving pan or a large heavy-based saucepan. Bring to the boil, half-cover, and simmer gently for 1 hour or until the shells are soft but not mushy. Tip into a large sieve or colander over a bowl to collect all the liquid: press the mixture lightly to extract the maximum liquor.

3 Scoop out the excess mush from inside the cooked shells with a spoon and discard. Slice the peel into thick or thin strands, or coarse or fine chunks.

4 Put the liquor, prepared peel, and reserved fruit juice back in the pan and add the sugar. Heat gently, stirring until the sugar has dissolved. Turn the heat up high, bring to the boil, and boil rapidly for 5–15 minutes or until the setting point is reached. Remove the pan from the heat while you test for a set (p89).

5 Skim off any surface scum with a skimmer, leave the marmalade to settle for a few minutes until it forms a skin, then stir to distribute the peel. Ladle into warm sterilized jars, cover with waxed paper discs, seal, and label. Store in a cool, dark place, and refrigerate after opening.

This is a slightly different method of making marmalade, in which the fruit is cooked with the lemon and lime zest first. The combination of these two citrus fruits makes this fresh-tasting marmalade extra zesty, with a distinctive bitter tang.

Lemon and lime marmalade

MAKES APPROX 2KG (4½LB) (6 MEDIUM JARS)

TAKES 3 HOURS 25 MINUTES

KEEPS 12 MONTHS

INGREDIENTS

4 large organic lemons (approx 550g/1¼lb), washed

6 large organic limes (approx 550g/1¼lb), washed

2 oranges, peeled

1kg (2½lb) granulated sugar

1 Zest all the fruits, or peel the zest from the fruit using a swivel peeler, remove any white pith from the peel, and shred the peel finely. Put the zest in a preserving pan or a large heavy-based saucepan. Remove all the white pith from the fruit using a sharp knife and reserve. Halve the fruits, scoop out the pips, and gather the pith and pips in muslin (or a clean new disposable kitchen cloth) to make a bag, and tie with string. Add to the pan. Roughly chop the fruit and add it to the pan.

2 Pour over 1.4 litres (2½ pints) of water and bring to the boil. Then turn down the heat and simmer for 1 hour or until the peel is soft. Remove the muslin bag of pips and pith and squeeze out any juice into the pan. Discard the bag.

3 Add the sugar and stir until it has dissolved. Bring back to the boil and boil rapidly for 20 minutes or until the setting point is reached. Remove the pan from the heat while you test for a set (p89).

4 Skim off any surface scum with a skimmer, leave the marmalade to settle for a few minutes until it forms a skin, then stir to distribute the peel. Ladle into warm sterilized jars, cover with waxed paper discs, seal, and label. Store in a cool, dark place, and refrigerate after opening.

This is a thick-textured marmalade, made the same way as a fruit cheese. If you prefer, you can chop the oranges, lemons, and apples in a food processor using the pulse button first, though the resulting texture will be much smoother.

Apple and ginger marmalade

MAKES APPROX 1.5KG (3LB 3OZ) (4 MEDIUM JARS PLUS 1 SMALL JAR)

TAKES 2 HOURS 40 MINUTES

KEEPS 6–9 MONTHS

INGREDIENTS

900g (2lb) cooking apples, peeled, cored, and roughly chopped

2 small organic oranges (approx 350g/12oz), washed, halved with pips removed, and thinly sliced

3 small organic lemons (approx 350g/12oz), washed, halved with pips removed, and thinly sliced

675g (1½lb) granulated sugar

2.5cm (1in) piece of fresh root ginger, peeled and grated

1 Put the apples, oranges, and lemons in a preserving pan or a large heavy-based saucepan and pour in 500ml (16fl oz) of water. Bring to the boil, then reduce to a simmer and cook for about 45 minutes–1 hour, or until the peel is very soft.

2 Add the sugar and stir until it has dissolved. Add the ginger, bring back to the boil, and cook over a medium heat for about 1 hour until the mixture is thick enough for a wooden spoon drawn across the bottom of the pan to leave a clear trail.

3 Ladle into warm sterilized jars, cover with waxed paper discs, seal, and label. Store in a cool, dark place, and refrigerate after opening.

Combining the three fruits results in a lovely balance of flavours, good colour, and a good set. You can make four-fruit marmalade by substituting a large organic lime for one of the lemons. Choose fruit that feels heavy, as it is likely to have more flesh and less pith.

Three-fruit marmalade

MAKES APPROX 2.25KG (5LB) (5 LARGE JARS)

TAKES 2¼ HOURS

KEEPS 12 MONTHS

INGREDIENTS

I organic grapefruit, washed

I organic orange, washed

2 organic lemons, washed

1.35kg (3lb) granulated sugar

1 Halve the fruit, squeeze to extract the juice, and strain the juice into a preserving pan or a large heavy-based saucepan, reserving the pips.

2 Scrape out any soft flesh from the citrus shells and add to the pan. Scoop out the membranes from the fruit shells and some of the white pith (especially from the grapefruit if very thick) and add to the pips. Gather the pips, membranes, and any removed pith in muslin (or a clean new disposable kitchen cloth) to make a bag, and tie with string.

3 Thinly shred the fruit peel and cut into short lengths, or finely chop in a food processor. Add to the pan with 1.7 litres (3 pints) of water and the muslin bag. Bring to the boil, reduce the heat, and simmer for 1½ hours or until the peel is really soft and the liquid has reduced by half.

4 Using a slotted spoon, squeeze the bag of pips against the side of the pan to extract as much liquid as possible, then discard. Add the sugar and stir over a gentle heat until dissolved. Bring to the boil and boil rapidly for about 15 minutes or until the setting point is reached. Remove the pan from the heat while you test for a set (p89).

5 Skim off any scum from the surface. Leave to stand for about 10 minutes, then stir well to redistribute the peel evenly through the marmalade. Ladle into warm sterilized jars, cover with waxed paper discs, seal, and label. Store in a cool, dark place, and refrigerate after opening.

The flavour of whisky in this marmalade greatly enhances those of the citrus fruits. Clementines aren't too high in pectin or acid, so lemon juice helps the set. Enjoy on hot buttered toast, or dilute with a little water and serve as a hot sauce on winter puddings.

Clementine and whisky marmalade

MAKES APPROX 1KG (2¼LB) (3 MEDIUM JARS)

TAKES 1¼ HOURS

KEEPS 9 MONTHS

INGREDIENTS

900g (2lb) organic clementines, scrubbed, rinsed, and halved, with pips removed

Juice of 2 large lemons

900g (2lb) granulated sugar

1–2 tbsp whisky, or you can use brandy

1 Either put the clementines in a food processor and chop using the pulse button until they are shredded but not turned to mush, or squeeze the juice from the fruit by hand and finely shred the skins with a sharp knife.

2 Put the chopped fruit in a preserving pan or a large heavy-based saucepan. Pour in 900ml (1½ pints) of water and bring to the boil, then reduce to a simmer and cook gently for 30 minutes or longer until the rind has softened.

3 Add the lemon juice and sugar and cook on a low heat, stirring continuously, until the sugar has dissolved. Turn the heat up, bring to the boil, then keep at a rolling boil for 20–30 minutes or until the setting point is reached. Remove the pan from the heat while you test for a set (p89).

4 Stir the whisky into the marmalade. Ladle into warm sterilized jars, cover with waxed paper discs, seal, and label. Store in a cool, dark place, and refrigerate after opening.

Savoury preserves are designed to get the taste buds tingling; this is where preserving gets exciting. These preserves are supremely versatile and almost foolproof to make. Whether it is a sweet and sour **relish**, a spicy, mellow, fiery, mild, fruity, or piquant **chutney**, or a crunchy, sharp **pickle**, there is a savoury preserve to suit all tastes. Autumn is the prime time to make these preserves, and all you need are some seasonal fruit and vegetables and a little imagination.

Chutneys

These preserves can be made with a huge variety of
seasonal summer and autumn fruit and vegetables.
The best chutneys use crops at their seasonal best,
and will never fail to impress.

Apples

An essential fruit for chutneys, as
its flavour blends supremely well
with all other ingredients.
Cooking apples produce
a smooth texture,
while dessert
apples are sweeter
and keep more of
their texture.

Pears

Delicious in chutneys if
teamed with ginger, or
fragrant spices such as
cardamom, cinnamon,
and allspice. All varieties
are good to use; choose
hard pears or windfalls
rather than over-ripe fruits.

Plums

All varieties, including
greengages and damsons,
make superb, richly flavoured
chutneys with lots of body.
Any combination of spices works
well with plums (pp172–73).

GOLDEN RULES
FOR SUCCESS

- Prepare all the ingredients
  meticulously (the final texture
  and quality of the preserve is
  dependent upon this approach).
- If possible, grind spices when
  required so they remain fresh.
- A long, gentle cooking time
  is essential.
- The secret ingredient is time:
  like fine wines, all chutneys
  improve with age, so leave
  to mature and mellow
  before using.

Rhubarb

A popular
choice with
cooks, as its tart flavour combines well
with dried fruit. Orange and ginger are
also classic partners with rhubarb.
Harvest in spring and early summer and
use the tender, less fibrous stems.

Figs

Their exotic taste and unctuous
texture is perfect for chutneys.
Choose under-ripe fruit and
flavour with citrus fruits, or perk
up with chillies and fennel seeds.

Aubergines

A must for Indian, Mediterranean, or South East Asian-inspired chutneys. Aubergines are both versatile and drink up spices to good effect. Choose aubergines with glossy skins and firm flesh.

Onions

Essential for all chutneys, onions meld with spices during cooking to give an appetizing taste. Red and white onions are both suitable; shallots give a milder flavour.

Peppers

Ripe red and yellow peppers add flavour, sweetness, colour, and texture to autumn chutneys. Tomatoes, chillies, garlic, onions, and courgettes are all natural partners. Slice or dice neatly.

Chillies

Fresh or dried, chillies give chutneys a lively kick. Wonderful with either fruit or vegetable chutneys, their heat varies greatly, so always taste first before adding them.

Green and red tomatoes

Red (ripe) and green (unripe) tomatoes are the ultimate classic chutney ingredient. They make sensationally good chutneys on their own or teamed with other ingredients.

Cranberries

This fruit makes vividly coloured, tangy winter chutneys. Use fresh or frozen berries, add warm spices, and a hint of chilli.

Peaches

Like nectarines, peaches produce refreshing, delicate chutneys. Make in summer with ripe, well-flavoured fruit and light spices. Walnuts, almonds, or pecans add texture and complement them well.

Marrows

Their creamy texture and mellow flavour make marrows a traditional favourite. Choose young marrows and add dried dates and robust spices for a classic chutney.

Making simple chutney

Chutneys are versatile sweet-sour mixtures of vegetables, fruit, spices, and dried fruits, cooked until soft, to eat with cold meats and cheese. This recipe shows the basic method, which can be made with all kinds of seasonal produce.

Plum chutney

MAKES APPROX 1.35KG (3LB) (3 LARGE JARS)

TAKES 1 HOUR 50 MINUTES– 2 HOURS

KEEPS 12 MONTHS

INGREDIENTS

1kg (2¼lb) plums

350g (12oz) cooking apples

250g (9oz) onions

125g (4½oz) raisins

300g (10oz) light soft brown sugar

1 tsp sea salt

1 tsp each allspice, cinnamon, and coriander, freshly ground if possible

1 dried chilli or ½ tsp dried chilli flakes

1 tsp fennel seeds (optional)

600ml (1 pint) white wine or cider vinegar

MATURING CHUTNEYS

Chutneys can taste harsh and flat if they are eaten straight away, so leave them to mature for 1–2 months before using.

1 Halve the plums, remove the stones, and quarter the fruit. Core, peel, and dice the cooking apples into bite-sized pieces, and peel and finely slice the onions.

2 Put all the ingredients into a preserving pan or a large heavy-based, stainless steel saucepan, then bring slowly to the boil, stirring to dissolve the sugar.

3 Simmer gently for 1½–2 hours until a wooden spoon drawn across the base of the pan leaves a trail. Stir frequently towards the end so the chutney doesn't burn.

4 The chutney should now look thick and glossy. Check the seasoning, add more salt if necessary, and pot into warm sterilized jars, making sure there are no air gaps.

5 Cover with discs of waxed paper, seal with cellophane covers and elastic bands, or non-metallic or vinegar-proof lids, label, and store in a cool, dark place.

This classic, versatile chutney is as tasty in a cheese sandwich as it is served with a curry or some cold meats. If you want to spice the chutney up a little, add a finely chopped red or green chilli. Choose fairtrade or organic mangoes.

Mango chutney

MAKES APPROX 1KG (2¼LB) (3 MEDIUM JARS)

TAKES 1¼ HOURS

KEEPS 6 MONTHS

INGREDIENTS

300ml (10fl oz) cider vinegar

200g (7oz) light muscovado sugar

2 large organic mangoes (approx 900g/2lb), stoned and flesh chopped into chunks

1 cooking apple (approx 200g/7oz), peeled, cored, and roughly chopped

1 onion, finely chopped

2.5cm (1in) piece of fresh root ginger, peeled and grated

½ tsp onion seeds (nigella seeds) (optional)

1 Put the vinegar and sugar in a preserving pan or a large heavy-based, stainless steel saucepan and cook on a low heat, stirring occasionally until the sugar dissolves.

2 Add the mango, apple, onion, ginger, and onion seeds, (if using), then raise the heat. Bring to the boil, then reduce the heat to a gentle simmer and cook for about 45 minutes until it is reduced and thickened and most of the liquid has been absorbed. Don't let it dry out too much. Stir continuously near the end of the cooking time so that the chutney doesn't catch on the base of the pan.

3 Ladle into warm sterilized jars with non-metallic or vinegar-proof lids, making sure there are no air gaps. Cover each pot with a waxed paper disc, seal, and label. Store in a cool, dark place. Allow the flavours to mature for 1 month, and refrigerate after opening.

A light, fresh chutney that is warmed up with spices. Use peaches when they are in full season for the best flavour. As with all chutneys, this is best left for at least one month for the flavours to mature before eating. It tastes delicious with pork or cheeses.

Peach chutney

MAKES APPROX 500G (1LB 2OZ) (1 LARGE JAR)

TAKES 2 HOURS

KEEPS 9 MONTHS

INGREDIENTS

4 small red onions, finely diced

7 medium-sized peaches (approx 675g/1½lb), stoned and diced

1 organic orange, washed, zested, and then segmented

1 organic lemon, washed, zested, and then segmented

Sea salt and freshly ground black pepper

360ml (12fl oz) cider vinegar

350g (12oz) granulated sugar

½ tsp ground cinnamon

5cm (2in) piece of fresh root ginger, peeled and finely chopped

½ tsp chilli flakes

1 Add the onions, peaches, and orange and lemon zest and segments to a preserving pan or a large heavy-based, stainless steel saucepan and stir to mix.

2 Add a pinch of salt and some black pepper, then pour in the vinegar and stir in the sugar. Sprinkle in the cinnamon, ginger, and chilli flakes and bring to a simmer, stirring until the sugar has dissolved.

3 Bring to the boil, then reduce to a fairly high simmer (not a roaring boil) and cook until the chutney thickens, about 1½ hours, and most of the liquid has been absorbed. Stir continuously near the end of the cooking time so that the chutney doesn't catch on the base of the pan.

4 Ladle into a warm sterilized jar with a non-metallic or vinegar-proof lid, making sure there are no air gaps. Cover with a waxed paper disc, seal, and label. Store in a cool, dark place. Allow the flavours to mature for 1 month, and refrigerate after opening.

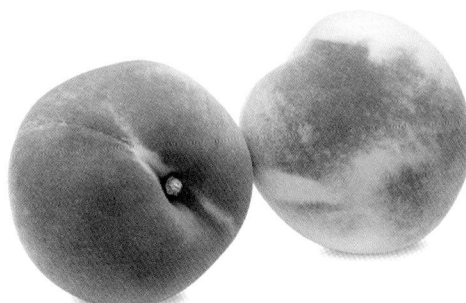

Peaches
Peach trees are hardy, but their blossom is susceptible to late frosts. They need to be grown under protection – an orangery, greenhouse, or conservatory – in cool climates, where they grow and crop well.

This colourful chutney-come-relish is a tangy alternative to cranberry sauce. It's quicker to make than other chutneys, and contains less sugar. It makes a perfect Christmas condiment or gift if made four weeks earlier. Once opened, use within one month.

Cranberry and apricot chutney

MAKES APPROX 1.25KG (2¾LB) (5 SMALL JARS)

TAKES 1 HOUR

KEEPS 4–6 MONTHS, REFRIGERATED

INGREDIENTS

350g (12oz) fresh or frozen cranberries

2 cooking apples (approx 350g/12oz), peeled, quartered, and cored

225g (8oz) dried apricots

1 medium onion (approx 175g/6oz), roughly chopped

1cm (½in) piece of fresh root ginger, peeled and grated

175g (6oz) light soft brown sugar

175ml (6fl oz) apple cider vinegar

Zest and juice of 1 organic orange, washed

1 cinnamon stick

¼ tsp ground coriander

¼ tsp ground cumin

¼ tsp dried chilli flakes

Pinch of sea salt

1 Put the cranberries, apples, and apricots in a food processor with the onion and ginger. Pulse lightly until finely chopped, then place in a preserving pan or a large heavy-based, stainless steel saucepan and add the rest of the ingredients.

2 Bring slowly to the boil, stirring until the sugar has dissolved. Reduce the heat to a gentle simmer and cook gently, uncovered, for 30–35 minutes or until the cranberries have softened and burst (frozen cranberries soften more quickly) and are thick and pulpy, and a wooden spoon drawn across the base of the pan leaves a trail. Stir frequently towards the end of cooking so the chutney doesn't burn.

3 Remove the cinnamon stick and spoon into warm sterilized jars with non-metallic or vinegar-proof lids, making sure there are no air gaps. Cover each pot with a waxed paper disc, seal, and label. Leave to cool, then store in the fridge to mature for at least 2 weeks before opening. Once opened, keep refrigerated.

Dried fruit, such as peaches, apricots, prunes, and dates, go well with apples to make delicious chutneys. The walnuts add extra texture as well as flavour. If you prefer sweet spiced chutney, substitute mixed spice for the curry powder.

Curried apple, peach, and walnut chutney

MAKES APPROX 1.8KG (4LB) (4 LARGE JARS)

TAKES 1¾ HOURS

KEEPS 12 MONTHS

INGREDIENTS

2 cooking apples (approx 350g/12oz), peeled, quartered, and cored

1 large onion (approx 225g/8oz), peeled

350g (12oz) dried peaches

175g (6oz) walnut pieces, roughly chopped

125g (4½oz) sultanas

400g (14oz) light soft brown sugar

2 tsp mild curry powder

Good pinch of sea salt

300ml (10fl oz) apple cider vinegar

1 Roughly chop the apples and onion into bite-sized pieces. Snip the peaches with scissors into similar-sized pieces. Put in a preserving pan or a large heavy-based, stainless steel saucepan with the remaining ingredients.

2 Bring slowly to the boil, stirring until the sugar has dissolved. Reduce the heat to a gentle simmer and cook for 1½ hours or until a wooden spoon drawn across the base of the pan leaves a trail. Stir frequently towards the end of cooking so the chutney doesn't burn.

3 Check the seasoning and add salt or more curry powder, if needed. Simmer gently for an extra minute, stirring, to cook out the spice.

4 Spoon into warm sterilized jars with non-metallic or vinegar-proof lids, making sure there are no air gaps. Cover each pot with a waxed paper disc, seal, and label. Store in a cool, dark place for at least 1 month before using. Once opened, keep refrigerated.

With its mixture of sweet and tangy flavours, this chutney is perfect served with oily fish, but it is also delicious served with bread and cheese or a salad. As with most chutneys, the flavours will develop and mellow if left to mature before serving.

Runner bean and courgette chutney

MAKES APPROX 1KG (2¼LB) (3 MEDIUM JARS)

TAKES 2 HOURS

KEEPS 9 MONTHS

INGREDIENTS

600g (1lb 5oz) runner beans, thinly sliced

4 courgettes, thinly sliced

350g (12oz) cooking apples, peeled, cored, and chopped

2 onions, finely chopped

450g (1lb) light soft brown sugar

1 tsp mustard powder

1 tsp turmeric

1 tsp coriander seeds

600ml (1 pint) cider vinegar

1 Put the beans, courgettes, apples, and onions in a preserving pan or a large heavy-based, stainless steel saucepan, then add the sugar, mustard powder, turmeric, and coriander seeds. Pour in the vinegar and stir.

2 Cook over a gentle heat, stirring until all the sugar has dissolved, then bring to the boil and cook at a rolling boil, stirring occasionally, for about 10 minutes. Reduce to a simmer and cook for about 1½ hours, stirring from time to time, until the mixture thickens. Stir continuously near the end of the cooking time so that the chutney doesn't catch on the base of the pan.

3 Ladle into warm sterilized jars with non-metallic or vinegar-proof lids, making sure there are no air gaps. Cover each pot with a waxed paper disc, seal, and label. Store in a cool, dark place. Allow the flavours to mature for 1 month, and refrigerate after opening.

You can use green courgettes, or any other squash, for this chutney, but yellow courgettes are ideal, as they have a great colour and creamy texture. You can also substitute green tomatoes for red if you have some unripe produce to use up.

Yellow courgette and tomato chutney

MAKES APPROX 1KG (2¼LB) (2 LARGE JARS)

TAKES 2¾ HOURS

KEEPS 12 MONTHS

INGREDIENTS

450g (1lb) yellow courgettes, trimmed and diced

250g (9oz) onions, roughly chopped

350g (12oz) ripe tomatoes, roughly chopped

350g (12oz) granulated sugar

300ml (10fl oz) white wine vinegar

1 garlic clove, peeled and finely chopped

1cm (½in) piece of fresh root ginger, peeled and finely chopped

¼ tsp dried chilli flakes

Good pinch of sweet paprika

Good pinch of ground white pepper

½ tsp sea salt

1 Put all the ingredients in a preserving pan or a large heavy-based, stainless steel saucepan.

2 Bring slowly to the boil, stirring to dissolve the sugar. Reduce the heat and simmer for 2½ hours until a wooden spoon drawn across the base of the pan leaves a trail. Stir frequently towards the end so the chutney doesn't burn. If necessary, turn up the heat towards the end of cooking and boil rapidly until thick and glossy.

3 Pack into warm sterilized jars with non-metallic or vinegar-proof lids, making sure there are no air gaps. Cover each pot with a waxed paper disc, seal, and label. Store in a cool, dark place. Allow the flavours to mature for 1 month, and refrigerate after opening.

The cooking method for this sweet, dark, sticky chutney is designed to be quicker than for other chutneys. The overall flavour combination is rounded, but the cardamom scent is still distinctive. It is an ideal accompaniment to roast pork.

Marrow and date chutney

MAKES APPROX 1KG (2¼LB)
(2 LARGE JARS)

TAKES 1¼ HOURS

KEEPS 12 MONTHS

INGREDIENTS

225g (8oz) marrow, peeled and chopped

225g (8oz) cooking apple, peeled and
roughly chopped

175g (6oz) onions, chopped

225g (8oz) ready-to-eat stoned dates,
chopped

1 tsp cardamom seeds, crushed

1 tsp ground cloves

2.5cm (1in) piece of fresh root ginger,
peeled and grated

300ml (10fl oz) cider vinegar

225g (8oz) granulated sugar

1 Put the marrow, apple, and onion in a preserving pan or a large heavy-based, stainless steel saucepan. Pour over a little water (about 3 tbsp), cover, turn up the heat, and simmer gently for 15–20 minutes or until the apple begins to turn pulpy. Top up with a little more water if it begins to dry out. Stir occasionally and don't let the mixture brown at all.

2 Add the dates, spices, ginger, vinegar, and sugar and cook on a low heat, stirring until the sugar has dissolved. Bring to the boil, then reduce the heat and cook, uncovered, for 15–20 minutes or until the mixture thickens and the liquid has been absorbed.

3 Ladle into warm sterilized jars with non-metallic or vinegar-proof lids, making sure there are no air gaps. Cover each pot with a waxed paper disc, seal, and label. Store in a cool, dark place. Allow the flavours to mature for 1 month, and refrigerate after opening.

Dates
The colour, flavour, and natural sweetness of dates blend well with most fruits and vegetables. They cook down to a substantial purée to give added texture and body to chutneys. Choose dried dates without added sugar or preservatives.

Sun-ripened vegetables blend with subtle herbs and spices in this tasty chutney. It has a good colour and sweet, rounded flavours that develop over time. If you prefer to mix and match the vegetables, keep the total overall weight the same.

Mediterranean chutney

MAKES APPROX 1.8KG (4LB)
(4 LARGE JARS)

TAKES 2½ HOURS

KEEPS 12 MONTHS

INGREDIENTS

450g (1lb) red peppers, deseeded, chopped, and diced

450g (1lb) aubergines, chopped into bite-sized cubes

450g (1lb) small courgettes, chopped into bite-sized cubes

1 red onion, finely chopped

450g (1lb) tomatoes, roughly chopped

600ml (1 pint) cider vinegar

450g (1lb) light soft brown sugar

1 tsp coriander seeds

1 tsp *herbes de Provence*

1 tsp fennel seeds (optional)

1 Put all the vegetables and tomatoes in a preserving pan or a large heavy-based, stainless steel saucepan.

2 Pour in the vinegar, then tip in the sugar and stir the mixture to coat the vegetables in the sugar. Add the spices and herbs and heat gently, stirring occasionally so that the sugar dissolves. Then turn the heat up and bring the ingredients to the boil.

3 Reduce to a simmer and cook gently for 2 hours or so until the liquid evaporates and the mixture thickens and becomes sticky. Stir continuously near the end of the cooking time so that the chutney doesn't catch on the base of the pan.

4 Ladle into warm sterilized jars with non-metallic or vinegar-proof lids, making sure there are no air gaps. Cover each pot with a disc of waxed paper, seal, and label. Store in a cool, dark place for 1 month to allow the flavours to mature, and refrigerate after opening.

A hint of curry powder and a teaspoon of onion seeds really lift the flavour of the rhubarb in this recipe. It's worth noting that this chutney should be left to mature for at least one month until the flavours have mellowed and married together before you use it.

Spiced rhubarb chutney

MAKES APPROX 1.4KG (3LB)
(3 LARGE JARS)

TAKES 1 HOUR 20 MINUTES

KEEPS 9 MONTHS

INGREDIENTS

900g (2lb) rhubarb, rinsed and chopped
    into 2.5cm (1in) pieces

225g (8oz) cooking apples, peeled, cored,
    and roughly chopped

3 medium onions, finely chopped

5cm (2in) piece of fresh root ginger,
    peeled and grated

1–2 tsp mild curry powder

1 tsp onion seeds (nigella seeds)

Pinch of sea salt

450ml (15fl oz) pickling vinegar or
    ready-spiced pickling vinegar

450g (1lb) light soft brown sugar

1 Put the rhubarb in a preserving pan or a large heavy-based, stainless steel saucepan and add the apple and onion. Add 1–4 tbsp of water and cook on a low heat until the rhubarb softens, about 10 minutes.

2 Stir in the ginger, curry powder, onion seeds, and sea salt. Pour in half the vinegar and simmer gently for about 30–40 minutes, stirring occasionally.

3 Dissolve the sugar in the remaining vinegar in a bowl and add this to the pan. Simmer gently until the mixture begins to thicken, about 10–15 minutes, stirring continuously so it doesn't catch on the base of the pan.

4 Ladle into warm sterilized jars with non-metallic or vinegar-proof lids, making sure there are no air gaps. Cover each pot with a disc of waxed paper, seal, and label. Store in a cool, dark place to allow the flavours to mature, and refrigerate after opening.

This sweet, jammy, mild-flavoured chutney is an ideal accompaniment to Brie, goat's cheese, or other soft cheeses. Stir a teaspoon or two of chilli flakes into the mixture at the end of cooking if you want to give it added spice.

Tomato and roasted pepper chutney

MAKES APPROX 1.35KG (3LB) (3 MEDIUM JARS)

TAKES 2 HOURS 20 MINUTES

KEEPS 9 MONTHS

INGREDIENTS

1 red pepper

1 orange pepper

1 yellow pepper

1.35kg (3lb) ripe tomatoes, plunged into boiling water for 1 minute and then peeled

2 onions, roughly chopped

450g (1lb) granulated sugar

600ml (1 pint) white wine vinegar

1 Preheat the oven to 200°C (400°F/Gas 6). Put the peppers in a roasting tin and cook for about 25–30 minutes until they begin to char slightly. Remove from the oven, put in a plastic bag, and leave to cool. (This will make the skins easier to remove.)

2 Pull away the stalks, remove the skin, deseed, and roughly chop. Put the skinned tomatoes, roasted peppers, and onions in a food processor and pulse briefly until chopped but not mushy. Alternatively, chop by hand.

3 Tip the mixture into a preserving pan or a large heavy-based, stainless steel saucepan with the sugar and vinegar. Cook on low heat, stirring continuously, until the sugar has dissolved. Bring to the boil, then reduce to a simmer and cook for about 1–1½ hours, stirring occasionally, until it starts to thicken and turn jammy. You may need to increase the heat a little towards the end of cooking. Stir continuously near the end so the chutney doesn't catch on the base of the pan.

4 Ladle into warm sterilized jars with non-metallic or vinegar-proof lids, making sure there are no air gaps. Cover each pot with a waxed paper disc, seal, and label. Store in a cool, dark place. Allow the flavours to mature for 1 month, and refrigerate after opening.

This is a true autumnal chutney, an inspired combination of plums, apples, and squashes, which harmonize beautifully – the plums and apples provide a fruity character, while the squash gives body and added texture. The chilli gives it a lively kick.

Plum and squash chutney

MAKES APPROX 1.5KG (3LB 3OZ) (4 MEDIUM JARS)

TAKES 2¼–3¼ HOURS

KEEPS 12 MONTHS

INGREDIENTS

For the spice bag

2 mace blades

1 heaped tsp coriander seeds

12 black peppercorns

12 cloves

2cm (¾in) peice of fresh root ginger, cubed

1 tsp ground ginger

500g (1lb 2oz) squash, peeled and cubed

500g (1lb 2oz) plums, stoned and roughly chopped

500g (1lb 2oz) cooking apples, peeled, cored, and diced

250g (9oz) onions, diced

250g (9oz) raisins or sultanas

250g (9oz) light soft brown sugar

400ml (14fl oz) cider or white wine vinegar

1½ tsp dried chilli flakes

½ tsp sea salt

1 Tie the ingredients for the spice bag in a piece of muslin or clean, new disposable kitchen cloth and place in a preserving pan or a large heavy-based, stainless steel saucepan. Put all the other ingredients in the pan and heat gently, stirring occasionally, until all the sugar has dissolved.

2 Bring to the boil, turn the heat down, and simmer for 2–2½ hours, stirring now and then until the liquid evaporates and the mixture thickens and becomes sticky, and a wooden spoon drawn across the base of the pan leaves a trail. Stir frequently near the end of the cooking time so the chutney doesn't catch on the base of the pan.

3 Ladle into warm sterilized jars with non-metallic or vinegar-proof lids, cover with waxed paper discs, seal, and label. Store in a cool, dark place. Allow the flavours to mature for 1–2 months, and refrigerate after opening.

Windfall or unripe pears can be turned into admirable chutneys to serve with cheese, cold ham, and savoury tarts. This is a mild, nicely rounded chutney. If you want a really good, spicy-sweet balance and mellow flavour, leave to mature for three months.

Pear chutney

MAKES APPROX 1.35KG (3LB) (4 MEDIUM JARS)

TAKES 2½–2¾ HOURS

KEEPS 12 MONTHS

INGREDIENTS

750g (1lb 10oz) pears, peeled, cored, and cut into 2cm (¾in) cubes

350g (12oz) onions, chopped

350g (12oz) green or red tomatoes, sliced

125g (4½oz) raisins, chopped

3 peppercorns, crushed

350g (12oz) demerara sugar

½ tsp cayenne pepper

½ tsp ground ginger

1 tsp sea salt

450ml (15fl oz) cider vinegar

1 Put all the ingredients into a preserving pan or a large heavy-based, stainless steel pan. Bring slowly to the boil, stirring to dissolve the sugar.

2 Reduce the heat and simmer gently, uncovered, for about 2 hours or until the mixture thickens and takes on a dark caramel colour, and a wooden spoon drawn across the base of the pan leaves a trail. Stir frequently towards the end of the cooking time so the chutney doesn't burn.

3 Ladle into warm sterilized jars with non-metallic or vinegar-proof lids, making sure there are no air gaps. Cover with waxed paper discs, seal, label, and store in a cool, dark place. Allow the flavours to mature for at least 1 month, and refrigerate after opening.

Serve these sweet, sticky onions simmered slowly in red wine with cheese, meat pâtés, or terrines. Add two teaspoons of chopped fresh thyme or rosemary leaves, or a pinch of chilli flakes, to the mix in step 2 for an added dimension of flavour.

Red onion marmalade

MAKES APPROX 700G (1½LB)
(2 MEDIUM JARS)

TAKES 1½ HOURS

KEEPS 3 MONTHS, REFRIGERATED

INGREDIENTS

2 tbsp olive oil

1kg (2¼lb) red onions (approx 6), peeled, halved, and sliced

Pinch of sea salt, and freshly ground black pepper to taste

150ml (5fl oz) red wine

3 tbsp balsamic vinegar

3 tbsp white wine vinegar

6 tbsp light soft brown sugar

1 Heat the oil in a preserving pan or a large heavy-based, stainless steel saucepan. Add the onions, the sea salt, and some freshly ground black pepper. Cook over a low-medium heat for about 30 minutes until the onions soften and turn translucent, stirring occasionally so they don't catch and burn. Slow cooking is essential at this point, as this is where the delicious caramelly taste is developed.

2 Raise the heat a little, add the wine and vinegars, and stir to combine. Bring to the boil, then reduce the heat, stir in the sugar, and cook on a low heat, stirring occasionally, for a further 30–40 minutes until most of the liquid has evaporated.

3 Remove the pan from the heat. Taste and adjust the seasoning as necessary (although the flavours will mature with time). Spoon into warm sterilized jars with non-metallic or vinegar-proof lids, making sure there are no air gaps. Cover with waxed paper discs, seal, label, and store in the fridge to allow the flavours to mature for 1 month. Keep refrigerated after opening.

The meltingly tender aubergine pieces, onion seeds, and gingery mix make this chutney taste very authentic. If you want a really fiery hot chutney, sprinkle in some cayenne pepper when you add the ginger. It is fabulous served with lamb or an Indian meal.

Hot-spiced aubergine chutney

MAKES APPROX 1.5KG (3LB 3OZ) (3 LARGE JARS)

TAKES 1 HOUR 30–40 MINUTES

KEEPS 12 MONTHS

INGREDIENTS

900g (2lb) aubergines, cut into cubes

2 red onions, roughly chopped

Pinch of sea salt

1 tbsp tomato purée

500ml (16fl oz) cider vinegar

450g (1lb) light soft brown sugar

175g (6oz) sultanas

Pinch of dried chilli flakes

1 cinnamon stick

2 tsp onion seeds (nigella seeds)

5cm (2in) piece of fresh root ginger, peeled and finely chopped or grated

1 Put the aubergine in a preserving pan or a large heavy-based, stainless steel saucepan. Add the red onions and a pinch of sea salt. Stir to combine, then stir in the tomato purée.

2 Pour in the vinegar and sugar and stir, then add the sultanas, chilli flakes, cinnamon stick, onion seeds, and ginger. Heat the ingredients gently, stirring occasionally until the sugar has dissolved. Turn the heat up and bring the mixture to the boil.

3 Reduce the heat to a simmer and cook gently on a low heat for about 1 hour, stirring occasionally so it doesn't burn. It is ready when it is thick and sticky and the vinegar has been absorbed. Stir continuously near the end of the cooking time so that the chutney doesn't catch on the base of the pan. Remove the cinnamon stick.

4 Ladle into warm sterilized jars with non-metallic or vinegar-proof lids, making sure there are no air gaps. Cover each pot with a waxed paper disc, seal, and label. Store in a cool, dark place. Allow the flavours to mature for 1 month, and refrigerate after opening.

A selection of vegetables is first simmered in Indian spices and vinegar to give this colourful, chunky chutney its classic flavours, while the dates add a characteristically grainy sweetness. For a hotter chutney, add one or two finely chopped fresh green chillies.

Indian-spiced vegetable chutney

MAKES APPROX 1.5KG (3LB 3OZ) (3 LARGE JARS)

TAKES 2½–3 HOURS

KEEPS 12 MONTHS

INGREDIENTS

900g (2lb) butternut squash, halved, peeled, and cut into bite-sized chunks

2 onions, finely chopped

225g (8oz) cooking apples, peeled, cored, and roughly chopped

3 courgettes, halved lengthways and chopped

50g (1¾oz) ready-to-eat stoned dates, chopped

450ml (15fl oz) cider vinegar

2 tbsp medium-hot curry powder (depending on your heat preference)

1 tsp ground cumin

2.5cm (1in) piece of fresh root ginger, peeled and grated or finely chopped

450g (1lb) granulated or light soft brown sugar

1 Put the squash, onions, cooking apples, courgettes, and dates in a preserving pan or a large heavy-based, stainless steel saucepan. Pour over the vinegar, add the spices, and ginger, and mix well.

2 Bring the mixture to the boil, then reduce the heat and simmer for 40–45 minutes or until the vegetables are soft, stirring occasionally.

3 Add the sugar, stir until it has dissolved, then continue to cook on a gentle simmer for 1–1½ hours or until the chutney is thick and the liquid has been absorbed. Stir continuously near the end of the cooking time so that the chutney doesn't catch on the base of the pan.

4 Ladle into warm sterilized jars with non-metallic or vinegar-proof lids, making sure there are no air gaps. Cover each pot with a waxed paper disc, seal, and label. Store in a cool, dark place. Allow the flavours to mature for 1 month, and refrigerate after opening.

This substantial, adaptable chutney gets better with age. Dried cranberries, figs, or dried apricots all complement apples well, and can be used instead of dried dates, if you prefer. For a darker colour, use light or dark soft brown sugar instead of white.

Apple, sultana, and date chutney

MAKES APPROX 1.8KG (4LB) (5 MEDIUM JARS)

TAKES 2¼ HOURS

KEEPS 9 MONTHS

INGREDIENTS

2kg (4½lb) cooking apples (approx 8–10), peeled, cored, and chopped

3 onions, peeled and finely chopped

2.5cm (1in) piece of fresh root ginger, peeled and finely chopped

115g (4oz) sultanas

125g (4½oz) ready-to-eat stoned dates, chopped

1 tsp mustard seeds

1 litre (1¾ pints) cider vinegar

500g (1lb 2oz) granulated sugar

1 Put the apples, onions, ginger, sultanas, dates, and mustard seeds in a preserving pan or a large heavy-based, stainless steel saucepan. Stir everything together, then pour in the cider vinegar and add the sugar.

2 Cook on a low heat, stirring until the sugar has dissolved, then bring to the boil, reduce the heat, and cook gently for about 1½ hours. Stir continuously near the end of the cooking time so that the chutney doesn't catch on the base of the pan. The mixture is ready when it is thick and sticky.

3 Ladle into warm sterilized jars with non-metallic or vinegar-proof lids, making sure there are no air gaps. Cover each pot with a waxed paper disc, seal, and label. Store in a cool, dark place. Allow the flavours to mature for 1 month, and refrigerate after opening.

The best ingredients for...
Pickles

Pickling transforms everyday fruits and vegetables into tangy condiments. All hard vegetables and firm fruits are suitable but those shown here are some of the best. Always keep them submerged in their liquor.

Gherkins
These specific varieties of short, knobbly cucumbers are essential for most traditional cucumber pickles (pp202–203). They can be pickled crunchy (cold method) or soft (hot method).

Shallots
Mild-flavoured sweet shallots are easy to grow and can be used instead of pickling onions for all pickles.

Runner beans
Their firm texture, appetizing crunch, and fresh flavour make runner beans great to pickle on their own or with other vegetables.

Chillies
Fresh chillies of all kinds are perfect for pickling whole (prick them with a fork to allow the vinegar to penetrate), and are an indispensible flavouring for many other pickles.

Pickling onions
Small, thin-skinned (silverskin) pickling onions are grown specifically for pickling. Pickle whole with bay leaves, chillies, and mustard seeds, or in mixed pickles.

Beetroots
Use summer or winter varieties (small-medium roots) and a well-spiced or flavoured vinegar. Good flavourings include tarragon, horseradish, and garlic.

Turnips
A popular Middle-Eastern pickle, turnips can be pickled on their own or with beetroot, which gives them a rosy pink hue. Add whole cloves of garlic.

Walnuts
Though they are time-consuming to prepare, pickled walnuts are a condiment like no other. Make in autumn with freshly harvested green walnuts.

Damsons
Pickled damsons develop a rich, sweet-sour flavour and become more delicious the longer they are stored. Use in chutneys or serve with meats, pâtés, or hard cheeses.

Limes
Choose ripe, fragrant organic limes for sharp, hot, tangy pickles. Spice with ginger, cumin, cloves, cardamom, fenugreek, and star anise.

Pears
Choose firm, flavourful pears for pickles (pp196–97). Combine with citrus zest, vanilla, warm spices, or exotic flavourings such as kaffir lime leaves or lemongrass.

Garlic
An essential addition to cucumber pickles, garlic is also delicious pickled on its own, either as a spiced or sweet pickle.

Fennel
This aniseed-flavoured, clean-tasting, crisp vegetable makes an excellent autumn pickle. It combines well with julienne strips of carrot and celeriac, or sliced red peppers and chillies.

OTHER INGREDIENTS
FRUITS
Apricots
Blackberries
Cherries
Citrus fruits
Figs
Gooseberries
Grapes
Greengages
Melons
Nectarines
Peaches
Plums
Quinces
Rhubarb
Watermelon rind

VEGETABLES
Aubergines
Carrots
Celeriac
Courgettes
Cucumber
French beans
Horseradish root
Mushrooms
Peppers
Radishes
Romanesco
White cabbage

Cauliflower
Choose tight-headed cauliflower with creamy white florets. Traditionally used for mustard pickles, they work well with South East Asian and Indian pickle flavourings.

Red cabbage
Cabbage makes a colourful, crisp pickle. Pick firm small- or medium-sized heads, and discard outer or damaged leaves. Flavour with caraway or cumin seeds.

Making hot pickles

Pickles are sharp, salty or sweet-sour condiments typically served with cold meats, hamburgers, and cheese, or with rice or spiced dishes. Hot pickled fruits are all made the same way, and add a new dimension to fruit preserves.

Spiced pear pickle

MAKES APPROX 900ML (1½ PINTS) (2 MEDIUM JARS)

TAKES 40 MINUTES

KEEPS 9 MONTHS

INGREDIENTS

1kg (2¼lb) firm, shapely pears such as 'Williams' or 'Conference' pears

For the syrup

350g (12oz) granulated sugar

175ml (6fl oz) cider vinegar

Zest of ½ organic lemon

2.5cm (1in) piece fresh root ginger, chopped

Seeds from 6 cardamom pods

1 Prepare the syrup first: put all the syrup ingredients into a preserving pan or a large heavy-based stainless steel saucepan and bring gently to the boil, stirring to dissolve the sugar. Simmer for 5 minutes, then remove from the heat.

2 Peel the pears, remove their cores, and cut them in half or quarters (the latter are easier to pack into jars).

3 Put the pears into the syrup so they are covered, and poach them gently until just soft, about 5–10 minutes. They are ready when a skewer can be inserted into the flesh. Remove each pear as soon as it is ready.

4 Pack the pears into warm sterilized jars. Return the pan of syrup and spices to the heat, bring back to the boil, and cook for 5 more minutes or so.

5 When the boiling syrup has reduced by about a third, pour it over the pears, filling the jars to the brim, so it completely covers the pears.

6 To keep the pears submerged, cover with a waxed paper disc. Seal with vinegar-proof lids, label, and store in a cool, dark place for 1 month before using. Refrigerate after opening.

This pickle has a lovely deep purple colour. It is made by cooking the beetroot in syrup, and the fragrance of star anise and cinnamon blend beautifully with the earthy taste of the vegetable. Its balance of sweetness and acidity improves with keeping.

Spiced beetroot pickle

MAKES APPROX 1KG (2¼LB)
(2 SMALL PRESERVING JARS)

TAKES 1–2¼ HOURS

KEEPS 6 MONTHS

INGREDIENTS

1kg (2¼lb) raw beetroots, unpeeled, of similar size

1 litre (1¾ pints) red wine vinegar

225g (8oz) granulated sugar

1 small bay leaf

1 cinnamon stick

1 star anise

4 black peppercorns

1 tsp sea salt

1 Wash the beetroots and trim any beet tops, taking care not to cut into the beetroots (or they will "bleed" when cooked). Leave the roots intact.

2 Put the remaining ingredients in a preserving pan or a large heavy-based, stainless steel pan. Heat gently, stirring until the sugar has dissolved, then bring to the boil. Add the beetroots, bring back to the boil, reduce the heat, cover tightly and simmer gently for 1–2 hours or until the beetroots are really tender when pierced with a skewer. Leave to cool in the liquid.

3 Lift out the beetroots with a slotted spoon. When cool enough to handle, cut off the roots and tops, peel, and dice. Wear rubber gloves to peel the beetroots, or you'll stain your hands. Pack into warm sterilized jars with non-metallic or vinegar-proof lids.

4 Strain the liquid and return it to the pan. Bring back to the boil and pour over the beetroots to cover them completely. Seal, leave to cool, label, and store in a cool, dark place. Allow the flavours to mature for 1 month, and refrigerate after opening.

Beetroots
These sweet-tasting vegetables are easy to grow, and they grow fast. Tender summer varieties sown in the spring are ready to pull in June and July.

Chillies and limes add a real kick to any pickle. This recipe is light on salt and vinegar, which gives it a strong, fresh citrus flavour that, combined with spices, delivers an authentic Asian taste. It is ideal as an accompaniment to curries and other spicy dishes.

Fresh lime pickle

MAKES APPROX 1KG (2¼LB)
(2 SMALL PRESERVING JARS)

TAKES 40–50 MINUTES,
PLUS STANDING TIME

KEEPS 3 MONTHS

INGREDIENTS

15 organic limes, washed and cut into
1cm (½in) cubes

10 small green chillies, sliced lengthways
(use more chillies if you like it hot, or
include the seeds)

1 tsp turmeric

1 tbsp sea salt

2 tbsp sunflower oil

1 tsp fenugreek seeds

1 tsp aniseed (or use cumin or fennel
seeds, or 2 star anise as a substitute)

1 tsp onion seeds (nigella seeds)

1 tsp hot chilli powder

5cm (2in) piece of fresh root ginger,
peeled and grated

2 tbsp granulated sugar

1 tbsp white wine vinegar

1 Put the limes, chillies, turmeric, and salt in a large glass or ceramic bowl, combine the ingredients well, and leave overnight at room temperature.

2 Heat the oil in a preserving pan or a large heavy-based, stainless steel saucepan and add the fenugreek, aniseed, onion seeds, chilli powder, and ginger and gently cook, stirring continuously, for 2–3 minutes. Add the lime and chilli mixture and combine well.

3 Cook gently for about 20 minutes until the mixture starts to thicken and soften.

4 Sprinkle in the sugar and stir until it dissolves. Add the vinegar and continue cooking for a further 5 minutes.

5 Allow to cool a little, then ladle into warm sterilized jars with non-metallic or vinegar-proof lids. Press the pickle down into the jars to remove air gaps and ensure that the limes sit in the sauce. Seal, label, and store in a cool, dark place. Allow the flavours to mature for 1 month, and refrigerate after opening.

The young, green walnuts used for this recipe must be thoroughly dried out before being potted and covered with pickling solution. This important process, known as "sunning", turns the walnuts black. Pickled walnuts are best served with blue cheese.

Pickled walnuts

MAKES APPROX 1.1KG (2½LB) (2 SMALL PRESERVING JARS)

TAKES 30–35 MINUTES, PLUS SOAKING AND DRYING TIME

KEEPS 12 MONTHS

INGREDIENTS

1kg (2¼lb) young, green walnuts

400g (14oz) sea salt

For the pickling solution

1 litre (1¾ pints) white wine vinegar

2.5cm (1in) piece of fresh root ginger, peeled and grated

75g (2½oz) light soft brown sugar

2 cinnamon sticks

1 Prick the walnuts all over with a pin or metal skewer. Pour 1 litre (1¾ pints) of warm water and half the salt into a large glass or ceramic bowl, mix well to make a brine, and add the walnuts. They should be completely covered by the water. Leave for 5 days in a cool place, stirring occasionally.

2 Drain the walnuts, then repeat the brining procedure again using fresh warm water and the rest of the salt. Leave for a further 5 days.

3 Drain the walnuts and spread them out on a clean tea towel or kitchen paper to dry out. This will take a minimum of 1–2 days, and will probably take up to 1 week. The walnuts will turn black during this time.

4 Pour all the ingredients for the pickling solution into a stainless steel saucepan and gently simmer for 15–20 minutes, stirring to dissolve the sugar. Put the dry walnuts into warm sterilized jars with non-metallic or vinegar-proof lids, then pour over the pickling solution. Ensure that the walnuts are completely covered by the solution. Seal, label, and store in a cool, dry place. Allow the flavours to mature for at least 6 weeks before eating, and refrigerate once opened.

These lightly caramelized onions in rich balsamic vinegar liven up any savoury dish. For easy peeling, pour boiling water over the shallots, leave them for a few minutes, then drain and peel them – the skins should come away effortlessly.

Pickled sweet shallots

MAKES APPROX 500G (1LB 2OZ) (1 SMALL PRESERVING JAR)

TAKES 35–40 MINUTES

KEEPS 6 MONTHS

INGREDIENTS

550g (1¼lb) shallots, peeled

A few stalks of thyme

1 tbsp olive oil

175ml (6fl oz) balsamic vinegar, plus extra if needed

1 Preheat the oven to 200°C (400°F/Gas 6). Put the shallots and thyme stalks in a roasting tin, then add the olive oil and coat the shallots evenly using your hands. Roast for about 20–25 minutes or until the shallots are beginning to soften (they should no longer be crunchy).

2 Pour the balsamic vinegar into a stainless steel pan, bring it to the boil, and cook for a few minutes until it reduces. Don't let it cook away for too long, or it will become too sticky. Add the shallots and thyme stalks and stir so they all get evenly coated in the reduced vinegar and the onions are sticky.

3 Spoon the shallots, along with the vinegar and fresh thyme, into a warm sterilized jar with a non-metallic or vinegar-proof lid. Pack the shallots in tightly and top up with extra balsamic vinegar so that the shallots are completely covered. Seal, label, and turn the jar upside down to combine the ingredients thoroughly. Store in a cool, dark place and leave for 2 weeks to mature. Refrigerate after opening.

Making cold pickles

Cold pickling is a simple process: vegetables are first salted to draw out moisture to avoid diluted vinegar and thus keep them crisp, and then they are pickled in cold vinegar. Use Jordanian pickling cucumbers or cornichons for this recipe.

Pickled gherkins

MAKES APPROX 1KG (2¼LB) (2 SMALL PRESERVING JARS)

TAKES 20 MINUTES, PLUS SALTING TIME

KEEPS 6 MONTHS OR LONGER

INGREDIENTS

500g (1lb 2oz) small pickling cucumbers (5–6cm/2–2½in long), washed and rubbed down (wash skins thoroughly, rub each with a cloth to dry and remove its fine down)

125g (4½oz) sea salt

3 or 4 peeled shallots

1 or 2 peeled garlic cloves (optional)

2–3 dried chillies (optional)

2–3 cloves (optional)

½ tsp coriander seeds, peppercorns, dill seeds, or 1 crumbled dried bay leaf

2 sprigs tarragon, dill, or thyme

1 washed vine leaf (optional)

Approx 750ml (1¼ pints) white wine vinegar

1 Snip off the stalk and any dried blossom from the end of the cucumbers. If your jars are large enough, leave the cucumbers whole, otherwise cut them into quarters lengthways, or into 3mm (⅛in) slices.

2 Put a layer of salt in a bowl, add a layer of cucumbers, then another layer of salt. Repeat the layers until all the cucumbers are used up, finishing with a layer of salt. Leave at room temperature for 24 hours.

3 Wash the cucumbers to remove all the salt and pack into clean sterilized jars, leaving 1cm (½in) of head space. Add the shallots or garlic cloves, spices, and herbs. Include fresh dill if you want a traditional flavour, and a vine leaf to keep the pickles crisp and crunchy. Fill the jars with enough vinegar to cover the cucumbers completely.

4 Seal the jars with non-metallic or vinegar-proof lids and label. Store in a cool, dark place for 3–4 weeks to mature before eating (remove the pickles with wooden tongs).

This sweet cucumber pickle is an all-time American favourite. The cucumbers are pickled in hot vinegar, which makes them soft rather than crunchy. Excellent with strong cheeses, and to jazz up meat sandwiches, hamburgers, and barbecued food.

Cucumber pickle

MAKES APPROX 1.25KG (2¾LB)
(1 MEDIUM PRESERVING JAR PLUS
1 SMALL PRESERVING JAR)

TAKES 1¼ HOURS,
PLUS STANDING TIME

KEEPS 6 MONTHS

INGREDIENTS

1 large cucumber, diced or sliced

1 large onion (white), peeled
  and chopped or sliced

1 small green pepper, finely sliced

1 tsp sea salt

300ml (10fl oz) cider vinegar

225g (8oz) light soft brown sugar

¼ level tsp celery seeds

¼ level tsp mustard seeds

¼ level tsp ground cloves

¼ level tsp dill

1 Put the cucumber, onion, and pepper in a large bowl, add the salt and mix thoroughly. Cover the bowl and leave to stand for a couple of hours.

2 Rinse the vegetables under cold water, drain, and put into a preserving pan or a large heavy-based, stainless steel saucepan. Add the vinegar and bring to the boil. Turn off the heat.

3 Add the remaining ingredients and stir to dissolve the sugar. Leave to cool. Ladle into sterilized jars with non-metallic or vinegar-proof lids, seal, and label. Store in a cool, dark place. Allow the flavours to mature for at least 1 month, and refrigerate after opening.

Cucumber
As the cucumber in this recipe is diced or sliced, either a ridge cucumber or smooth salad cucumber (as shown here) is suitable.

This crunchy, sharp cold pickle requires no cooking and could not be simpler to make. It is excellent as part of a mixed hors d'oeuvres, with cheese sandwiches, or served with vegetarian meals. Vary the vegetables, if you wish, using suitable pickling varieties (pp194–95).

Mixed vegetable pickle

MAKES APPROX 500G (1LB 2OZ)
(1 SMALL PRESERVING JAR)

TAKES 30 MINUTES,
PLUS STANDING TIME

KEEPS 3 MONTHS, REFRIGERATED

INGREDIENTS

60g (2oz) sea salt

1 small cauliflower, chopped into florets

1 large onion, roughly chopped

2 carrots, peeled and sliced

10 cherry tomatoes

5 jalapeño peppers, left whole (optional)

600ml (1 pint) ready-spiced
   pickling vinegar

1 tsp coriander seeds

1 tsp mustard seeds

1 Put the salt in a large bowl, add 600ml (1 pint) of water, and mix thoroughly. Add all the vegetables, cover the bowl, and leave to stand overnight. If you find that your prepared vegetables weigh more than 500g (1lb 2oz), you may need to make up more brine: always use a ratio of 60g (2oz) salt per 600ml (1 pint) of water.

2 Mix the vinegar in a jug with the coriander and mustard seeds and put to one side.

3 Rinse the vegetables under cold water, drain, and dry well with a clean tea towel or kitchen paper. Layer and pack them into a sterilized jar with a non-metallic or vinegar-proof lid and pour over the spiced vinegar to cover them completely. Top up with more of the vinegar mix if needed, then seal and label. Keep at room temperature for 2 days, then put in the fridge and leave for at least 1 week before eating. Keep refrigerated once opened.

Originally known as "Indian pickle", this classic recipe is irresistible and has long been a firm favourite. Its characteristic yellow colour and flavour is due to a mixture of turmeric and mustard. This preserve livens up any cold meats or cheese.

Piccalilli

MAKES APPROX 2.25KG (5LB)
(3 MEDIUM PRESERVING JARS)

TAKES 35 MINUTES,
PLUS STANDING TIME

KEEPS 6 MONTHS

INGREDIENTS

1 large cauliflower, cut into florets

2 large onions, peeled, quartered, and sliced finely, or use pickling onions

900g (2lb) mixed vegetables such as courgettes, runner beans, carrots, and green beans, cut into bite-sized pieces

60g (2oz) sea salt

2 tbsp plain flour

225g (8oz) granulated sugar (increase this quantity slightly if you don't like the pickle too sharp)

1 tbsp turmeric

60g (2oz) English mustard powder

900ml (1½ pints) ready-spiced pickling vinegar

1 Put all the vegetables in a large non-metallic bowl. Dissolve the salt in 1.2 litres (2 pints) of water and pour the brine over the vegetables. Put a plate on top of the vegetables to keep them submerged and leave for 24 hours.

2 The next day, drain the vegetables in a colander and rinse in cold water. Bring a large pan of water to the boil, add the vegetables, and blanch for about 2 minutes. Do not overcook them, as they should be crunchy. Drain and refresh in cold water to halt the cooking process (pp58–59).

3 Put the flour, sugar, turmeric, and mustard powder in a small bowl and mix in a little of the vinegar to make a paste. Put it in a large stainless steel saucepan along with the remaining vinegar, bring to the boil, and stir continuously so no lumps appear. Reduce the heat and simmer for about 15 minutes.

4 Add the vegetables to the sauce and stir well so they are all coated. Ladle into warm sterilized jars with non-metallic or vinegar-proof lids, making sure there are no air gaps, seal, and label. Store in a cool, dark place. Allow the flavours to mature for 1 month, and refrigerate after opening.

This vibrant, slightly sweet pickle is crunchy and pleasantly spiced. A wide-necked kilner jar is the best sort of jar to use for this cold pickling method so that the vegetables can fit easily. Serve with traditional Lancashire hot pot, cold meats, or salad.

Red cabbage pickle

MAKES APPROX 1.1KG (2½LB)
(2 SMALL PRESERVING JARS)

TAKES 30 MINUTES,
PLUS STANDING TIME

KEEPS 3 MONTHS, REFRIGERATED

INGREDIENTS

675g (1½lb) red cabbage,
  cored and shredded

1 red onion, sliced

3 tbsp sea salt

600ml (1 pint) white wine vinegar

125g (4½oz) light muscovado sugar,
  or use caster sugar

1 tsp mustard seeds

1 tsp coriander seeds

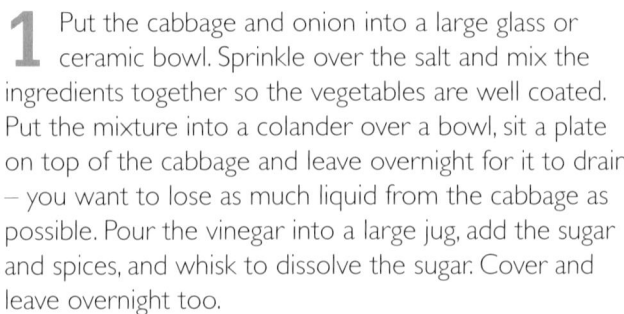

1 Put the cabbage and onion into a large glass or ceramic bowl. Sprinkle over the salt and mix the ingredients together so the vegetables are well coated. Put the mixture into a colander over a bowl, sit a plate on top of the cabbage and leave overnight for it to drain – you want to lose as much liquid from the cabbage as possible. Pour the vinegar into a large jug, add the sugar and spices, and whisk to dissolve the sugar. Cover and leave overnight too.

2 Rinse the cabbage and onion under cold water to remove the salt, then dry the vegetables thoroughly with a clean tea towel or kitchen paper.

3 Layer the vegetables in warm sterilized jars with non-metallic or vinegar-proof lids, packing them down. Give the vinegar a stir and pour over the vegetables so that they are completely covered. Seal, label, and store in a cool, dark place for 1 week. Then leave in the fridge for at least 1 month before using to allow the flavours to develop and mellow. Keep refrigerated once opened.

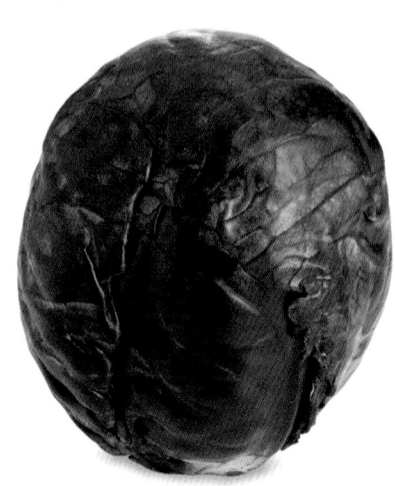

Red cabbage
Dense-headed red (Dutch) cabbages have delicious, peppery-tasting leaves. They are grown from May onwards and harvested throughout the autumn.

Use up a glut of beetroots with this easy, colourful pickle. Roasting them intensifies their flavour but, if you prefer, cook them in a saucepan of salted water for 40 minutes, or until soft if pierced with a knife. Leave for at least one month before using.

Pickled beetroot

MAKES APPROX 1KG (2¼LB)
(2 SMALL PRESERVING JARS)

TAKES 1–1½ HOURS

KEEPS 6 MONTHS

INGREDIENTS

1kg (2¼lb) raw beetroots, scrubbed

600ml (1 pint) pickling vinegar or
    ready-spiced pickling vinegar

50g (1¾oz) caster sugar (optional)

Pinch of chilli flakes (optional)

1 Preheat the oven to 200°C (400°F/Gas 6). Put the beetroots in a roasting tin and roast in the oven for 50 minutes–1½ hours or until the beetroots are soft when tested with a knife. Remove from the oven and leave to cool.

2 When cool enough to handle, peel away the skins from the beetroots and quarter or slice them. Pack into warm sterilized jars with non-metallic or vinegar-proof lids, then pour over the vinegar so it covers the beetroot completely (stir the sugar into the vinegar before you pour it if you like a slightly sweeter pickle). Add the chilli flakes (if using) and then seal and label.

3 Give the jars a little shake so that the ingredients mingle together, and store in a cool, dark place. Allow to mature for one month, and refrigerate after opening.

Making relish

As its name implies, relish packs a tangy punch of flavour. Made from diced fruit or vegetables, it is part pickle, part chutney, but cooked for a shorter time than a chutney. It is a classic accompaniment to barbecued food and burgers.

Sweetcorn and pepper relish

MAKES APPROX 1KG (2¼LB) (2 SMALL PRESERVING JARS)

TAKES 35–40 MINUTES

KEEPS 3 MONTHS

INGREDIENTS

4 fresh sweetcorn cobs

2 medium red peppers, or 1 green and 1 red pepper, deseeded and finely diced

2 celery sticks, sliced finely

1 red chilli, deseeded and finely sliced (optional)

1 medium onion, peeled and finely sliced

450ml (15fl oz) white wine vinegar

225g (8oz) granulated sugar

2 tsp sea salt

2 tsp mustard powder

½ tsp ground turmeric

1 Strip the kernels from the cobs by holding them upright and running a large sharp knife down the sides. Blanch the kernels in a saucepan of boiling water for 2 minutes, then drain well.

2 Put the sweetcorn and the other ingredients in a large saucepan and bring to the boil, stirring to dissolve the sugar. Then simmer gently, stirring frequently, for 15–20 minutes or until the mixture has thickened slightly and has only a little liquid left in the bottom of the pan when you draw a wooden spoon across it.

3 Check the seasoning is right, then pot into warm sterilized jars. The relish should be a spoonable consistency and wetter than a chutney.

4 Seal with non-metallic or vinegar-proof lids, leave to cool, and label. Store in a cool, dark place. Like all relishes, this can be eaten immediately or stored. Once opened, store in the fridge.

This flavoursome mix of sweet tomatoes, vegetables, and hot spices is excellent as a condiment or stirred into a meat dish such as ragù sauce. If you prefer some chunks in your relish, chopping by hand is the best option.

Vegetable and tomato relish

MAKES APPROX 750G (1LB 10OZ) (1 MEDIUM PRESERVING JAR)

TAKES 1 HOUR 30–40 MINUTES

KEEPS 6 MONTHS

INGREDIENTS

1kg (2¼lb) ripe tomatoes, skinned if you prefer

2 onions, roughly chopped

3 courgettes, roughly chopped

1 yellow pepper, deseeded and roughly chopped

2 garlic cloves

2 red chillies, stalks removed (or more if you like it hot)

2 tbsp tomato purée

1 tsp English mustard powder

300ml (10fl oz) malt or cider vinegar

150g (5½oz) granulated sugar

1 Either chop the tomatoes, onions, courgettes, pepper, garlic, and chilli by hand or process in separate batches in a food processor. Whiz until chopped using the pulse button, taking care that the vegetables aren't chopped too fine.

2 Put the chopped vegetables in a preserving pan or a large heavy-based, stainless steel saucepan. Stir in the tomato purée and mustard powder, then add the vinegar and sugar. Simmer, stirring continuously, until the sugar has dissolved, then turn the heat up and cook steadily for 40 minutes–1 hour, stirring frequently, or until the mixture begins to thicken.

3 Ladle into a warm sterilized jar with non-metallic or vinegar-proof lids, seal, and label. Store in a cool, dark place. Allow to mature for 1 month, and refrigerate after opening.

Sweet, sticky, and spicy, this relish, with its lovely hints of orange, is perfect served with a curry, but it's important that the flavours are allowed to mature and mellow for at least one month before opening a jar to use.

Carrot and coriander relish

MAKES APPROX 450G (1LB)
(1 SMALL PRESERVING JAR)

TAKES 50 MINUTES–1 HOUR

KEEPS 3 MONTHS

INGREDIENTS

500g (1lb 2oz) carrots, grated

1 tsp mustard seeds

2 tsp coriander seeds, crushed

1 tsp cardamom seeds (taken from pods)

2.5cm (1in) piece of fresh root ginger, peeled and grated

Juice and zest of 1 organic orange, washed

120ml (4fl oz) cider vinegar

125g (4½oz) granulated sugar or light soft brown sugar

1 Put the carrots in a preserving pan or a large heavy-based, stainless steel saucepan, then add the mustard seeds, coriander seeds, and cardamom seeds and stir.

2 Add the ginger and orange juice and zest, then pour in the vinegar and sugar and stir. Slowly simmer, stirring until the sugar has dissolved, then continue cooking for 10 minutes or so, stirring occasionally, until the carrots have softened. Then raise the heat a little and cook for 15–20 minutes or until most of the liquid has disappeared. Stir frequently so the mixture doesn't burn or stick on the base of the pan.

3 Ladle the relish into a warm sterilized jar with a non-metallic or vinegar-proof lid, seal, and label. Allow to mature for 1 month, and refrigerate after opening.

Carrots
If you grow your own carrots and sow a selection of early and maincrop varieties from March to June, you should be able to harvest them from June to the end of October.

This is a sweet relish with a hint of spice – perfect to serve with cheeses or beef. If you want to save time making the relish, pre-cook the beetroots the night before. Add a handful of coriander seeds or a chopped fresh chilli with the shallots, if you wish.

Beetroot relish

MAKES 1KG (2¼LB)
(2 SMALL PRESERVING JARS)

TAKES 2¼ HOURS

KEEPS 9 MONTHS

INGREDIENTS

1.35kg (3lb) raw beetroots

1 tsp caster sugar

450g (1lb) shallots, finely chopped

600ml (1 pint) cider or white wine vinegar

1 tbsp pickling spices, placed in a muslin pickling/spice bag

450g (1lb) granulated sugar

1 Put the beetroots in a preserving pan or a large heavy-based, stainless steel saucepan, pour over enough water to cover them, and add the caster sugar. Bring to the boil and simmer for 1 hour or until the beetroot is soft and cooked. Drain and leave to cool. When cool enough to handle, peel and dice into small, neat pieces.

2 Put the shallots and vinegar in the rinsed-out preserving pan or saucepan and cook for 10 minutes on a low heat. Add the chopped beetroots and the muslin bag of pickling spices. Give the mixture a stir, add the granulated sugar, and cook gently until the sugar has all dissolved. Bring to the boil and cook at a rolling boil for 5 minutes, then reduce the heat to a simmer and cook for about 40 minutes or until the mixture thickens.

3 Remove the spice bag, then ladle into warm sterilized jars with non-metallic or vinegar-proof lids, making sure there are no air gaps. Seal, label, and store in a cool, dark place. Allow the flavours to mature for 1 month, and refrigerate after opening.

This tangy relish is full of fresh, fruity flavours and warm aromatic spices. The cranberries provide texture, the nectarines give a soft base, and the onion delivers crunch. Use raisins or sultanas instead of cranberries, if you prefer.

Sweet and sour nectarine and cranberry relish

MAKES APPROX 800G (1¾LB)
(2 SMALL PRESERVING JARS)

TAKES 1¼–1½ HOURS

KEEPS 3 MONTHS

INGREDIENTS

1 tbsp olive oil

2 red onions, finely chopped

Pinch of sea salt

1 tsp chilli flakes

450g (1lb) nectarines, stoned and chopped

125g (4½oz) dried cranberries,
  or use sour cherries

1 tsp coriander seeds

Pinch of ground cinnamon

Pinch of allspice

300g (10oz) light soft brown sugar

150ml (5fl oz) white wine vinegar

1 Heat the oil in a preserving pan or a large heavy-based, stainless steel saucepan. Add the onions and sea salt and cook until soft.

2 Stir in the chilli flakes. Add the nectarines and cranberries, spices, sugar, and vinegar and stir until the sugar has dissolved. Bring to the boil, stirring occasionally, then reduce to a simmer and cook on a low heat for 40 minutes–1 hour or until the mixture begins to thicken. Stir frequently towards the end of cooking so the mixture doesn't stick to the bottom of the pan. Add a little hot water if it becomes too dry.

3 Ladle into warm sterilized jars with non-metallic or vinegar-proof lids, seal, and label. Store in a cool, dark place. Allow the flavours to mature for 1 month, and refrigerate after opening.

Sharp and lightly spiced, this relish works well with lamb burgers. It tastes tart just after being made, so leave for one month to settle, let the flavours meld together, and allow the sweetness to come through.

Sweet courgette relish

MAKES APPROX 1.5KG (3LB 3OZ) (2 MEDIUM PRESERVING JARS)

TAKES 1 HOUR 25 MINUTES

KEEPS 6 MONTHS

INGREDIENTS

900g (2lb) courgettes, finely chopped by hand or in a food processor

1 large onion, very finely chopped by hand or in a food processor

500ml (16fl oz) cider vinegar

350g (12oz) granulated sugar

2 tsp English mustard powder

1 tsp turmeric

1–2 tsp chilli flakes

2 tsp cornflour

2 tsp coriander seeds

1 Put the courgettes and onion in a preserving pan or a large heavy-based, stainless steel saucepan. Pour over the cider vinegar and stir to mix.

2 Add the sugar, mustard powder, turmeric, chilli flakes, cornflour, and coriander seeds, and stir over a gentle heat until the sugar has dissolved. Bring to the boil, reduce the heat, and cook, stirring occasionally, for 40 minutes– 1 hour or until the mixture has thickened. The relish is ready when it is the consistency of a burger relish (pp210–11).

3 Ladle into warm sterilized jars with non-metallic or vinegar-proof lids, seal, and label. Store in a cool, dark place. Allow the flavours to mature for 1 month, and refrigerate after opening.

Courgettes
These summer vegetables grow extremely quickly. They are thirsty plants and are best kept moist in a rich soil, mulched if possible. Try varieties such as 'Black Forest', 'Defender', 'Jemma', and 'Zucchini'.

Bottled delights include fruits in syrup, cordials, and syrups, ketchups, and sauces, and that most luxurious – and, arguably, most delicious and easiest – preserve of all, fruits in alcohol. All home-made bottled preserves are better than those you can buy, as they are in every way purer-, cleaner-, and richer-tasting. They occupy a special place in the preserving tradition, and are to be treasured. For long keeping, bottled preserves are heat-processed; see pp18–19 for information on how to do this, and general bottling know-how.

The best ingredients for...
Bottling

Almost all fruits bottle well, whether in syrup or alcohol, or made into natural additive-free syrups, juices, and cordials. You will be spoilt for choice as to which glorious seasonal fruits to bottle.

Figs
Choose aromatic, ripe, but not squashy, green or black thin-skinned figs to bottle in syrup (add lemon juice to balance their alkaline nature), or add to rumtopf. Flavour with vanilla or ginger. In season from summer to autumn.

Greengages
This variety of plum is widely acknowledged to have the finest flavour and texture. Greengages are in season briefly in August; bottle in syrup to capture the best of this heavenly fruit.

Blueberries
Like other berry fruits, blueberries are excellent bottled in syrup, added to a rumtopf, or made into health-giving, antioxidant- and vitamin-rich cordials.

Nectarines
Like peaches and apricots, nectarines are delicious as cordials, bottled in syrup, or steeped in alcohol. Choose sun-ripened, freshly picked fruit.

Cherries
Fresh, ripe dessert or 'Morello' cherries taste luscious if bottled in syrup or added to a rumtopf, and even better if steeped in brandy and left for three months to mature.

Pears
Lke quinces, pears are lovely bottled in syrup and flavoured with ginger, star anise, cinnamon, or cardamom, or in brandy or eau-de-vie to make fruit liqueurs.

Raspberries
A classic fruit to add to a rumtopf. Raspberries also make superlative liqueurs and cordials, as their flavour is more pronounced and fruity than if bottled in syrup.

Plums

All varieties of plums, including cookers and dessert plums, bottle well in syrup. Like all stone fruits, it's easier to remove the stones, slice into halves, then bottle.

Clementines

A sweet citrus fruit, clementines have a loose skin and web-like pith that are easily removed for bottling in syrup or alcohol, or as a cordial.

Kumquats

These winter fruits are not true citrus fruits. They have thin, soft skins and are exquisite bottled in alcohol, as they are too tart to eat raw.

BOTTLING METHODS

When bottling in hot syrup, heat process fruits (p19) for the following times. The chart also lists whether fruits are suitable for cordials and syrups and bottling in alcohol.

INGREDIENTS	BOTTLED IN HOT SYRUP		CORDIALS AND SYRUPS	ALCOHOL
	Oven method Minutes at 150°C/300°F/Gas 2	Water bath method Minutes simmering; heat from warm (38°C/100°F) to simmering (88°C/190°F) in 25–30 minutes		
Apples	30–40	2	Yes	No
Apricots	40–50	10	Yes	Yes
Blackberries	30–40	2	Yes	Yes
Blackcurrants	30–40	2	Yes	Yes
Blueberries	30–40	2	Yes	Yes
Boysenberries	30–40	2	Yes	Yes
Cherries	40–50	10	Yes	Yes
Chestnuts	50–60		No	No
Citrus fruits	30–40	10	Yes	Yes
Cranberries	30–40	2	Yes	Yes
Figs (with lemon juice)	40	60–70	No	Yes
Gooseberries	40–50	10	Yes	Yes
Kumquats	30–40	10	No	Yes
Loganberries	30–40	2	Yes	Yes
Melon (with lemon juice)	40–50		No	No
Mulberries	30–40	2	Yes	Yes
Nectarines and peaches	50–60 (halved)	20	Yes	Yes
Pears	60 (halved)	40	Yes	Yes
Plums (all types)	50–60 (halved)	20	No	Yes
Quinces	40–50	30	Yes	Yes
Raspberries	30–40	2	Yes	Yes
Red- and white currants	30–40	2	Yes	Yes
Rhubarb	40-50	10	Yes	No
Strawberries	30–40	2	Yes	Yes
Tayberries	30–40	2	Yes	Yes
Watermelon (with lemon juice)	40–50		No	No

BOTTLED WHOLE TOMATOES

Unlike other vegetables, tomatoes bottle exceptionally well and retain all their flavour. Using the ripest small tomatoes (1kg/2¼lb), remove the stalks and toss in a bowl with 2 tbsp of lemon juice, 2 tsp of salt, and 1 tsp of caster sugar. Pack the tomatoes tightly into 2 warm sterilized medium preserving jars, squashing them down without bruising them. Divide any remaining lemon juice mixture between the 2 jars, and seal. Heat process in a pre-heated moderate oven (150°C/ 300°F/Gas 2) for 1 hour–1 hour 10 minutes or a warm water bath (88°C/190°F) for 40 minutes. Leave to cool, check the seal, and store in a cool, dark place for up to 12 months.

Bottling fruits in syrup

Bottled fruits have a charm and appeal of their own. All fruits can be bottled, and many are better bottled than frozen. Sugar alone will not preserve them, so both fruit and jars must be heat-processed for successful storage (p19).

Peaches in syrup

MAKES APPROX 450ML
(15FL OZ) (2 SMALL
PRESERVING JARS)

TAKES 15 MINUTES, PLUS
PROCESSING TIME

KEEPS 12 MONTHS
IF HEAT-PROCESSED

INGREDIENTS

Approx 115g (4oz)
  granulated sugar

4–5 just-ripe peaches

Cracked peach kernels (optional)

SUGAR SYRUP

Depending on the tartness
of the fruit you have, and how
sweet you want it to taste,
choose a light, medium, or
heavy syrup for bottling:

Light syrup 115g (4oz) sugar
per 600ml (1 pint) water
Medium syrup 175g (6oz)
sugar per 600ml (1 pint) water
Heavy syrup 250g (10oz)
sugar per 600ml (1 pint) water

The syrup can also be flavoured
with spices such as star anise,
cinnamon, and cloves, or use
scented geranium leaves or a
split vanilla pod.
  Put the sugar and water into
a pan and bring to the boil over
a gentle heat, stirring to dissolve
the sugar. Boil for 1–2 minutes.

1 Make a light, medium, or heavy sugar syrup first (see box, left). Put the sugar and 600ml (1 pint) of water into a pan, bring gently to the boil, and boil for 1–2 minutes.

2 Skin the peaches (dip in boiling water for 30 seconds if they don't peel easily). Cut in half, remove the stones, and reserve a few stones if you want to use the kernels (p21).

3 Place the warm sterilized jars in a deep roasting tray. Pack in the fruit, leaving 1cm (½in) of space at the top. Add the kernels (if using) and fill to the brim with hot syrup.

4 Bang the jars lightly and swivel them to remove air bubbles. Top up with syrup. Fit the rubber-sealed or screw lids (loosen by a quarter of a turn) and process (p19).

5 Tighten the clips or lids (or screw on plastic screw-band lids) immediately after processing. Leave the jars for 24 hours, then test the seals, and store in a cool, dark place.

Antioxidant-rich berries such as these are a boost to your immune system. Serve them with a vanilla-flavoured crème fraîche, or drained with turkey, game, or ham instead of the usual cranberry sauce. Once opened, refrigerate and consume within one week.

Berries in lime syrup

MAKES APPROX 1 LITRE (1¾ PINTS)
(2 SMALL PRESERVING JARS)

TAKES 1 HOUR 5 MINUTES

KEEPS 12 MONTHS IF HEAT-PROCESSED

INGREDIENTS

450ml (15fl oz) heavy syrup (p222)

¼ organic lime, either thinly pared or as finely grated zest

225g (8oz) cranberries, washed

225g (8oz) blueberries, washed

1 Make the heavy syrup, adding the lime zest to the saucepan at the beginning.

2 Pat the berries dry with kitchen paper and mix them together. Put the sterilized jars on a cloth or wooden board. Pack the fruit into the warm sterilized jars as tightly as possible without squashing them and leaving 1cm (½in) of space at the top.

3 Pour the boiling syrup, including the lime zest, over the berries, adding enough to cover the fruit completely. Tap the jars gently on the board or work surface to remove any air bubbles. Push down any berries that float to the surface with the back of a sterilized spoon, then fit the rubber band or metal lid seal and clamp on the lid. If using screw-band jars, loosen by a quarter of a turn.

4 Process for the required time (p221) using one of the methods on page 19, then tighten or put on the screw-band if necessary. Leave for 24 hours, then test for a seal. (If using kilner jars with metal lids, you will know immediately or soon after processing if you have a seal, as the lid becomes slightly concave and is firm with no "give" when pressed. You may even hear a "pop" as the seal forms.) Store in a cool, dark place, and refrigerate after opening.

This is a labour of love, as it takes a while to peel the chestnuts. You can make half the quantity if the effort is too much! If you add the split vanilla pods to the sugar syrup when you make it, you can ensure that more of the vanilla flavour is imparted.

Chestnuts in vanilla syrup

MAKES APPROX 1 LITRE (1¾ PINTS) (2 SMALL PRESERVING JARS)

TAKES 1 HOUR 55 MINUTES

KEEPS 12 MONTHS IF HEAT-PROCESSED

INGREDIENTS

400–600ml (14fl oz–1 pint) medium syrup (p222), using light soft brown sugar

2 vanilla pods, split

900g (2lb) fresh chestnuts

Chestnuts
If you forage for sweet chestnuts (*Castanea salvia*) in autumn, wear gardening gloves to extract the nuts from their husks and discard any that are damaged or cracked.

1 Make the heavy syrup, adding the vanilla pods to the saucepan at the beginning if you wish.

2 Make a nick in the skin of each chestnut and place in a saucepan. Cover with water, bring to the boil, then simmer for 20 minutes. Remove the pan from the heat.

3 Peel off the hard outer skin and the thin brown inner skin from each chestnut with a small sharp knife. If the chestnuts start to cool down, pop them back on the hob for a minute to heat up. They won't peel at all well if cold.

4 Pack the nuts into warm sterilized jars, leaving 1cm (½in) of space at the top, and tuck a split vanilla pod inside each jar. Bring the syrup to the boil and pour it over the nuts so they are completely covered (make more syrup if necessary). Tap the jars gently on a work surface to remove air bubbles. Fit the rubber band or metal lid seal and clamp on the lid. If using screw-band jars, loosen by a quarter of a turn.

5 Process for the required time (p221) using one of the methods on page 19, then tighten or put on the screw-band if necessary. Leave for 24 hours, then test for a seal. (If using kilner jars with metal lids, you will know immediately or soon after processing if you have a seal, as the lid becomes slightly concave and is firm with no "give" when pressed. You may even hear a "pop" as the seal forms.) Store in a cool, dark place, and refrigerate after opening.

Although figs lose their vibrant colour, turning greener if bottled, being macerated in honey syrup with lemon zest enhances their flavour. They are delicious served as a dessert with thick Greek yoghurt or cream, but also as a starter with cool, salty feta cheese.

Fresh figs in honey syrup

MAKES I LITRE (1¾ PINTS)
(2 SMALL PRESERVING JARS)

TAKES I HOUR

KEEPS 12 MONTHS IF HEAT-PROCESSED

INGREDIENTS

250ml (8fl oz) clear honey

2 thinly pared strips of washed organic
   lemon zest (about 1cm/½in wide)

Juice of I lemon (2 tbsp)

Approx 16 small ripe figs
   (or 12 larger ones)

1 Put the honey, 500ml (16fl oz) of cold water, and the lemon zest and juice in a saucepan. Heat gently, stirring until the honey has dissolved. Bring to the boil and boil for 3 minutes.

2 Meanwhile, wash and dry the figs. Add to the syrup and boil for 2 minutes. Using a slotted spoon, pack the fruit tightly into warm sterilized jars without squashing them too much. Lift the zest from the syrup and discard. Pour the hot syrup over the figs to cover completely. Tap each jar gently on a wooden board or work surface to remove any air bubbles.

3 Fit the rubber band or metal lid seal and clamp on the lid. If using screw-band jars, loosen by a quarter of a turn.

4 Process for the required time (p221) using one of the methods described on page 19. Then tighten the screw-band, if necessary. Leave for 24 hours and test for a seal. (If using kilner jars with metal lids, you will know immediately or soon after processing if you have a seal as the lid becomes slightly concave and is firm with no "give" once pressed. You may even hear a "pop" as the seal forms.) Store in a cool, dark place. Once opened, store in the fridge.

The fruit in this recipe is bottled in water, so sweeten it to taste depending on whether you are planning to put it in a pie, crumble, or purée it for a mousse or fruit fool. Make sure you toss the apple slices completely in the lemon juice, or they will discolour.

Bottled rhubarb and apples

MAKES APPROX I LITRE (1¾ PINTS) (2 SMALL PRESERVING JARS)

TAKES I HOUR

KEEPS 12 MONTHS IF HEAT-PROCESSED

INGREDIENTS

450g (1lb) rhubarb

2 medium cooking or cookable dessert apples (approx 350g/12oz)

4 tbsp lemon juice

1 Trim the rhubarb and cut it into short lengths. Peel, core, and slice the apples. Toss the slices immediately in the lemon juice.

2 Pack the fruit in layers in warm sterilized jars set well apart on a baking sheet. Place the sheet of unsealed jars immediately in the oven at 130°C (250°F/Gas ½) and cook for 50 minutes.

3 Remove one jar at a time and quickly pour in enough boiling water to cover the fruit and reach the brim of the jar. Seal tightly immediately. Repeat with the remaining jar. Leave to stand for 24 hours, then test for a seal (p19). Store in a cool, dry place. Refrigerate after opening.

Apples
If you have a glut of 'Anne Elizabeth', 'Blenheim Orange', 'Pippin' varieties, or cooking apples, you can omit the rhubarb and make this recipe using just the apples.

Try these bottled quinces served with spice-flavoured or vanilla ice cream, clotted cream, or crème fraîche. They are also delicious chopped or puréed and served as an accompaniment to game, pork, or duck.

Quinces in spiced syrup

MAKES APPROX I LITRE (1¾ PINTS)
(2 SMALL PRESERVING JARS)

TAKES 1¼ HOURS

KEEPS 12 MONTHS IF HEAT-PROCESSED

INGREDIENTS

900g (2lb) quinces, scrubbed

I tbsp lemon juice

275g (9½oz) caster sugar

2 star anise, I cinnamon stick, or 2 cloves

1 Place the quinces in a large saucepan, add 600ml (1 pint) of water, bring to the boil, and boil for 2 minutes to soften them. Lift out of the pan with a slotted spoon and plunge into cold water. Reserve the pan of water. Peel, core, and quarter the quinces and put immediately into a bowl of cold water with the lemon juice (to prevent the quince flesh discolouring).

2 Stir the sugar into the reserved pan of water. Heat the pan gently until the sugar dissolves, then stir well. Drain the quince quarters and add them, and the star anise, to the syrup. Bring to the boil, reduce the heat, cover and poach gently for 12–15 minutes or until just tender.

3 Pack the quinces tightly into the warm sterilized jars, leaving 1cm (½in) of space at the top. Bring the syrup back to the boil and pour over the fruit to cover it completely. Tap the jar gently on a wooden board to remove air bubbles. Fit the rubber band or metal lid seal and clamp on the lid. If using screw-band jars, loosen by a quarter turn.

4 Process for the required time (p221) using one of the methods on page 19, then tighten or put on the screw-band if necessary. Leave for 24 hours, then test for a seal. (If using kilner jars with metal lids, you will know immediately or soon after processing if you have a seal, as the lid becomes slightly concave and is firm with no "give" when pressed. You may even hear a "pop" as the seal forms.) Store in a cool, dark place, and refrigerate after opening.

Quinces
A relative of pears and apples, quinces have a similar shape, often with down on their skin, and hard, fragrant flesh. Japonica is a small ornamental quince that can be used instead for this recipe.

You can use any soft citrus fruits for this recipe or, if you prefer to use oranges rather than clementines, cut all the rind and pith off six oranges, cut into slices, and follow the recipe. Serve with fresh cream for an instant delicious dessert.

Clementines in caramel syrup

MAKES APPROX 1 LITRE (1¾ PINTS)
(1 LARGE PRESERVING JAR)

TAKES 25 MINUTES

KEEPS 12 MONTHS IF HEAT-PROCESSED

INGREDIENTS

175g (6oz) granulated sugar

10 small clementines, peeled, with the white pith scraped off with a knife

1 Put the sugar and 100ml (3½fl oz) of cold water in a medium saucepan. Stir well, then heat without stirring or boiling until the sugar has all dissolved. Bring to the boil and boil rapidly for 5–10 minutes or until a rich golden brown.

2 Cover your hand with a cloth (as the caramel will splutter) and pour in 200ml (7fl oz) of hot water. Stir until the caramel has dissolved and bring back to the boil.

3 Pack the fruit into a warm sterilized jar tightly without squashing it, leaving 1cm (½in) of space at the top.

4 Fill to the brim with the hot caramel syrup. Tap the jar down lightly on the work surface and swivel to and fro to remove any air pockets. Top up with extra syrup if needed so the fruit is completely covered. Fit the rubber band or metal lid, seal, and clamp on the lid. If using screw-band jars, loosen by a quarter of a turn.

5 Process for the required time (p221) using one of the methods described on page 19, then tighten the screw-band, if necessary. Leave for 24 hours and test for a seal. (If using kilner jars with metal lids, you will know immediately or soon after processing if you have a seal as the lid becomes slightly concave and is firm with no "give" once pressed. You may even hear a "pop" as the seal forms.) Store in a cool, dark place. Once opened, store in the fridge.

These fruits are bottled in apple juice, so there is no added sugar. (You can use this method for any recipe where light syrup is called for.) Otherwise, use the recipe for light syrup on page 222 instead if you prefer. The fruit must be ripe for maximum flavour.

Red summer fruits in apple juice

MAKES APPROX 1 LITRE (1¾ PINTS) (2 SMALL PRESERVING JARS)

TAKES 1¼ HOURS

KEEPS 12 MONTHS IF HEAT-TREATED

INGREDIENTS

450g (1lb) mixed red fruits (e.g. cherries, strawberries, raspberries, and redcurrants)

450ml (15fl oz) pure apple juice

1 Halve and stone the cherries, or leave whole but stoned. If using strawberries, hull them, leave small ones whole, and halve or quarter large ones. Remove the redcurrants from their stalks using the prongs of a fork.

2 Put the apple juice in a saucepan and bring to the boil. Boil for 2 minutes.

3 Mix the fruits together. Put the warm sterilized jars on a cloth or wooden board. Pack the fruits into them as tightly as possible without squashing them, leaving 1cm (½in) of space at the top.

4 Pour the boiling juice over the fruits to cover them completely (if berries float up, submerge them completely using the back of a sterilized spoon). Tap the jars gently on a wooden board to remove air bubbles. Fit the rubber band or metal lid seal and clamp on the lid. If using screw-band jars, loosen by a quarter turn.

5 Process for the required time (p221) using one of the methods on page 19, then tighten or put on the screw-band if necessary. Leave for 24 hours, then test for a seal. (If using kilner jars with metal lids, you will know immediately or soon after processing if you have a seal, as the lid becomes slightly concave and is firm with no "give" when pressed. You may even hear a "pop" as the seal forms.) Store in a cool, dark place, and refrigerate after opening.

Watermelon needs lemon juice added to it to make it suitable for bottling, so don't omit it. For even more flavour, try adding a few slices of orange to the syrup as you make it, then distribute the pieces among the melon in the jars before you pour over the syrup.

Watermelon with fresh ginger

MAKES APPROX 1 LITRE (1¾ PINTS) (2 SMALL PRESERVING JARS)

TAKES 1 HOUR 10 MINUTES

KEEPS 12 MONTHS IF HEAT-PROCESSED

INGREDIENTS

1 small watermelon

2.5cm (1in) piece fresh root ginger

140g (5oz) granulated sugar

2 tbsp lemon juice

1 Cut the melon in half, remove the seeds, and either scoop the flesh into balls using a melon baller, or remove the skin and cut the flesh into bite-sized cubes.

2 Peel the ginger and cut into wafer-thin slices using a mandolin, the slicer blade on a grater, or a sharp knife.

3 Make the syrup (p222) using 300ml (10fl oz) of water and the ginger, sugar, and lemon juice. Add the melon and boil for 2 minutes. Place the warm sterilized jars on a wooden board or cloth. Using a slotted spoon, pack the fruit tightly into the jars without squashing it, and leaving 1cm (½in) of space at the top.

4 Fill the jars to the brim with the hot syrup, then tap the jars lightly on a board to remove air bubbles. Top up with extra syrup if needed to cover the fruit completely. Fit the rubber band or metal lid seal and clamp on the lid. If using screw-band jars, loosen by a quarter of a turn.

5 Process for the required time (p221) using the oven heat processing method (p19), then tighten or put on the screw-band if necessary. Leave for 24 hours, then test for a seal. (If using kilner jars with metal lids, you will know immediately or soon after processing if you have a seal, as the lid becomes slightly concave and is firm with no "give" when pressed. You may even hear a "pop" as the seal forms.) Store in a cool, dark place, and refrigerate after opening.

Bottling fruits in alcohol

Fruits preserved in alcohol – brandy, rum, whisky, vodka, gin, or Eau de vie – taste deliciously boozy. Serve with coffee, or with the fragrant liquor on ice cream or desserts. This method suits juicy, thin-skinned berries, plums, and cherries.

Cherries in brandy

MAKES APPROX 750ML (1¼ PINTS) (3 SMALL PRESERVING JARS)

TAKES 10 MINUTES

KEEPS 12 MONTHS OR LONGER

INGREDIENTS

500g (1lb 2oz) just-ripe cherries (sweet or 'Morello') in perfect condition, washed and de-stalked

Approx 175g (6oz) caster sugar

Approx 350ml (12fl oz) brandy

1 Carefully place the washed cherries in some wide-necked, sterilized preserving jars, packing them in tightly while taking care not to squash or bruise them.

2 Add enough sugar to fill one third of the jar and top with alcohol. (As a general guide, use ¼–⅓ sugar and ¾–⅔ alcohol to fruit.)

3 Tap the jar gently on a board, turn it to and fro to release any air bubbles, and seal. The sugar will gradually dissolve – give the jar an occasional shake or turn it upside down to help it dissolve.

4 Store in a cool,
dark place for
2–3 months to mature
before opening.

The idea of rumtopf (which literally means "rum pot") is that you start with your favourite fresh fruits in season and add other fruits as they become available until the pot is full. If you don't have a real rumtopf jar, use any sterilized earthenware jar with a lid.

Rumtopf

MAKES 1 RUMTOPF JAR OR EARTHENWARE JAR

TAKES 10 MINUTES EACH TIME

KEEPS BEST EATEN WITHIN 12 MONTHS

INGREDIENTS

A selection of fresh soft, ripe fruit (e.g. berries, currants, grapes, pears, and stone fruits)

Granulated sugar (for quantity, see method)

Rum (for quantity, see method)

1 Peel fruits such as pears if necessary, halve and remove the cores or stones, then cut into slices if the fruit is large. Halve small fruits such as cherries, apricots, or plums. Leave berries, grapes, and currants whole.

2 Weigh the prepared fruits and measure out half their weight in sugar. Put the fruit in a sterilized rumtopf jar with the sugar, mix well, and leave to stand for 1 hour.

3 Pour in just enough rum to cover the fruit. Cover with a sterilized saucer or plate, pressing it down to keep the fruit submerged (if your pot has quite a narrow neck, use 3 or 4 demitasse saucers overlapping).

4 Cover the jar opening with cling film, then put the lid on and store in a cool, dark place.

5 As you grow or buy more fruits, mix them with half their weight in sugar, add them to the pot, top up with rum, and cover as before. When you've added all you wish (it doesn't have to be full), leave for at least 1 month in a cool place before eating, although it tastes best after 3 months of maturing.

Pears
The fruit for a rumtopf should be ripe, but not over-ripe, and flavoursome. Pear varieties such as 'Comice' and 'Conference' are full of flavour.

If you like sweet spices, try adding a cinnamon stick or a star anise to the jar as you pot up the fruit. You can also use this method for preserving damsons and greengages. Once opened, store the jar in the fridge and eat within two weeks.

Plums in brandy

MAKES APPROX 1 LITRE (1¾ PINTS)
(2 SMALL PRESERVING JARS)

TAKES 10 MINUTES

KEEPS 12 MONTHS

INGREDIENTS

Approx 500g (1lb 2oz) plums

Approx 175g (6oz) granulated sugar

Approx 350ml (12fl oz) brandy

1 Prick the fruits with a fork or darning needle. If the plums are quite large, halve them and stone them instead. Pack the fruits into sterilized jars, adding as many fruits as you can without squashing or bruising them.

2 Add enough sugar to fill about one third of the jar. Pour over enough brandy to fill the jar completely. Tap the jars gently on a wooden board and turn them to and fro to release any air bubbles, then seal. Invert the jars a few times to mix the sugar around a bit.

3 The sugar will gradually dissolve. Give the jars a quick shake whenever you remember to help this process.

4 Store in a cool, dark place for 2–3 months to allow the flavours to mature. Refrigerate after opening.

Plums
The size, colour, and sweetness of plums vary widely.
Choose dessert varieties such as 'Opal', 'Cambridge Gage',
or 'Victoria', or culinary plums such as 'Marjorie's Seedling'.

The addition of a few split cardamom pods gives these fruits a lovely fragrance. The fruit is stunning served with bitter chocolate ice cream, while the liquor makes a delicious orange liqueur. Use brandy instead of vodka if you prefer.

Kumquats in vodka

MAKES APPROX 1 LITRE (1¾ PINTS) (1 LARGE PRESERVING JAR)

TAKES 10 MINUTES

KEEPS 12 MONTHS

INGREDIENTS

500g (1lb 2oz) kumquats, washed, scrubbed, and dried

6 cardamom pods, split (optional)

Approx 175g (6oz) caster sugar

Approx 360ml (12fl oz) vodka

1 Use a cocktail stick to prick the fruit all over, then pack in a sterilized preserving jar, adding as many as you can without squashing or bruising them.

2 Add the cardamom pods (if using) and enough sugar to fill about one third of the jar. Pour on enough vodka to fill the jar completely. Tap the jar gently on the work surface and swivel to and fro to release any air bubbles. Seal with a tight-fitting lid.

3 Invert the jar a few times to mix the sugar around a bit. The sugar will gradually dissolve. Give the jar a shake occasionally for the first couple of days to help this process.

4 Store in a cool, dark place for 2–3 months to mature. Once opened, refrigerate and eat within 2 weeks.

This recipe uses less sugar, but gives a good flavour; if you like very sweet liqueurs, double the quantity of sugar. If you want to use damsons, use a wide-necked preserving jar, then strain the flavoured gin into a bottle. You can also use vodka instead of gin.

Sloe gin

MAKES APPROX 500ML (16FL OZ)
(1 LARGE BOTTLE)

TAKES 20 MINUTES

KEEPS 12 MONTHS

INGREDIENTS

Approx 225g (8oz) sloes, fresh or frozen

85g (3oz) caster sugar

4 juniper berries, slightly crushed

A few drops natural almond extract

Approx 350ml (12fl oz) gin

1 Wash the sloes and prick each one with a darning needle. If using frozen sloes, there is no need to prick the skins; just allow the berries to defrost at room temperature. Place the fruits in a sterilized cordial bottle, special sloe gin bottle, or an empty gin bottle.

2 Add the sugar, juniper berries, and the almond extract. Top up with gin.

3 Seal, then shake the bottle by tilting it up and down a few times to mix the ingredients. Leave in a cool, dark place for 3 months, shaking the bottle occasionally.

4 Strain the liqueur into a sterilized bottle, cork, and use as required. You can use the macerated sloes to serve with ice cream or to add to an apple pie (remember they have stones). They can also be made into a chocolate biscuit cake in place of raisins for a grown-up treat.

Sloes
Traditionally sloes are picked after the first frosts so their skins are softened and give the gin more flavour. A practical alternative is to freeze the sloes for a few hours (pp62–63).

Use just-ripe, slightly firm pears for this recipe. Over-ripe fruit will become unpalatably soft once bottled and stored. Wine is not strong enough to preserve the fruit without processing to seal the jars, so they have to be heat-processed.

Mulled pears

MAKES APPROX 1 LITRE (1¾ PINTS) (2 SMALL PRESERVING JARS)

TAKES 1 HOUR 15 MINUTES

KEEPS 12 MONTHS IF HEAT-PROCESSED

INGREDIENTS

115g (4oz) granulated sugar

2 tsp lemon juice

550ml (16½fl oz) red wine, plus extra if needed

1 cinnamon stick

2 star anise

2 cloves

6 pears, peeled, cored, and halved

1 Put the sugar in a large saucepan (large enough for the pears to sit in one layer) with the lemon juice, 250ml (8fl oz) of the wine, and the spices. Bring to the boil over a medium heat, stirring until the sugar has dissolved, then boil for 2 minutes without stirring. Add the pears and cook gently for 2 minutes, turning them over once.

2 Place warm sterilized preserving jars on a cloth or wooden board. Lift the fruit out of the syrup with a slotted spoon and pack tightly into the jars without squashing it, leaving 1cm (½in) of space at the top.

3 Add the rest of the wine to the syrup. Bring back to the boil for a few seconds. Pour the syrup into a heat-proof jug (discard the cinnamon stick) and pour over the fruit. If necessary, top up with a little extra wine so the fruit is completely covered. Fit the rubber band or metal lid seal and clamp on the lid. If using screw-band jars, loosen by a quarter of a turn.

4 Process for the required time (p221) using one of the methods described on page 19, then tighten or put on the screw-band if necessary. Leave for 24 hours, then test for a seal. (If using kilner jars with metal lids, you will know immediately or soon after processing if you have a seal, as the lid becomes slightly concave and is firm with no "give" when pressed. You may even hear a "pop" as the seal forms.) Store in a cool, dark place, and refrigerate after opening.

Apricots seeped in almond liqueur is a marriage made in heaven. If you want to preserve them whole, prick with a darning needle and poach in a single layer in the syrup for one to two minutes, shaking the pan to turn the fruit. Serve with cream or ice cream.

Apricots and almonds in amaretto

MAKES APPROX 1 LITRE (1¾ PINTS) (1 LARGE PRESERVING JAR)

TAKES 20 MINUTES

KEEPS 12 MONTHS

INGREDIENTS

85g (3oz) granulated sugar

450g (1lb) apricots, halved and stoned

60g (2oz) blanched almonds

Approx 250ml (8fl oz) amaretto

1 Put the sugar and 150ml (5fl oz) of cold water in a large saucepan. Heat gently, stirring continuously until the sugar has dissolved.

2 Remove half the apricots and reserve, and place the remaining apricots in a single layer in the pan. Bring the syrup and fruit to the boil and boil for 1 minute until the fruit has softened slightly, but still holds its shape well. Remove with a slotted spoon and place in a warm sterilized jar. Add half the almonds. Repeat with the remaining apricots and nuts.

3 Bring the syrup back to the boil, then pour it over the fruit. Top up with amaretto to cover completely. Leave to cool, cover tightly, and invert gently a few times to mix the syrup and liqueur. Store in a cool, dark place for 4 weeks for the flavours to develop. Refrigerate after opening.

Making soft fruit drinks

Home-made syrups, cordials, and juices make the most of seasonal fruit and taste much fruitier than those you can buy. Use this syrup to flavour milkshakes and smoothies, as a sauce for ice creams, and stirred into fruit salads.

Berry syrup

MAKES APPROX 500ML (16FL OZ) (2 SMALL BOTTLES)

TAKES 25 MINUTES

KEEPS 1–2 MONTHS, REFRIGERATED, (6 MONTHS FROZEN)

INGREDIENTS

450g (1lb) ripe blackberries or loganberries, washed if needed

Approx 350g (12oz) caster sugar (see method)

1 tsp citric acid

1 Place the fruit in a saucepan with a thin film of water in the bottom, and simmer very gently for the shortest time possible to extract the juice (about 3–5 minutes). Squash the fruit with a potato masher or the back of a wooden spoon as it cooks.

2 Strain the purée through a muslin-lined sieve or jelly bag into a clean bowl (to give a clearer syrup). Press the pulp in the sieve very gently to extract any remaining juice.

EXTRACTING THE GOODNESS IN FRUIT

To retain as much of a fruit's natural goodness, always use a very gentle heat to extract its juice. The amount of water needed to do this depends on the juiciness of the fruit, but use as little water as possible:
▪ For soft, juicy berry fruits such as strawberries, use a thin film of water at the bottom of the pan.
▪ For thicker-skinned or fleshier fruits such as blackcurrants, use approx 150ml (5fl oz) of water per 450g (1lb) of fruit.

3 Pour the juice into a measuring jug. Calculate and measure the amount of sugar needed (350g/12oz of sugar per 500ml/16fl oz of juice), then add it to the juice with the citric acid. Stir until the sugar has dissolved.

4 Once the sugar has completely dissolved, immediately pour the fruit syrup into warm sterilized bottles using a sterilized funnel, and then seal the bottles.

5 Store in the fridge if consuming immediately. Syrups can also be frozen in freezer pots, in which case, leave 2.5cm (1in) of space at the top of each pot.

Elderflowers impart a delicious muscat flavour, and this easy-to-make refreshing summer cordial has become deservedly popular. Serve chilled as a non-alcoholic aperitif, or to flavour gooseberry fools and fruit salads.

Elderflower cordial

MAKES APPROX 600ML (1 PINT) (1 LARGE BOTTLE)

TAKES 25 MINUTES, PLUS STANDING TIME

KEEPS 3 MONTHS, REFRIGERATED

INGREDIENTS

12 elderflower heads

1 large organic lemon, washed

750g (1lb 10oz) granulated sugar

2½ tbsp citric acid

1 Shake the elderflowers well to remove any insects and put them into a large bowl.

2 Pare off the zest from the lemon in thick strips and thinly slice the fruit. Put the zest and lemon slices in the bowl with the elderflowers.

3 Put the sugar and 600ml (1 pint) of water in a large saucepan and heat slowly, stirring gently, until the sugar has dissolved. Then bring to the boil.

4 Pour the boiling syrup over the elderflowers and lemon and stir well, then stir in the citric acid. Cover with a clean cloth and leave to stand for 24 hours.

5 Strain through a muslin-lined sieve (or use a new clean disposable kitchen cloth) into a clean bowl, then pour into a sterilized bottle using a sterilized funnel. Seal, label, and store in the fridge. Its high sugar and citric acid content means this cordial will keep in a cool, dark place, but it is better refrigerated.

Elderberries on their own offer a rather flat taste, but if mixed with blackberries they have a rich autumnal flavour that's lovely topped up with boiling water for a hot toddy on a chilly evening. Once opened, use within two weeks.

Elderberry and blackberry cordial

SPECIAL EQUIPMENT
JELLY BAG OR MUSLIN

MAKES APPROX 600–800ML (1–1¼ PINTS) (1 LARGE OR 2 SMALL BOTTLES)

TAKES 20 MINUTES, PLUS COOLING TIME

KEEPS 1–2 MONTHS, REFRIGERATED

INGREDIENTS

350g (12oz) elderberries, removed from their stalks with the prongs of a fork

350g (12oz) blackberries

Caster sugar (see method)

1 tbsp lemon juice

1 cinnamon stick

1 tsp citric acid

1 Put the elderberries in a preserving pan or large saucepan with the blackberries and 150ml (5fl oz) of water. Heat gently, covered with a lid, for 5–6 minutes or until the juices run freely. Leave to cool for about 5 minutes or so and crush the fruit with a potato masher or the back of a large spoon.

2 Strain the berries and juice through a suspended jelly bag or a muslin-lined sieve into a clean bowl. Squeeze or press to extract maximum juice. Measure the juice and add an equal quantity of sugar (600g/1lb 5oz sugar to 600ml/1 pint of juice).

3 Pour the juice and sugar back into the pan with the lemon juice and cinnamon. Stir, then heat gently until the sugar dissolves, then bring back to the boil and boil for 1 minute.

4 Discard the cinnamon, skim off any scum from the surface, stir in the citric acid, and pour immediately into warm sterilized bottles using a sterilized funnel. Seal, label, and leave to cool, then store in the fridge. Shake before use.

Elderberries
Pick elderberries in early autumn, when they are fully ripe and the clusters of berries are just beginning to droop with the weight of fruit.

This cordial has a delicate menthol flavour. If you like a stronger taste – and have a rampant crop of mint – double the weight of leaves (but keep the other ingredients the same). Serve with sparkling or still water, or mixed with vodka and crushed ice.

Fresh mint cordial

MAKES APPROX 400ML (14FL OZ)
(1 SMALL BOTTLE)

TAKES 20 MINUTES,
PLUS INFUSING TIME

KEEPS 1 MONTH, REFRIGERATED

INGREDIENTS

50g (1¾oz) peppermint, Moroccan mint, or spearmint (garden mint) leaves

300g (10oz) granulated sugar

A few drops of natural green food colouring

A few drops of natural peppermint extract (only if using spearmint)

1 Put the leaves in a large bowl, add the sugar, and pound with the end of a rolling pin or a pestle to bruise and crush them to a paste.

2 Pour over 300ml (10fl oz) of boiling water, stir, cover, and leave to infuse for at least 2 hours or until the mixture is completely cold.

3 Strain through a sieve into a saucepan, pressing and squeezing the mint to extract the maximum flavour. Heat the pan over a moderate heat, stirring until the sugar has dissolved. Then bring to the boil and boil for 2 minutes. Stir in a few drops of natural green food colouring and peppermint extract, if using.

4 Pour immediately into a warm sterilized bottle using a sterilized funnel, seal, label, and leave to cool, then store in the fridge. Shake before use.

Mint
There are many varieties of this profusely spreading perennial herb. Spearmint or garden mint (as shown here) is most widely grown, but Moroccan or peppermint are more pungent so they are great for cordials and tisanes.

Always a favourite, this lime cordial has a good balance of sweetness and sharpness and is not overly syrupy, so it mixes well with water. You can use the same method to make lemon or orange cordial (use half juice, half water and an equal quantity of sugar).

Lime cordial

MAKES APPROX 500ML (16FL OZ)
(1 LARGE OR 2 SMALL BOTTLES)

TAKES 20 MINUTES

KEEPS 3 MONTHS, REFRIGERATED

INGREDIENTS

6–8 large organic limes, washed

500g (1lb 2oz) caster sugar

1 tsp citric acid

1 Thinly pare the zest from 2 of the limes. Squeeze the juice from all the limes and strain it to remove any pips or flesh (you should have about 250ml/8fl oz of lime juice).

2 Pour 250ml (8fl oz) of water into a saucepan and add the lime zest and sugar. Stir well, then heat gently without stirring until the sugar dissolves. Bring to the boil and simmer for 5 minutes. Strain through a sieve into a clean pan and discard the lime zest.

3 Stir in the strained lime juice and bring back to the boil. Remove from the heat and stir in the citric acid.

4 Pour immediately into warm sterilized bottles using a sterilized funnel. Seal, label, and leave to cool, then store in the fridge. Shake before use.

This version of barley water is concentrated, so it can be topped up with still – hot or cold – or sparkling water for a refreshing or soothing drink. You can also use the cooked barley for a salad or instead of rice for a pilaf (discard the fruit zest first).

Orange barley water

MAKES APPROX 600ML (1 PINT)
(1 LARGE OR 2 SMALL BOTTLES)

TAKES 20 MINUTES

KEEPS 2 WEEKS, REFRIGERATED

INGREDIENTS

2 organic oranges, washed

1 small organic lemon, washed

85g (3oz) pearl barley

200g (7oz) caster sugar

1 Pare the zest of one orange and the lemon and place in a bowl. Squeeze the juice from all the fruit and strain the juice to remove any pips or flesh (you should have about 250ml/8fl oz of juice).

2 Put the barley in a small saucepan, cover with cold water, and bring to the boil. Then strain through a sieve and discard the water. Return the barley to the pan, add 600ml (1 pint) of boiling water and the pared fruit rind, stir, and bring back to the boil. Reduce the heat, cover, and simmer gently for 40 minutes. Then strain the barley (reserving the grains if you are using them) and return the liquid to the pan.

3 Add the sugar to the strained barley water, stir once, then heat gently without stirring until the sugar has dissolved. Boil for 2 minutes, stirring once or twice, then add the strained fruit juice and bring back to the boil.

4 Pour immediately into warm sterilized bottles using a sterilized funnel. Seal, label, and leave to cool, then store in the fridge. Shake before use.

The rose gives this syrup a heady, aromatic kick. Dilute to taste with still or sparkling water, or serve drizzled over ice cream or set jelly creams. If you are not keen on a rose flavour, replace the petals and rosewater with thinly pared orange rind strips.

Rhubarb and rose petal syrup

SPECIAL EQUIPMENT
JELLY BAG OR MUSLIN

MAKES APPROX 500ML (16FL OZ)
(1 LARGE OR 2 SMALL BOTTLES)

TAKES 40–50 MINUTES

KEEPS 1 MONTH, REFRIGERATED

INGREDIENTS

450g (1lb) pink or red-stemmed rhubarb, cut into short lengths

350g (12oz) granulated sugar

8 scented pink rose petals

2 tbsp rosewater

1 tsp citric acid

1 Put enough water in a heavy-based saucepan to just cover the base. Add the rhubarb, sugar, and rose petals. Bring to the boil, stir gently, cover, reduce the heat, and cook gently for 20–30 minutes until really pulpy, stirring once or twice.

2 Strain the pulp in a jelly bag or a muslin-lined sieve set over a measuring jug or bowl. Press the pulp to extract maximum juice. Return the juice to the pan and bring back to the boil.

3 Remove from the heat and stir in the rosewater and citric acid to the strained juice. Pour immediately into warm sterilized bottles using a sterilized funnel. Seal, label, and leave to cool, then store in the fridge. Shake before use.

Rose petals
Old-fashioned roses such as 'Damask', 'Gallica', 'Alba', or 'Centifolia', are the best kinds to use in the kitchen. Pick them before they start to fade, and use them quickly.

This syrup makes a really refreshing drink when topped up with sparkling or still water, or lemonade. It also makes a delicious milkshake. Or try it drizzled over vanilla ice cream with fresh, skinned peaches for a variation on peach melba.

Raspberry and vanilla syrup

MAKES APPROX 500ML (16FL OZ) (1 LARGE OR 2 SMALL BOTTLES)

TAKES 35 MINUTES

KEEPS 1–2 MONTHS, REFRIGERATED

INGREDIENTS

450g (1lb) ripe raspberries

1 vanilla pod, split

250g (9oz) caster sugar

1 tsp citric acid

1 Put the raspberries and 200ml (7fl oz) of water in a saucepan. Heat gently over a low heat until the juices run. Crush the fruit with a potato masher or the back of a large spoon.

2 When the fruit is really soft, strain through a muslin-lined sieve (or use a new clean disposable kitchen cloth) into a clean bowl. Squeeze or press to extract the maximum juice. Return the juice to the rinsed-out pan. Add the vanilla pod to the pan with the sugar. Stir, then heat gently, without stirring, until the sugar dissolves. Bring to the boil and boil for 5 minutes or until syrupy.

3 Remove from the heat, discard the vanilla pod, and stir in the citric acid.

4 Pour immediately into warm sterilized bottles using a sterilized funnel. Seal, label, and leave to cool, then store in the fridge. Shake before use.

Extremely versatile, this syrup tastes delicous in milkshakes or on top of ice cream too. It is also wonderful added to chilled sparkling wine or champagne as an aperitif, or poured over some whole or sliced strawberries in pretty glasses as a sumptuous dessert.

Strawberry syrup

MAKES APPROX 500ML (16FL OZ) (1 LARGE OR 2 SMALL BOTTLES)

TAKES 25–35 MINUTES

KEEPS 1–2 MONTHS, REFRIGERATED

INGREDIENTS

450g (1lb) ripe strawberries

1 tbsp lemon juice

1 vanilla pod, split with seeds scraped out and reserved

200–250g (7–9oz) caster sugar

1 tsp citric acid

1 Hull and slice the berries and place in a saucepan with 200ml (7fl oz) of water and the lemon juice. Heat gently over a low heat until the juices run. Crush the fruit with a potato masher or the back of a large spoon.

2 When the fruit is really soft, strain through a muslin-lined sieve (or use a new clean disposable kitchen cloth). Squeeze or press to extract maximum juice. Return the juice to the rinsed out pan. Add the vanilla pod and seeds to the pan with the sugar. Whisk to distribute the vanilla seeds, then heat gently until the sugar dissolves, without stirring. Bring to the boil and boil for 5 minutes.

3 Remove the pan from the heat, take out the vanilla pod, and stir in the citric acid.

4 Pour immediately into warm sterilized bottles using a sterilized funnel. Seal, label, and leave to cool, then store in the fridge. Shake before use.

Agave syrup is a natural sugar substitute. It's sweeter than sugar, so you usually need less of it. If you prefer, flavour the tomato juice with a dash of Worcestershire sauce or Tabasco and a sprinkling of celery salt when serving.

Tomato juice

MAKES APPROX 1 LITRE (1¾ PINTS) (2 LARGE BOTTLES OR 1 LARGE PRESERVING JAR)

TAKES 40 MINUTES–1 HOUR 10 MINUTES

KEEPS 1 WEEK, REFRIGERATED (OR 12 MONTHS IF HEAT-PROCESSED)

INGREDIENTS

1.35kg (3lb) ripe tomatoes, quartered

Salt and freshly ground black pepper

1–2 tsp agave syrup or caster sugar

1 Put the tomatoes in a preserving pan or a large heavy-based saucepan. Heat gently over a low heat, pressing them down firmly until their juices start to run. Turn up the heat slightly and simmer for 30 minutes, stirring occasionally, until the tomatoes are pulpy.

2 Purée the pulp in a blender or food processor then rub the purée through a sieve back into the rinsed-out pan. Season to taste with salt, pepper, and agave syrup or sugar. Bring back to the boil.

3 Pour immediately into warm sterilized bottles or jars using a sterilized funnel. Cool, seal, label, store in the fridge, and use within 1 week.

4 For longer-term keeping, process for the 20 minutes using the water bath method on page 19, then tighten or put on the screw-band, if necessary. Leave for 24 hours and test for seal. (If using a kilner jar with a metal lid, you will know immediately or soon after processing if you have a seal as the lid becomes slightly concave and is firm with no "give" once pressed. You may even hear a "pop" as the seal forms.) Store in a cool, dark place for up to 1 year. Once opened, store in the fridge and use within 1 week.

If you have a glut of apples, increase the quantities to make as much of this juice as you like. If you have an electric fruit juicer, simply juice the fruit and follow the method from step 3, but ensure that you boil the juice for one minute.

Apple juice

SPECIAL EQUIPMENT
JELLY BAG OR MUSLIN

MAKES APPROX 1 LITRE (1¾ PINTS)
(2 LARGE BOTTLES OR 1 LARGE
PRESERVING JAR)

TAKES 25–50 MINUTES

KEEPS 1 WEEK, REFRIGERATED (OR
12 MONTHS IF HEAT-PROCESSED)

INGREDIENTS

2kg (4½lb) mixed sweet eating apples
  (such as 'Cox's Orange Pippin', 'Egremont
  Russet', 'Gala'), cut into eighths (don't
  peel or core)

1 Put the apples in a preserving pan or a large heavy-based saucepan with 500ml (16fl oz) of water. Bring the water to the boil, reduce the heat immediately, cover, and cook very gently for 20–30 minutes until the fruit is really soft, stirring occasionally. The time will depend on the type of apples and the size of the pieces.

2 Strain through a jelly bag overnight, or through a muslin-lined sieve (or use 2 clean new disposable kitchen cloths), pressing to extract maximum juice (it will be cloudier this way, but much quicker).

3 Place the juice in a saucepan. Bring to the boil. Pour immediately into warm sterilized jars or bottles using a sterilized funnel. Cool, seal, label, store in the fridge, and use within 1 week.

4 For longer-term keeping, process for 20 minutes using the water bath method on page 19, then tighten or put on the screw-band, if necessary. Leave for 24 hours and test for a seal. (If using a kilner jar with a metal lid, you will know immediately or soon after processing if you have a seal as the lid becomes slightly concave and is firm with no "give" once pressed. You may even hear a "pop" as the seal forms.) Store in a cool, dark place for up to 1 year. Once opened, store in the fridge and use within 1 week.

The best ingredients for...

Ketchups and sauces

The best ketchups and sauces are made from a few readily available fruits and vegetables. Make them in season from gluts of ripe fruit, bunches of fresh summer herbs, and freshly harvested vegetables.

Chillies

All varieties of chillies, fresh or dried (or a combination of both), enliven and add extra flavour and depth to ketchups and sauces. Alternatively, make into fiery chilli sauces. Varieties shown here are (clockwise from left) Scotch bonnet, piri piri, dried chipotle, and poblano.

Basil

With its lush, soft leaves, this tender annual (which grows best in pots), is at its peak in mid-summer. Turn the fresh leaves into pesto sauces.

Tomatoes

A glut of ripe or over-ripe meaty tomatoes is perfect for tomato ketchup. Any well-flavoured variety is suitable (beefsteak or plum varieties are especially good).

Mushrooms

Choose large, open-capped mushrooms such as organic portabello mushrooms (shown here) or wild field mushrooms, if you can find them. They yield lots of liquor when cooked down (pp260–61).

Garlic

Choose large plump bulbs for ketchups and sauces. Combine with chilli and tomato or Indian or Asian flavourings for more pungent garlic ketchups.

Plums

All plums make excellent sweet-savoury ketchups. Make them in late summer or early autumn when plums are plentiful. You don't need perfect fruit, but cut out blemished or bruised parts.

OTHER INGREDIENTS

FRUITS
Apples
Blackberries
Cranberries
Damsons
Elderberries
Gooseberries
VEGETABLES
Horseradish root
Peppers
Shallots
HERBS (for pestos)
Mint
Parsley

Onions

These are essential for a well-flavoured ketchup or sauce, as they add body and texture. Use white and red onions or, for a milder onion flavour, use shallots.

Rocket

A salad leaf, rocket is ready to harvest within four weeks of sowing. Late spring and early and late summer are best. Pick when the leaves are small and tender enough to use for pesto sauces.

Coriander

A tender summer herb. Sow repeatedly from late spring and through the summer, harvest the young leaves before the plant self-seeds, and use for aromatic pesto sauces.

Making ketchups and sauces

Ketchups and sauces are another way of enjoying a bumper harvest. Thick ketchups (p262) can be used as a condiment, while thin ketchups such as this are used as a concentrated flavouring in soups, sauces, gravies, and savoury dishes.

Mushroom ketchup

MAKES APPROX 300ML (10FL OZ) (1 SMALL BOTTLE) DEPENDING ON JUICINESS OF MUSHROOMS

TAKES 2½ HOURS, PLUS SALTING TIME

KEEPS 9 MONTHS

INGREDIENTS

2kg (4½lb) fresh field or large open cultivated mushrooms, wiped and finely chopped

30g (1oz) sea salt

1 tsp black peppercorns

1 tsp allspice berries

½ tsp cloves

½ cinnamon stick

1 small shallot

A few pieces dried cep

300ml (10fl oz) red or white wine vinegar

6 salted anchovies, rinsed (or 2 tbsp dark soy sauce)

2 mace blades

2 tsp brandy (optional)

1 Put the chopped mushrooms in a large bowl. Sprinkle over the salt, toss together with your hands to mix well, cover, and leave for 24 hours, squashing the mushrooms down occasionally.

2 Grind the peppercorns, allspice, cloves, and cinnamon in a pestle and mortar, peel and finely chop the shallot, measure the vinegar, and select a few dried ceps. Check the mushrooms; they should have now reduced to a third of their original volume.

3 Put the mushrooms, their juice, the ground spices, and the shallot in a saucepan with the vinegar, anchovies, dried ceps, and mace. Bring to the boil, cover, and simmer very gently for 1 hour.

4 Strain the cooked ingredients through a fine nylon sieve set over a clean bowl. Press the mixture hard against the sides of the sieve to extract as much liquor as possible.

5 Tip the contents of the sieve onto a square of muslin, gather up the corners, and squeeze the muslin ball tightly to extract the last of the liquor. Check the quantity; if the liquor is more than 300–400ml (10–14fl oz), return to the pan and cook until its volume reduces to approximately 300ml (10fl oz).

6 Pour the liquor into a warm sterilized bottle, add the brandy (if using) and seal. Store in a cool, dark place. Once opened, keep refrigerated for 4–6 months.

Making ketchup from home-grown tomatoes is very satisfying, and you know that it's full of goodness without chemical additives. This authentic-tasting ketchup has a tasty balance of sweetness, acidity, and spice. Once opened, use within two weeks.

Tomato ketchup

MAKES APPROX 750ML (1¼ PINTS) (2–3 SMALL JARS)

TAKES 1 HOUR–1 HOUR 20 MINUTES

KEEPS 3 MONTHS

INGREDIENTS

1kg (2¼lb) ripe tomatoes, roughly chopped

1 carrot, chopped

1 small onion, chopped

1 celery stick, chopped

Good pinch of ground cloves

1 large bay leaf

2 mace blades

1 tsp sea salt

150ml (5fl oz) red wine vinegar

60g (2oz) light soft brown sugar

1 Put all the ingredients except the sugar in a preserving pan or a large heavy-based, stainless steel saucepan. Bring to the boil, reduce the heat, cover and simmer for 30 minutes. Remove the lid and cook for a further 15 minutes, stirring occasionally.

2 Discard the mace and bay leaf. Purée the mixture in a blender or food processor, then rub it through a nylon sieve back into the rinsed-out pan.

3 Stir in the sugar, bring back to the boil and boil, stirring all the time, for 5 minutes until the sauce is the consistency of thick cream.

4 Pour into warm sterilized screw-topped jars with non-metallic or vinegar-proof lids. Cover with waxed paper discs, cool, seal, and label. Store in a cool, dark place for up to 3 months. Once opened, store in the fridge and use within 2 weeks. Shake before use.

This fiery blend of ingredients gives a wonderful kick to everything from scrambled eggs to cheese on toast, kebabs to cold meat. The tamarind gives a lovely sharpness to the sauce, but you can omit it for a sweeter version, if you prefer.

Hot chilli sauce

MAKES APPROX 600ML (1 PINT) (2 SMALL JARS)

TAKES 1 HOUR–1 HOUR 20 MINUTES

KEEPS 1 MONTH, REFRIGERATED

INGREDIENTS

4 fresh red bird's eye (thin) chillies, stalks removed

1 dried chipotle chilli

4 ripe tomatoes, quartered

1 carrot, chopped

1 small onion, chopped

1 celery stick, chopped

2 tbsp agave syrup or clear honey

1 tbsp tomato purée

2 tbsp red wine vinegar

1 tsp tamarind paste

150ml (5fl oz) organic apple juice

Salt and freshly ground black pepper

1 Put all the ingredients except the salt and pepper in a preserving pan or a large heavy-based, stainless steel saucepan. Bring to the boil, reduce the heat, cover, and simmer gently, stirring occasionally, for 45 minutes or until pulpy.

2 Purée in a blender or food processor with 5 tbsp of water, stopping and scraping down the sides as necessary, then rub through a sieve into a bowl. Season to taste.

3 Pour the sauce into warm sterilized jars with non-metallic or vinegar-proof lids, top with waxed paper discs, seal, and store in the fridge for up to 1 month.

Chillies
Bird's eye chillies are extremely hot: be extra careful when handling them, wash your hands and knives after chopping them, and don't touch your eyes (the capsaicin responsible for the heat is a severe skin irritant). Chipotle chillies are dry-smoked, medium-hot jalepeño chillies with a sweet chocolatey flavour, and add depth to a chilli sauce.

Pesto is most often made with fresh basil and pine nuts, but this combination of coriander and walnuts is equally delicious. Toss with pasta, smear under the skin of chicken before grilling, flavour dips and dressings, or spread on crostini.

Coriander and walnut pesto sauce

MAKES APPROX 175G (6OZ) (1 SMALL JAR)

TAKES 10 MINUTES

KEEPS 2 WEEKS, REFRIGERATED

INGREDIENTS

1 small bunch of coriander (approx 30g/1oz)

1 large garlic clove, lightly crushed

30g (1oz) walnut pieces

A good grinding of black pepper

A good pinch of salt

30g (1oz) Parmesan cheese, freshly grated

5 tbsp olive oil

1 Trim the stalks off the coriander (these can be reserved for flavouring soup or curry).

2 Put the coriander leaves in a food processor with the garlic, walnuts, black pepper, salt, cheese, and 1 tbsp of the oil. Blend the ingredients, stopping to scrape down the sides of the bowl as necessary.

3 With the machine still running, gradually add 3 tbsp of the remaining oil, a little at a time, until you have a glistening thinnish paste. (Alternatively, pound the herbs and garlic using a pestle and mortar. Gradually add the nuts, crushing them to a paste with the herbs. Add the pepper and salt then work in a little of the cheese, then a little of the oil, and continue until both are used up and you have a glistening paste.)

4 Spoon into a sterilized jar, top with the remaining 1 tbsp of oil to prevent air getting in, screw on the lid, and store in the fridge. If you don't use all the pesto in one go, cover the remainder with another 1 tbsp of olive oil and screw the lid back on tightly.

The lovely peppery flavour of rocket tastes wonderful with the tang of blue cheese and the creamy texture of almonds in this pesto. It is best served folded through fresh linguine or spaghetti cooked al dente.

Rocket, almond, and blue cheese pesto

MAKES APPROX 185G (6OZ) (1 SMALL JAR)

TAKES 15 MINUTES

KEEPS 2 WEEKS

INGREDIENTS

30g (1oz) rocket, washed

1 garlic clove, lightly crushed

30g (1oz) blue cheese, crumbled or diced, depending on the texture

45g (1½oz) blanched, toasted almonds

7 tbsp extra virgin olive oil

Freshly ground black pepper and salt to taste

1 Put the rocket in a food processor with the garlic, cheese, almonds, and 2 tbsp of the olive oil. Coarsely blend the ingredients, stopping to scrape down the sides of the bowl as necessary.

2 With the machine still running, gradually add 4 tbsp of the remaining olive oil, a little at a time, until you have a glistening paste. (Alternatively, pound the rocket and garlic using a pestle and mortar. Gradually add the cheese and nuts, working them into a thick paste. Add the olive oil, a tablespoon at a time, working it in until you have a glistening paste.)

3 Season to taste with freshly ground black pepper and salt. Spoon into a sterilized jar, top with the remaining 1 tbsp of olive oil to prevent air getting in, screw on the lid, and store in the fridge.

Rocket
It's easy to sow and grow rocket seeds. Keep picking the leaves when they are about 6cm (2½in) long to encourage new leaves to grow.

This is a version of the traditional pesto that derives from Genoa, Italy. It is delicious with the addition of a small handful of fresh mint too – just add the mint leaves to the mix of ingredients when you blend them.

Basil and pine nut pesto

MAKES APPROX 200G (7OZ) (1 SMALL JAR)

TAKES 10 MINUTES

KEEPS 2 WEEKS

INGREDIENTS

65g (2½oz) basil

1 large garlic clove, lightly crushed

30g (1oz) pine nuts

A good grinding of black pepper

30g (1oz) Parmesan cheese, freshly grated

7 tbsp extra virgin olive oil

Salt to taste

1 Pull all the leaves off the basil stalks. Discard the stalks and put the leaves in a food processor with the garlic, pine nuts, black pepper, cheese, and 2 tbsp of the olive oil. Coarsely blend the ingredients, stopping to scrape down the sides of the bowl as necessary.

2 With the machine still running, gradually add 4 tbsp of the remaining olive oil, a little at a time, until you have a glistening coarse paste. (Alternatively, pound the herbs and garlic using a pestle and mortar. Gradually add the pine nuts, crushing them to a paste with the herbs. Add the pepper and salt, then work in a little of the cheese, then a little of the olive oil, and continue until both are used up and you have a glistening paste.)

3 Season to taste with salt. Spoon into a sterilized jar, top with the remaining 1 tbsp of olive oil to prevent air getting in, screw on the lid, and store in the fridge.

Basil
To encourage bushy growth and ensure a continuous harvest, basil leaves should be picked regularly and their tips pinched out.

Serve this hot sauce with beef, ox tongue, sausages, beetroots, and salted or smoked fish. The horseradish root should not be cooked or it loses its pungency, but making a sauce base such as this helps its keeping qualities and gives a more mellow flavour.

Horseradish sauce

MAKES APPROX 360ML (12FL OZ) (2 SMALL JARS)

TAKES 15–20 MINUTES, PLUS COOLING TIME

KEEPS 2 MONTHS, REFRIGERATED

INGREDIENTS

300ml (10fl oz) white wine vinegar

1 bay leaf

12 peppercorns

2 tbsp caster sugar

2 cloves

8 tbsp double cream at room temperature, plus extra for serving (optional)

150g (5½oz) freshly grated horseradish

Salt to taste

1 Put the vinegar, bay leaf, peppercorns, sugar, and cloves in a small saucepan. Bring to the boil, stirring until all the sugar has dissolved, and then boil rapidly until the volume has reduced by half – about 5 minutes. Stir in the cream and boil for 1 minute.

2 Strain the liquid through a sieve into a bowl, allow to cool, then stir in the grated horseradish and season with salt.

3 Spoon the sauce into sterilized jars with non-metallic or vinegar-proof lids, top with waxed paper discs, seal, label, and store in the fridge for up to 2 months. Thin with a little extra cream, if needed, when serving.

Horseradish root
A perennial root with an exhilarating, pungent flavour, horseradish is easy to grow (it spreads, so needs space). Once established, dig up as required, scrub clean, and keep in the fridge.

Use this authentic-tasting sauce in several ways: as a dip, as a baste for grilled or roasted duck, chicken, or pork, to replace hoi-sin sauce to smear on Chinese pancakes with crispy duck or to flavour stir-fries. Once opened, store in the fridge and use within two weeks.

Chinese-style plum sauce

MAKES APPROX 600ML (1 PINT) (3 SMALL JARS)

TAKES 1 HOUR 10 MINUTES

KEEPS 3 MONTHS

INGREDIENTS

½ tsp wasabi paste or English mustard

150ml (5fl oz) rice (or white) wine vinegar

500g (1lb 2oz) ripe dark red or blue plums, halved and stoned

1 onion, chopped

1 garlic clove, crushed

60g (2oz) dark soft brown sugar

5 tbsp clear honey

2 tbsp dark soy sauce

1 tsp Chinese five-spice powder

2 tbsp sake or dry sherry

1 Mix the wasabi paste or mustard and vinegar in a large saucepan until blended. Add the plums, onion, and garlic. Bring to the boil, reduce the heat, part cover, and simmer gently for 10–15 minutes until pulpy.

2 Purée in a blender or food processor, then return to the pan and stir in the remaining ingredients.

3 Bring to the boil, stirring all the time, then reduce the heat and simmer, uncovered, for 25 minutes, stirring occasionally until thick and rich.

4 Spoon into warm sterilized jars, top with waxed paper discs, allow to cool, seal, and label and store in a cool, dark place for up to 3 months.

Preserving in oil is a rewarding way of preserving food, and adds another dimension to enjoying produce: the results are delectable and mouthwatering. Traditionally, it was standard practice (especially in Mediterranean countries) to store vegetables, olives, and occasionally cheeses, under olive oil. These days, this technique is best considered as a short-term method of preservation (p10), and all produce stored in this way should be refrigerated.

The best ingredients for...
Preserving in oil

Mediterranean vegetables are particularly well suited to this method of preservation, which brings out the best of their sun-ripened flavours. Other firm or crunchy vegetables work well too, as do olives and feta cheese.

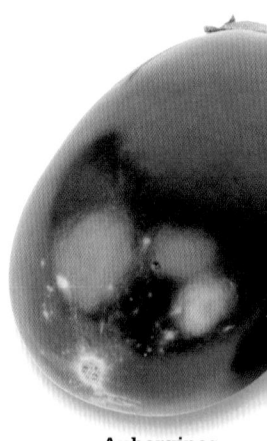

Aubergines
Choose small or medium firm, freshly picked aubergines for cooking and storing under oil (their flesh acts as a sponge, and can easily become too soft).

Tomatoes
Before they can be preserved in oil, tomatoes must be dried first; but the combination of dried tomatoes and olive oil is heavenly.

Feta cheese
This traditional Greek cheese is made from ewe's or goat's milk. As it is a brined and naturally acidic cheese, it can be safely stored under olive oil.

Garlic
Choose large, plump, freshly harvested bulbs of garlic and cook and store them under olive oil either as whole cloves or a purée.

Peppers
Choose ripe, firm, unblemished red and yellow peppers. 'Bell Boy', 'Romano', and 'Hungarian wax' are all good varieties. Peppers are at their best in late summer or early autumn.

Olives
There are many flavoursome varieties of green (unripe) and black (ripe) table olives. As they are already cured in salt, they are safe to store under oil.

Asparagus

Freshly picked asparagus with green stalks and green or purple tips, which are in season from April to June, are best for preserving in oil (rather than white asparagus).

OTHER INGREDIENTS

VEGETABLES
Carrots
Cauliflower
Celeriac
Celery
Chillies
French beans
Pickling onions
Romanesco
Salsify
Shallots

CHEESES
Labna (strained yoghurt cheese)
Soft goat's cheeses

Globe artichokes (baby)

These tall, stately vegetables crop for 3–4 years, are a great delicacy, and are best preserved in oil. Pick small, tender heads from July to September.

Mushrooms

Any varieties, cultivated or wild, are delicious preserved in oil. Choose small specimens and clean wild mushrooms thoroughly first.

Fennel

The crunchy texture and aniseed flavour of fennel lends itself to storing in oil. Choose plump fleshy bulbs (take off any outside stringy layers).

Courgettes

Choose small, tender, firm courgettes 10–15cm (4–6in) long. Pick them as fresh as possible and preserve without delay (the flowers are not suitable for preserving in oil).

Preparing vegetables in oil

This way of preserving vegetables means they are cooked first in vinegar to acidify them (p9) before being stored under oil and refrigerated. Serve with a drizzle of fresh oil, torn basil leaves or chopped parsley, and good bread.

Italian-style vegetables

MAKES APPROX 675G (1½LB) (2 MEDIUM JARS)

TAKES 30 MINUTES

KEEPS 1–2 MONTHS, REFRIGERATED

INGREDIENTS

600g (1lb 5oz) mixed seasonal vegetables (e.g. aubergines, fennel, romanesco florets, courgettes, small shallots, celery, carrots, French beans, peppers, button mushrooms)

Approx 500ml (16fl oz) white wine vinegar

2 tsp granulated sugar

2 tsp sea salt

Approx 150ml (5fl oz) extra virgin olive oil

Seasonings – choose from

1 tsp dried fennel seeds

1 tsp dried oregano

1 fresh or dried bay leaf

1 sprig rosemary

1 sprig lemon thyme

Pinch of chilli flakes

1 Wash, peel as necessary, and dice or slice each vegetable into evenly sized pieces about 1cm (½in) thick. Leave small shallots and mushrooms whole.

2 Put a batch of vegetables in a stainless steel saucepan and add enough vinegar until it is just covering the vegetables. Add the sugar and salt and bring to the boil.

3 When the soft vegetables have been boiled for 2–3 minutes and firmer vegetables until al dente, about 5–10 minutes, pat dry on kitchen paper and allow cool.

4 Loosely pack the vegetables into sterilized jars and add the seasonings. Cover with olive oil and press the vegetables down lightly to remove any air pockets.

5 Top up with oil, then seal and store in the fridge. Leave for at least 1 week before opening. Top up with extra oil once opened so the vegetables are always covered with 1cm (½in) of oil.

Make this recipe when tomatoes are in season. Choose fleshy varieties with fewer seeds, such as Italian plum tomatoes. The tomatoes absorb the oil, making them soft and unctuous. Use in salads, with pasta, as a tapas, or serve with mozzarella cheese.

Oven-dried tomatoes in oil

MAKES APPROX 450G (1LB)
(1 SMALL PRESERVING JAR)

TAKES 20 MINUTES, PLUS DRYING TIME

KEEPS 2 WEEKS, REFRIGERATED

INGREDIENTS

1.8kg (4lb) ripe tomatoes (approx 12 tomatoes), cut into quarters (or sixths, if the tomatoes are large)

2 tbsp caster sugar

3 tsp dried oregano

Sea salt and freshly ground black pepper

3 tbsp white wine vinegar

200ml (7fl oz) extra virgin olive oil, plus extra if needed

1 tsp dried chilli flakes

1 Preheat the oven to 60–80°C (150–175°F/Gas ¼–½). Put the tomatoes in a large bowl and sprinkle over the sugar, 2 tsp of the oregano, and a sprinkling of sea salt and pepper. Carefully tumble it all together so the tomatoes are evenly covered. Discard any liquid in the bowl.

2 Arrange the tomatoes in 2–3 large roasting tins or some baking trays, ensuring they don't touch. Leave in the oven for 7–12 hours (leave overnight if necessary) until shrunk to at least half their size and feel leathery and dry. Leave the door of an electric oven slightly ajar using a skewer so air can circulate. Then allow to cool completely.

3 Put the vinegar and olive oil in a medium saucepan, heat gently, and bring to the boil. Add the chilli flakes and the rest of the oregano, then turn off the heat and allow to cool.

4 Pack the cold tomatoes in a sterilized jar, pressing them in fairly tightly, and pour over the olive oil mixture. Add more olive oil if needed to ensure all the tomatoes are completely covered. Seal and store in the fridge. Once opened, keep refrigerated, top up with oil if necessary so the tomatoes are always completely covered, and use within 2 weeks.

Tomatoes
The best tomatoes to use are Italian plum tomatoes, as they are fleshy and don't have as much juice as other tomatoes. This means they will dry out more easily.

This is one of the most heavenly ways to eat and preserve newly harvested garlic. Simply squeeze the cloves from their skins and use for garlic toast, in mashed potato and other dishes, or served with barbecued, grilled, or roasted meat and poultry.

Simple garlic confit

MAKES APPROX 225G (8OZ)
(1 SMALL JAR)

TAKES 1 HOUR–1¼ HOURS

KEEPS 3 WEEKS–1 MONTH,
REFRIGERATED

INGREDIENTS

2 large bulbs of fresh garlic with plump
    cloves, with the cloves separated

90–150ml (3–5fl oz) extra virgin olive oil,
    plus extra as needed

1 sprig thyme

1 bay leaf

Large pinch of sea salt

2 tbsp balsamic or sherry vinegar

1 Pack the unpeeled cloves of garlic into a small snug-fitting ovenproof dish, pour in enough olive oil to cover the garlic, tuck in the thyme and bay leaf, and sprinkle over the salt.

2 Cook in a low oven at 150°C (300°F/Gas 2) for 45 minutes–1 hour or until the cloves are soft (this will depend on the size of the cloves).

3 To store, cool, transfer the cooked cloves to a sterilized jar and add the vinegar, stirring the contents to ensure all the cloves are well coated. Fill the jar with the garlic-infused oil they were cooked in, topping up with extra fresh oil if needed. Store in the fridge, ensuring that the cloves are always completely covered in oil, and use within 1 month.

Garlic
If you plant individual cloves (pointed end up) in autumn, pressing them into the soil with their tips just showing 10cm (4in) apart, they will be ready to harvest the following July.

Baby artichokes are a great delicacy, and the whole of the inner choke can be used. They taste delicious when kept under olive oil. Serve as an antipasti, with avocado or mozzarella cheese salads, or add to fresh pasta with home-made pesto.

Baby artichokes in oil

MAKES APPROX 500G (1LB 2OZ)
(1 SMALL PRESERVING JAR)

TAKES 45 MINUTES

KEEPS 2 MONTHS, REFRIGERATED

INGREDIENTS

10 baby artichokes

300ml (10fl oz) white wine vinegar

1 tbsp sea salt

For the marinade

450ml (15fl oz) extra virgin olive oil

75ml (2½fl oz) white wine vinegar

Handful of black peppercorns

1 Trim the artichoke stalks and snap off the hard outside leaves (about 5–6 layers) until you reach the paler, more tender leaves. Cut about 2.5cm (1in) off the spiny tips and discard. Then slice in half and, using a teaspoon, carefully remove the choke and discard.

2 Put the vinegar, salt, and 300ml (10fl oz) of water in a preserving pan or heavy-based, stainless steel saucepan and bring to the boil. Add the prepared artichokes and blanch for 3–5 minutes in the simmering vinegar mix; they should still retain plenty of bite. Drain and leave to cool, then cut lengthways into quarters.

3 Prepare the marinade: put the olive oil, vinegar, and peppercorns into a saucepan and bring to the boil. Add the artichokes and bring back to the boil, then turn the heat off and leave it to cool with the artichokes still sitting in the marinade.

4 Using a slotted spoon, remove the cooled artichokes and put them into a sterilized jar with a non-metallic or vinegar-proof lid. Pour the marinade over the top so the artichokes are completely covered (or you can strain the oil mixture if you prefer). Seal, label, and store in the fridge. Once opened, keep refrigerated, top up with oil if necessary so the artichokes are always covered, and use within 2 months.

Storing this tangy, salty cheese under olive oil prolongs its shelf life, adds flavour, and stops it drying out. Add to summer salads, crumble over sliced beef tomatoes with a little of the oil drizzled over the top, or tuck into pitta bread with salad and olives.

Feta cheese in oil

MAKES 400ML (14FL OZ)
(1 SMALL PRESERVING JAR)

TAKES 10 MINUTES

KEEPS 4 MONTHS, REFRIGERATED

INGREDIENTS

150ml (5fl oz) good-quality extra virgin olive oil, plus extra to top up if needed

Juice of 2 lemons

Handful of thyme or oregano, leaves only

1 tsp green peppercorns (optional)

Freshly ground black pepper

200g (7oz) Greek feta cheese, cut into bite-sized cubes

1 Put the olive oil, lemon juice, thyme or oregano, and peppercorns (if using) in a large bowl and stir carefully to mix. Season with some freshly ground black pepper (you won't need salt, as the feta cheese is salty).

2 Put the feta cheese in a sterilized jar and pour over the oil mixture. Press the cheese down lightly to remove any air pockets, then top up with more oil if needed until all the cubes are completely covered. Seal, label, and store in the fridge. Once opened, keep refrigerated, top up with more oil if necessary so the feta cheese is completely covered, and use within 4 months.

It is difficult to imagine a better way to enjoy ripe peppers than this. Roasting them amplifies their sweetness and concentrates their flavour, while the olive oil enhances their unctuous texture. Perfect with pasta, as a topping for bruschetta, or in salads.

Mixed peppers in oil

MAKES APPROX 750ML (1¼ PINTS) (2 MEDIUM PRESERVING JARS)

TAKES 40 MINUTES

KEEPS 3 WEEKS–1 MONTH, REFRIGERATED

INGREDIENTS

3 red peppers

3 orange peppers

3 yellow peppers

1 tsp dried oregano

Sea salt and freshly ground black pepper

2 tbsp extra virgin olive, plus extra to top up

2 tbsp cider vinegar

1 Preheat the oven to 200°C (400°F/Gas 6). Put the peppers in a roasting tin and cook for about 25–30 minutes until they begin to char slightly. Remove from the oven, put in a plastic bag, and leave to cool. (This will make the skins easier to remove.)

2 Pull away the stalks, remove the skin, deseed, and and tear or slice the peppers into chunky strips. Put into a bowl with the oregano and season with sea salt and black pepper. Mix the oil with the vinegar, then pour over the peppers and stir carefully.

3 Spoon the peppers into sterilized jars and add all the juices. Top up with olive oil to cover completely. Seal, label, and store in the fridge. Once opened, keep refrigerated, top up with oil if necessary so the peppers are always covered, and use within 1 month.

Courgettes are delicious chargrilled on the barbecue, then dressed with oil; this recipe produces similar results (if you can cook them slowly over the embers of a barbecue, they will be extra tasty). Use as a starter with fresh herbs and finely chopped preserved lemon.

Griddled courgettes in oil

MAKES APPROX 500ML (16FL OZ)
(1 SMALL PRESERVING JAR)

TAKES 30 MINUTES

KEEPS 3 WEEKS–1 MONTH,
REFRIGERATED

INGREDIENTS

450g (1lb) baby courgettes,
   sliced thinly lengthways

3 tbsp olive oil

Pinch of sea salt, and freshly ground
   black pepper

200ml (7fl oz) extra virgin olive oil, plus
   extra to top up if needed

Juice of 2 lemons in a bowl

1 Put the courgettes in a large bowl and add the 3 tbsp of olive oil along with the sea salt and black pepper. Toss the ingredients together using your hands, until everything is evenly covered.

2 Heat a griddle pan until hot, then carefully add the courgette slices, a few at a time, and cook for about 3 minutes on each side or until golden. Then place in the bowl of lemon juice, toss well, and leave to cool in the juice.

3 Remove the courgette slices from the lemon juice, layer them in a sterilized jar and pour over the olive oil to cover them completely. Press the vegetables down lightly to remove any air pockets. Seal and label the jar and store in the fridge. Once opened, keep refrigerated, top up with more oil if necessary so the courgettes are always completely covered, and use within 1 month.

The meaty texture of griddled aubergines makes a succulent accompaniment to cold meats, salads, or vegetarian dishes. The vinegar helps to cut through the oily richness of the vegetables and lends a piquant edge to their flavour.

Griddled aubergines in oil

MAKES APPROX 500ML (16FL OZ)
(1 SMALL PRESERVING JAR)

TAKES 40 MINUTES,
PLUS STANDING TIME

KEEPS 3 WEEKS–1 MONTH,
REFRIGERATED

INGREDIENTS

2 medium-sized aubergines, sliced
   lengthways, about 5mm (¼in) thick

Sea salt to sprinkle

200ml (7fl oz) extra virgin olive oil, plus
   extra if needed and for brushing

1 tsp thyme leaves

2 tbsp white wine vinegar

1 Layer the aubergine slices in a colander, covering each layer with a generous sprinkling of sea salt. Leave for 30 minutes to extract any excess water. Then rinse under cold water and pat dry thoroughly with a clean tea towel or kitchen paper.

2 Heat a griddle pan until hot. Brush each side of the aubergine slices with a little olive oil and add a few at a time to the griddle pan. Cook each side for 2–4 minutes or until golden. Remove and put to one side.

3 Put the oil and thyme into a stainless steel saucepan and cook gently for about 2 minutes, just enough to cook the herbs. Turn the heat down, stir in the vinegar, and add the aubergines. Bring to the boil, then turn the heat off and leave the contents of the pan to cool completely.

4 When cool, carefully remove the aubergines and put them into a sterilized jar. Strain the marinade and pour it over the aubergines to completely cover them, topping up with more oil if needed. The aubergines should be completely immersed in the oil. Press them down gently to remove any air pockets. Seal and label the jar and store in the fridge. Once opened, keep refrigerated, top up with more oil if necessary so the aubergines are always completely covered, and use within 1 month.

Aubergines
These are decorative plants that grow well in pots but need constant warmth. Choose plump small or medium-sized aubergines with shiny skins that spring back when pressed.

Storing olives under oil is traditionally the best way to extend their shelf life and keep them plump and succulent. Adding flavourings and spices to the oil enhances them further. Buy good-quality olives (taste them first to check their flavour).

Mixed spiced olives in oil

MAKES APPROX 500ML (16FL OZ) (1 SMALL PRESERVING JAR)

TAKES 10 MINUTES

KEEPS 4 MONTHS, REFRIGERATED

INGREDIENTS

2 tsp extra virgin olive oil

3 tbsp white wine vinegar

1 tsp coriander seeds

1 tsp fennel seeds, crushed

1 tsp cumin seeds, crushed

Finely grated zest of 1 organic orange, washed

Pinch of chilli flakes

Sea salt and freshly ground black pepper

150g (5½oz) large juicy black olives, unpitted

150g (5½oz) large juicy green olives, unpitted

1 Mix together the olive oil, white wine vinegar, coriander seeds, fennel seeds, cumin seeds, orange zest, and chilli flakes. Season well with sea salt and some black pepper.

2 Put the olives in a sterilized jar. Pour in the marinade mixture and top up with olive oil until the olives are completely covered. Seal, label, and store in the fridge. Once opened, keep refrigerated, top up with oil if necessary so the olives are always covered, and use within 4 months.

Since the season for asparagus is so short, it makes sense to preserve them in oil for a little longer. Asparagus has a unique flavour that is greatly intensified when griddled; serve with salads, chop and stir into pasta or risotto, or enjoy on its own.

Asparagus in oil

MAKES APPROX 500ML (16FL OZ) (1 SMALL PRESERVING JAR)

TAKES 20 MINUTES

KEEPS 3 WEEKS, REFRIGERATED

INGREDIENTS

350g (12oz) medium asparagus spears, trimmed to the height of your jar

200ml (7fl oz) extra virgin olive oil, plus extra if needed for coating and topping up

Sea salt and freshly ground black pepper

Juice of 2 lemons in a small bowl

1 Smother the asparagus in a little olive oil to coat them using your hands and season them well with sea salt and black pepper.

2 Heat a griddle pan until hot then add the asparagus spears in batches and turn occasionally. Cook each batch for about 5 minutes or until they are beginning to char slightly and soften but not become limp.

3 Toss the asparagus spears in the lemon juice and leave to cool in the juice. Then stand them upright in a sterilized jar, tips upright. Pack them in tightly and top up with the oil to cover them completely. Seal, label, and store in the fridge. Once opened, keep refrigerated, top up with oil if necessary so the asparagus spears are always covered, and use within 3 weeks.

Asparagus
Home-grown asparagus is the ultimate treat and is easy to grow. Plant asparagus crowns in spring, let them build up their strength for 2 years, and thereafter they will produce more and more succulent fabulous-tasting spears every year.

These mushrooms are lightly blanched first to soften them before being stored under oil. Use mixture of different types of mushroom, or wild foraged mushrooms in season. They make delightful picnic food, or stir into pasta or casseroles, or use as a pizza topping.

Mushrooms in oil

MAKES APPROX 500ML (16FL OZ)
(1 SMALL PRESERVING JAR)

TAKES 20 MINUTES

KEEPS 3 WEEKS–1 MONTH,
REFRIGERATED

INGREDIENTS

450g (1lb) mushrooms, sliced or left whole
   if small, wiped of any soil or grit,
   but not washed

2 tbsp cider vinegar

1 tsp thyme leaves

Sea salt and freshly ground black pepper

150ml (5fl oz) extra virgin olive oil, plus
   extra to top up if needed

1 Put the mushrooms in a saucepan of boiling salted water and blanch for 3 minutes. Then drain well and put to one side to cool completely.

2 Mix the vinegar with the thyme in a small bowl and season well with sea salt and black pepper. Then toss the mushrooms in the flavoured vinegar to coat them.

3 Spoon the mushrooms and flavoured vinegar into a sterilized jar with a non-metallic or vinegar-proof lids. Pour in the olive oil to cover the mushrooms, and seal. If the jars are not completely full, invert them a few times so the oil coats the mushrooms completely. Label and store in the fridge. Once opened, keep refrigerated, top up with oil if necessary so the mushrooms are always completely covered, and use within 1 month.

Mushrooms
Small mushrooms are best for this dish, rather than large or open-capped mushrooms. Organic chestnut mushrooms are ideal, as they have less moisture and more flavour than white button mushrooms.

Simple salting, curing, and charcuterie techniques produce some of the world's best-loved foods. Most modern, centrally heated homes do not have cellars cold enough to employ traditional salting, wet-curing, and dry-curing methods, but with a fridge we can still enjoy home-cured fish and meat, make our own sausages, and learn the art of simple charcuterie. Fastidious hygiene cannot be stressed enough when using these techniques, and is critical for the successful preservation of meat and fish.

The best ingredients for...
Simple salting, curing, and charcuterie

With these ingredients, there is something to suit everyone's taste. Whichever produce you choose to preserve, it is crucial that you buy the best quality ingredients, especially meat and fish.

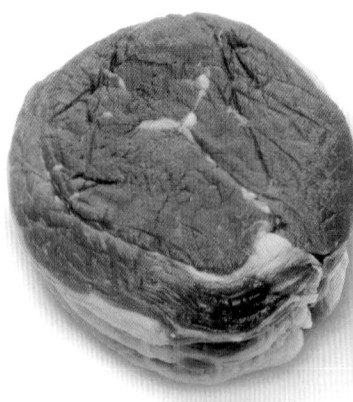

Brisket of beef
This inexpensive, richly flavoured cut of beef is ideal for salting and curing. Choose meat from cattle that have been fed on grass and traditionally reared.

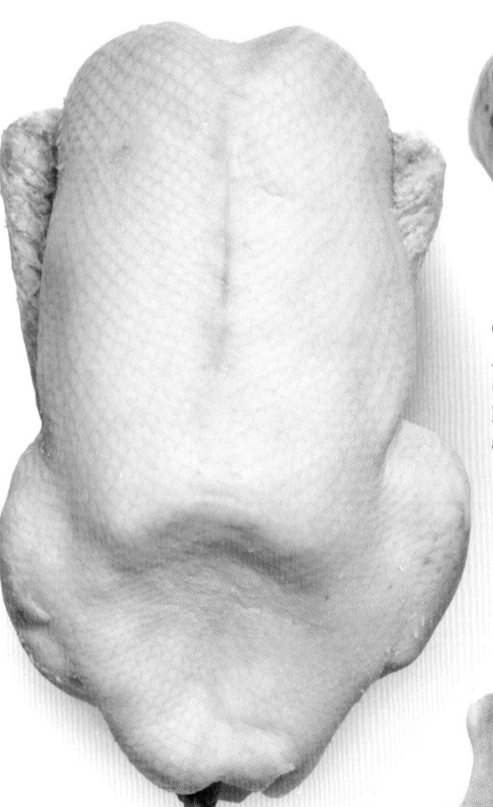

Gammon joint
A leg of pork can be salted to make ham (pp304–305). For home brining, remove the bone first. Choose traditionally bred pork and avoid watery, intensively reared meat.

Pork belly
This cheap but delicious cut of pork is ideal for making streaky bacon (pp308–309). Intensively reared pork is too lean and lacks flavour, so choose traditionally bred meat.

Pork loin
A prime cut, used to make back bacon. Choose traditionally bred pork (intensively reared pork is not of a sufficiently good quality).

Goose

This bird has the richest flavour and most fat of all traditional poultry (its fat is highly prized for roasting). Use the whole bird (jointed) or legs for succulent confit.

Duck legs
For successful charcuterie, poultry needs ample natural fat as well as delicious flesh. Duck legs provide plenty of both. Avoid intensively raised birds and buy good-quality produce.

Pickling cucumber

Pickling cucumbers, either smooth- or warty-skinned, are transformed by lactic-fermentation when salted (the lactic acid produced both preserves the vegetable and promotes the growth of healthy flora in the gut).

Lemons

When salted, lemons (and limes) become piquant (pp296–97), and store well. No kitchen should be without them. Choose firm, ripe organic or Sicilian lemons.

Red cabbage

Salting (pp292–93) transforms cabbage into a superfood, immune booster, cancer preventative, and digestive aid through lactic-fermentation. Pick firm, tight-balled cabbages.

Fish

Many fish stocks are now threatened, so choose locally caught, sustainably fished, or organic farmed fish. Select glisteningly fresh, bright-eyed fish and firm, sweet-smelling fish fillets. Cure in sea salt (pp298–99), or cure in brine and pickle (pp300–301).

Herring

Pollack

Cod

OTHER INGREDIENTS

VEGETABLES
French beans
Radishes
Runner beans
FISH
(buy sustainably sourced)
Coley (saithe)
Hake
Halibut
Pilchards
Sardines
Whiting
MEAT
(buy free-range or organic)
Leg of lamb
Leg of mutton
Ox tongue
Pig's head
Pork liver
Poultry livers
Rabbit
Shoulder of pork
Silverside of beef
Topside of beef

Salting vegetables

Preserving certain vegetables in salt relies on their natural lactic bacteria reacting with salt and fermenting. This process is known as lacto-fermentation. Home-made sauerkraut has a much better flavour than bought versions.

Sauerkraut

MAKES APPROX 1.35KG (3LB) (2 MEDIUM PRESERVING JARS)

TAKES 30–45 MINUTES, PLUS FERMENTATION TIME

KEEPS 1–2 MONTHS, REFRIGERATED

INGREDIENTS

2.5–3kg (5½–6½lb) hard white or red cabbage, or half red and half white cabbage

Approx 60g (2oz) coarse sea or rock salt (see method)

1 tbsp caraway seeds

FERMENTING TIPS

The ideal temperature is 20–22°C (68–72°F). At this temperature the sauerkraut is ready in 3–4 weeks. It takes less time if it is warmer, and longer if it is colder (5–6 weeks at 13–16°C/55–60°F). Fermentation will stop and the cabbage will spoil above 24°C (76°F) or below 13°C (55°F).

If your sauerkraut develops a pinkish hue on its surface, goes dark, or is very soft and mushy, it has not fermented properly and shouldn't be eaten. You may have used too little salt, there were air pockets in the jar, the cabbage was not completely submerged, it was stored too long, or the temperature was too high.

---

1 Remove the outer leaves of the cabbage, slice in half, remove the cores, quarter, and shred finely using a sharp knife, or in the food processor. Weigh the shredded cabbage and calculate the amount of salt you will need: approximately 60g (2oz) of salt per 2.5kg (5½lb) of cabbage.

2 Place the cabbage in a large clean bowl and sprinkle the salt evenly over it. Using your hands, work the salt thoroughly into the cabbage – imagine you are making pastry – until it begins to feel wet. Leave for a few minutes for the salt to soften the cabbage and draw out its juices.

3 Pack into a very large sterilized crock or jar. Add 5cm (2in) of cabbage at a time and scatter with the caraway seeds. Pack each layer down with a clean tamper, eg. the end of a rolling pin, a large pestle, or a jam jar. Leave 7.5cm (3in) of space at the top. Add any juices from the bowl and top up with cold brine (1½ tbsp of salt to 1¾ pints of boiled water) to cover the cabbage.

4 Put the jar on a tray, place clean muslin over the cabbage, and put a snug-fitting plate or saucer on top. Place a large jar or sandwich bag filled with water on top of the plate.

5 Leave in a well-ventilated place at room temperature (see box, left). Check every day that the cabbage is submerged. Remove any scum regularly and replace with clean muslin.

6 Fermentation is complete when all the bubbling has ceased. Pot up into sterilized jars, seal, and store in the fridge.

The traditional Korean cabbage dish, kimchi, has numerous variations, and this is one of the simplest. For the best flavour, leave for a few days in the fridge to marinate. Use as an accompaniment to rice dishes, meat, chicken, fish, or cheese.

Kimchi

MAKES APPROX 450–600G (1LB–1LB 5OZ)

TAKES 25 MINUTES, PLUS STANDING AND MARINATING TIME

KEEPS 2 WEEKS, REFRIGERATED

INGREDIENTS

1 small head Chinese leaves

2 tbsp sea salt

4 spring onions, chopped

2.5cm (1in) piece of fresh root ginger, peeled and grated

1 garlic clove, crushed

4 tbsp rice vinegar

1 tbsp Thai fish sauce (nam pla)

Juice of 1 lime

2 tbsp sesame oil

2 tbsp toasted sesame seeds

2 tbsp sambal oelek

1 Cut the head of Chinese leaves into quarters lengthways, then into 5cm (2in) chunks. Place in a colander over a bowl. Add the salt, toss well, and leave to stand overnight at room temperature.

2 Wash the Chinese leaves thoroughly to remove the salt, tossing it with your hands to rinse thoroughly. Drain and dry on kitchen paper.

3 Place the Chinese leaves in a freezer box (large enough to hold up to 600g/1lb 5oz of Chinese leaves) with a lid. Add the remaining ingredients and toss together thoroughly.

4 Place the lid on the box and leave at room temperature overnight to marinate, then chill in the fridge and use within 2 weeks.

Salted cucumbers taste different from those pickled in vinegar. Use small ridge cucumbers, or grow your own and pick them while still small (smooth salad cucumbers are too watery). Once opened, eat within two weeks.

Salted cucumbers with dill

MAKES APPROX 1KG (2¼LB)
(1 LARGE PRESERVING JAR)

TAKES 30 MINUTES

KEEPS 2 WEEKS, REFRIGERATED

INGREDIENTS

30g (1oz) sea salt

4 tbsp dill, chopped

1 tbsp tarragon, chopped

1 tsp black peppercorns

1 tsp celery seeds

2 ridge cucumbers, about 18cm (7in) long, quartered lengthways, or up to 8 smaller pickling ones, left whole

4 pickling onions or shallots, peeled and thickly sliced

1 Put the salt in a saucepan with 600ml (1 pint) of water and heat gently, stirring until all the salt has dissolved. Then bring to the boil.

2 Place half the fresh herbs, peppercorns, and celery seeds in the base of a 1 litre (1¾ pint) preserving jar. Pack the quartered cucumbers and onion slices in tightly on top of them, then add the rest of the flavourings.

3 Pour over enough boiling salted water to cover the cucumbers completely. Seal and store in a cool, dark place for 4–6 weeks before opening. Once opened, store in the fridge.

Preserving lemons

The Middle-Eastern tradition of preserving lemons in salt softens their skins and mellows their flavour to give a unique pickled tang. Use sparingly in stews, salads, salsas, sauces, and vinaigrettes, or double the quantities and give as a gift.

Preserved lemons

MAKES APPROX 450G (1LB) (1 SMALL PRESERVING JAR)

TAKES 10 MINUTES, PLUS MATURING TIME

KEEPS 6–9 MONTHS, REFRIGERATED

INGREDIENTS

4 organic lemons, washed

115g (4oz) coarse sea salt

A few bay leaves, ½ tsp black peppercorns, 1 dried chilli, a few cloves, or coriander or cumin seeds (optional)

Freshly squeezed juice of 2 extra lemons

1 Cut two-thirds of the way through each lemon with a sharp knife, then make a similar cut again at right angles to the first cut. The 2 deep cuts should produce 4 quarters that are joined at the base.

2 Open each lemon out slightly, pour salt into the crevices, and pack tightly into a sterilized preserving jar. Distribute your choice of herbs and spices, if using, among the lemons (these will look lovely if the lemons are to be given as gifts). Add the rest of the salt to the jar.

3 Pour the lemon juice into the filled jar; if there is not quite enough, top up with boiled, cooled water. Seal and leave at room temperature. The salt will form a brine; invert the jar from time to time to distribute the salt and juice. Leave for 3–4 weeks for the lemon rinds to soften.

Lemons in brine
Once opened, store in the fridge, ensuring the lemons remain immersed in the brine. To use, take a piece of lemon, scrape off the flesh, rinse the peel under cold water, and use as required.

Salting fish

'Gravadlax' is a traditional Scandinavian method of preserving salmon, and it makes a stunning starter. If you use wild salmon, freeze it overnight first and then thaw it in the fridge. This kills any potential parasites in the fish.

Gravadlax

MAKES 1KG (2¼LB)

TAKES 20 MINUTES, PLUS CURING TIME

KEEPS 3–4 DAYS, REFRIGERATED (2 MONTHS FROZEN)

INGREDIENTS

85g (3oz) caster sugar

30g (1oz) dill, chopped

1 tbsp lemon juice

75g (2½oz) fine sea salt

1 tsp freshly ground black pepper

2 x 500g (1lb 2oz) thick fillets very fresh organic farmed or sustainably sourced salmon

PLAIN SALTED FISH

Salting fish is an easy way to keep white and oily fish fillets fresh in the fridge for 1 to 2 days before cooking them. The salt draws moisture from the fish, which develops its flavour and firms up its texture.

Dip evenly-sized fish fillets in sea salt and shake off the excess. Refrigerate thin fillets for 5–10 minutes, medium-thick fillets for 10–15 minutes, and thick fillets for 15–30 minutes. Rinse in water, dry with kitchen paper, cover with cling film, and refrigerate for up to 2 days.

1 Combine the sugar, dill, lemon juice, salt, and pepper in a small bowl and mix all the ingredients together well.

2 Lay one fillet of salmon, skin side down, on a clean tray. Spread all the curing mix evenly over the whole fillet.

3 Place the other fillet on top, flesh side down. Wrap the fillets tightly in cling film and weigh them down with a plate and 1–2 cans. Refrigerate for 48 hours to cure.

4 Turn the fish every 12 hours to compress each fillet and drain off the fluid so the fillets firm up. Remove, unwrap, and pat dry with kitchen paper.

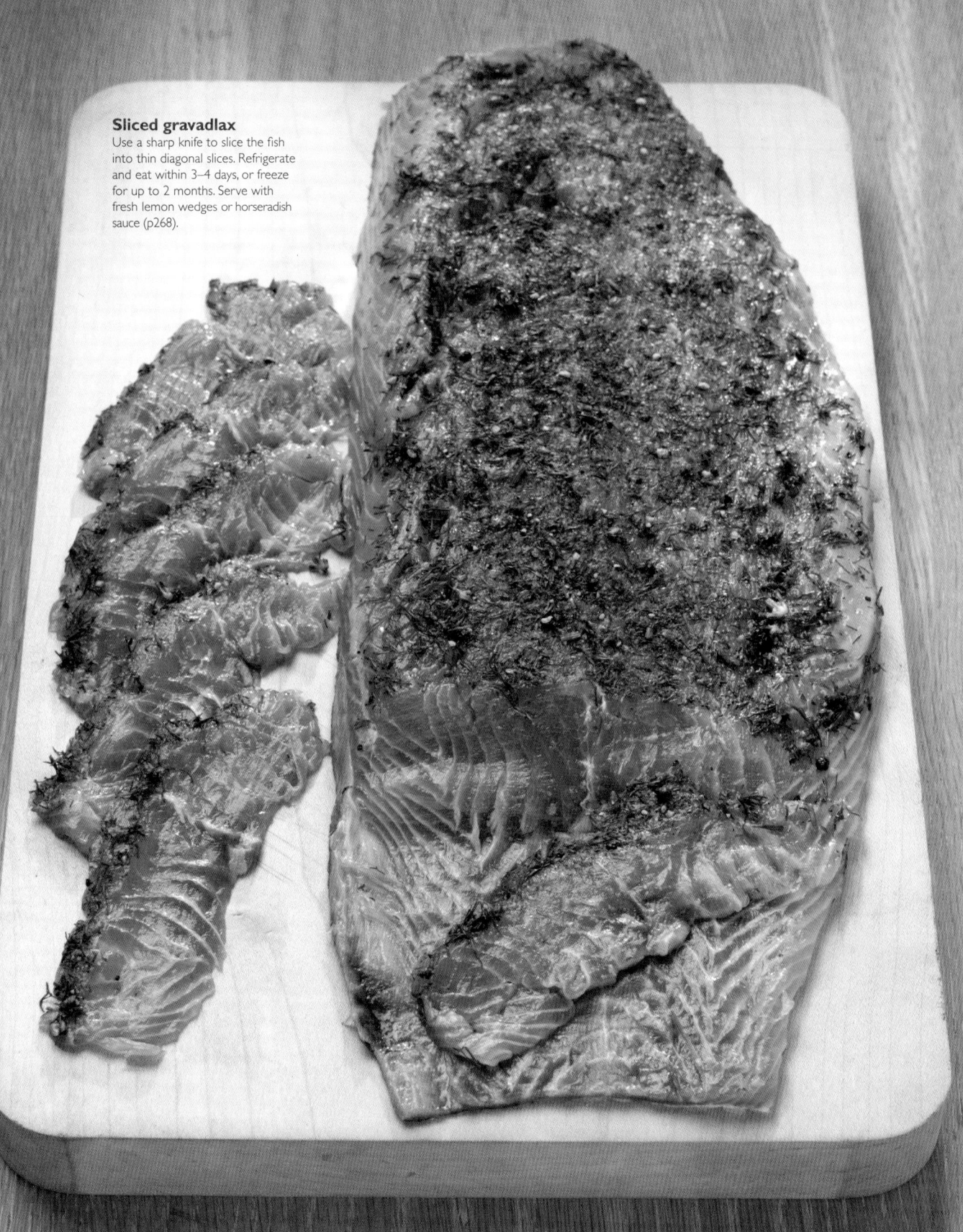

Sliced gravadlax
Use a sharp knife to slice the fish into thin diagonal slices. Refrigerate and eat within 3–4 days, or freeze for up to 2 months. Serve with fresh lemon wedges or horseradish sauce (p268).

Curing fish

Pickling fish in vinegar in effect "cooks" the fish and dissolves any tiny bones. Make the flavourings as mild or sharp as you want (for a mild pickle, use half the quantity of vinegar). Rollmops are delicious as a cold starter.

Rollmops

MAKES APPROX 750ML (1¼ PINTS) (1 MEDIUM PRESERVING JAR)

TAKES 20–25 MINUTES, PLUS SALTING TIME

KEEPS 1 MONTH, REFRIGERATED

INGREDIENTS

6–8 very fresh herring fillets, descaled and trimmed, with any visible bones removed

For the brine

60g (2oz) sea salt per 450ml (15fl oz) cold water

For the spiced vinegar

450ml (15fl oz) cider or white wine vinegar

1 tbsp light soft brown sugar

6 black peppercorns

6 allspice berries

1 mace blade

3 bay leaves

1 dried chilli

Plus

1 red onion, peeled, halved, and finely sliced

6–8 pickled gherkins (pp202–203)

1 Put the fillets in a glass dish. Dissolve the salt in the water, pour the brine over the fish and leave to soak for 2–3 hours. Then drain and pat dry with kitchen paper.

2 Put the vinegar, sugar, and spices into a stainless steel saucepan, bring slowly to the boil, simmer for 1–2 minutes, and then leave the mixture to cool.

3 Lay the fillets skin side down on a clean board. Place a slice of onion and gherkin at the tail end of each and roll them up. Secure each rollmop with a cocktail stick.

4 Pack into a snug-fitting sterilized preserving jar or crock. Pour the cold spiced vinegar and its spices over the rollmops so that they are completely submerged.

5 Top up with vinegar if
needed. Seal and store
in the fridge for 3–4 days to
mature. Always keep the
fish submerged in vinegar.

Whether just cured or also marinated for added richness and flavour, these quick salted herrings can either be served in salads with beetroot, radicchio, and soured cream or horseradish sauce (p268), or in slivers as instant hors d'oeuvres.

Quick salted herrings

MAKES 2–4 SERVINGS OR 1 SMALL PRESERVING JAR

TAKES 30 MINUTES, PLUS CURING TIME

KEEPS 1 WEEK, UNMARINATED, 2 WEEKS MARINATED

INGREDIENTS

2 boned, very fresh, herring fillets with heads removed

Small slivers of organic lemon peel (optional)

Olive oil to cover

For the cure mix

2 tsp fine sea salt

2 tsp caster sugar

1 tsp brandy

Freshly ground black pepper

2 tsp chopped dill

1 Clean the herrings if necessary and trim away any excess skin and fins.

2 Place one fillet skin side down on a clean plate. Mix all the ingredients for the cure mix and spread them evenly over the fillet. Lay the second fillet on top, skin side up, to make a sandwich.

3 Cover the fillets with cling film, put a heavy weight on top, and leave in the fridge for 24 hours to cure. Turn the fillets after 12 hours (the cure will turn to liquid, which can be drained off).

4 The herrings can be eaten at this point, if you wish. Transfer them to a clean dry plate, cover with cling film, and store in the fridge.

5 To marinate the herring for extra flavour, slice the fillets into slivers, removing any surplus skin (or all the skin, if you prefer).

6 Pack into a small sterilized jar or crock, add the lemon peel (if using), cover completely with olive oil, and return to the fridge. Leave for 48 hours before eating.

Escabeche means "pickled" in Spanish, and is a popular way of preparing fish. Some people prefer using oily fish, but try using white, meaty fish, as the result has a cleaner, less rich flavour. Coley is used here, as it's inexpensive and sustainable.

Escabeche

MAKES 4–6 SERVINGS

TAKES 45 MINUTES, PLUS MARINATNG TIME

KEEPS 3 DAYS, REFRIGERATED

INGREDIENTS

675g (1½lb) thick coley fillet, skinned

3 tbsp plain flour

Salt and freshly ground black pepper

2 tsp chopped thyme plus a few leaves for garnishing (or 1 tsp dried thyme, and garnish with a little chopped parsley)

6 tbsp olive oil

1 onion, thinly sliced into rings

1 large garlic clove, crushed

1 large carrot, cut into thin matchsticks

1 red pepper, halved, deseeded, and cut in thin strips

1 celery stick, cut into thin matchsticks

2.5cm (1in) piece fresh root ginger, grated

2–4 large green chillies, deseeded and sliced

250ml (9fl oz) white wine vinegar

¼ tsp sea salt

½ tsp caster sugar

6 tbsp olive oil, plus extra for drizzling

1 Cut the coley into 5cm (2in) pieces. Mix the flour with a little salt and pepper and the herbs, and use this mix to coat the fish.

2 Heat half the oil in a frying pan and fry the fish quickly on all sides until brown and just cooked – about 4 minutes. Place in a large, shallow serving dish.

3 Wipe out the pan, heat the remaining oil, and fry the onion, garlic, carrot, pepper, and celery gently for 5 minutes, stirring until just tender but still with some "bite". Remove from the pan with a slotted spoon and reserve.

4 Add the remaining ingredients to the pan, bring to the boil, reduce the heat, and simmer for 5 minutes. Stir in the vegetables, then spoon the mixture over the fish. Allow to cool slightly, then cover and leave to marinate overnight. Either serve that day at room temperature, drizzled with olive oil and sprinkled with a few fresh thyme or parsley leaves, or store in the fridge for up to 3 days (bring back to room temperature before garnishing and serving).

Wet-cured meat

There are many ways to cure pork legs into hams, but this is a good basic method that produces a mild, sweet cure. The fridge must be kept very cold (below 5°C/41°F) and the meat completely submerged during brining.

Simple wet-cured ham

MAKES 2.5KG (5½LB)

TAKES 10–15 MINUTES, PLUS BRINING, DRYING, AND COOKING TIME

KEEPS 4–5 DAYS, COOKED

INGREDIENTS

2.5kg (5½lb) horseshoe cut of pork with skin on

For the cure mix

700g (1lb 9oz) curing salt

30g (1oz) light soft brown sugar

25g (scant 1oz) ascorbic acid (vitamin C powder)

For cooking and finishing the ham

2 small glasses of cider

1 dried bay leaf

12 black peppercorns

6 cloves

ROASTING THE HAM

Once cooked, the ham can be finished in the oven with a sweet glaze: mix 2 level tbsp each of maple syrup, honey, and mustard, or 5 tbsp of marmalade, spread the glaze over the ham, and roast for 30–40 minutes in a hot oven (200°C/400°F/Gas 6).

1 Put 6 litres (12½ pints) of water in a large plastic box with a lid, add the curing ingredients, and stir until dissolved. The cure will fizz and may smoke a little.

2 Completely submerge the meat in the cure. Put a clean glass paperweight or plate on top to ensure the meat stays submerged. Seal and refrigerate for 25 days.

3 Lift the meat out of the brine. Dry with kitchen paper. Place on a rack on a tray (to catch drips), truss into a round with string, and store in the fridge for 3–4 days.

4 Soak in cold water for 1 hour. Bring a large saucepan of fresh water to the boil. Add the ham, cider, and aromatics, bring to the boil, cover, and barely simmer for 3–3½ hours.

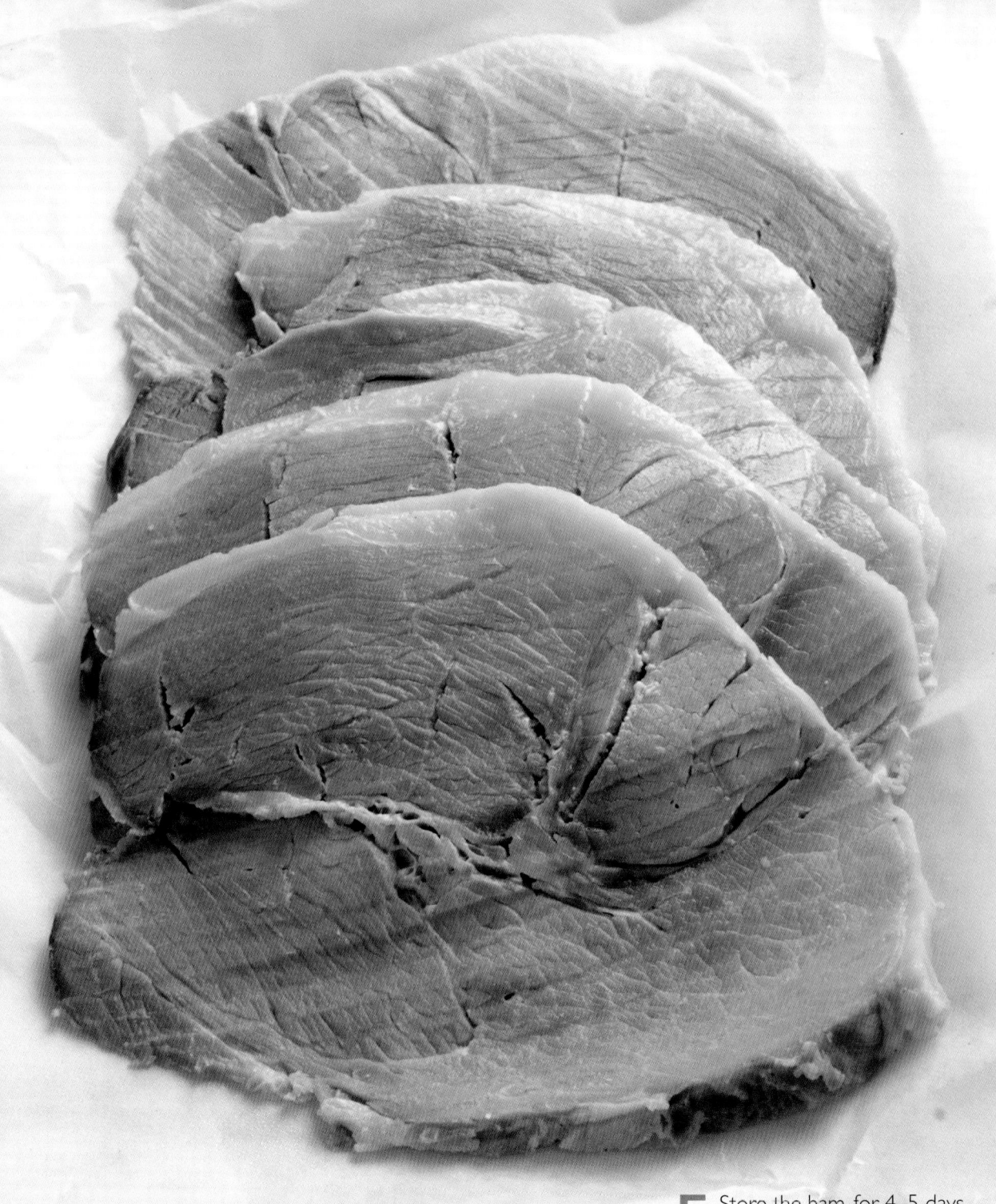

5 Store the ham, for 4–5 days in the fridge, or freeze for 2–3 months. (The uncooked cured ham may be stored for 1–3 days in the fridge, or frozen for 1–2 months.) Slice thinly to serve.

Salting beef is a splendid technique for preserving cheaper cuts of meat. The process of curing gives the meat an entirely different flavour and texture. Serve as a starter with salad and relishes, or in rye bread for the best-ever salt beef sandwiches.

Salted beef

MAKES 1KG (2¼LB)

TAKES 3–5 HOURS, PLUS CURING TIME

KEEPS 7 DAYS, REFRIGERATED

INGREDIENTS

1kg (2¼lb) rolled brisket with the cod fat (layer of gristle) removed

6 crushed juniper berries

1 bay leaf

1 sprig thyme or rosemary

2 carrots, roughly chopped

1 large onion

For the cure mix

400g (14oz) sea salt

200g (7oz) light muscovado sugar

15g (½oz) ascorbic acid (Vitamn C powder)

10–12cm (4–5in) piece of fresh root ginger, peeled and crushed in a garlic press or pestle and mortar

20g (¾oz) coarsely ground black pepper

1 Ensure that the meat is rolled tightly with string. Put the curing ingredients in a preserving pan or large, heavy-based saucepan with 5 litres (8¾ pints) of water. Bring slowly to the boil, stirring to dissolve the salt and sugar. Turn off the heat, add the juniper berries, bay leaf, and thyme or rosemary, and leave to cool.

2 Place the meat in a deep dish or plastic box, and add the spiced brine. Place in the fridge for 4–6 days. Check the meat is completely submerged at all times. Turn the meat halfway through.

3 Take the meat out of the cure, rinse well, and discard the cure. Put the beef in a large, heavy-based saucepan with the carrots and onion, cover with cold water, bring to the boil, and then simmer, covered, for 3 hours, topping up with boiling water if the water gets low. The water should barely tremble, and the meat should be cooked until it begins to flake away.

4 If serving hot, leave to settle in its cooking liquor for 30 minutes, then cut into thick chunks and serve with potato purée and crisp stir-fried cabbage.

5 If serving cold, leave to cool in its liquor, drain, wrap in greaseproof paper, put a plate and a 1–2kg (2¼–4½lb) weight on top, and leave overnight in the fridge. Slice into thin slices to serve.

If your fridge is large enough – and cold enough – to store the meat while it is curing, this is a fantastic way to enhance the flavour of turkey. The meat will be beautifully moist when cooked, which results in a dish worthy of a Christmas buffet.

Salted turkey

MAKES 2KG (4½LB)

TAKES 2 HOURS 20 MINUTES, PLUS CHILLING, SOAKING, DRYING, AND CURING TIME

KEEPS 7 DAYS, REFRIGERATED

INGREDIENTS

2kg (4½lb) turkey crown, bone in

250g (9oz) fine sea salt

50g (1¾oz) granulated sugar

Zest of 1 organic orange, washed

Zest of ½ organic lemon or lime, washed

1 bay leaf

1 small sprig rosemary

75ml (2½fl oz) vodka or gin (optional)

If roasting

A little olive oil

Sea salt and freshly ground black pepper

Slices of bacon or pancetta (optional, if roasting)

If pot-roasting

2 carrots, chopped

1 large onion

1 celery stick, chopped

A little olive oil and butter

1 Keep the turkey in the fridge while you make the brine. Put the salt, sugar, and 5 litres (7 pints) of water into a very large stockpot or preserving pan and bring to the boil. Take the pan off the heat and add the aromatics (and alcohol, if using). Allow to cool, then transfer to a large, clean plastic washing-up bowl, stainless steel bowl, or similar, and store in the fridge until very cold.

2 Submerge the turkey completely in the cold brine. Put back in the fridge (check the fridge temperature is 5°C/ 41°F) and keep in the brine for 8 days.

3 Take the turkey out of the brine, rinse it, and soak in fresh, very cold water in the fridge for 30 minutes. Discard the brine. Dry the meat with kitchen paper, sit on a clean plate lined with fresh kitchen paper, and return to the fridge to dry further for 1–3 hours.

4 To roast the meat, drizzle over a little olive oil, season with salt and black pepper, cover with bacon or pancetta (if using), and roast in a preheated oven 190°C (375°F/Gas 5) for 1¼–1½ hours or until the juices run clear. There is no need to baste the meat. To pot-roast the meat, put a layer of carrot, onion, and celery in the bottom of a casserole. Brown the turkey in a little butter and oil and place on top of the vegetables. Add enough water to cover the vegetables, cover tightly and cook in a preheated oven at 160°C (325°F/Gas 3) for 1½–1¾ hours until the juices run clear.

Dry-curing meat

Rubbing meat with salt and leaving it to dry and mature is the oldest technique of preserving meat. This is the best way of preparing breakfast bacon. For the best results, use organic or free-range pork from a traditional breed.

Dry-cured bacon

MAKES 2KG (4½LB)

TAKES 15 MINUTES, PLUS CURING TIME

KEEPS 10 DAYS REFRIGERATED (2–3 MONTHS FROZEN)

INGREDIENTS

2kg (4½lb) boneless loin of pork from a carcass hung for 3–4 days prior to being butchered, if possible

For the cure mix

80g (2¾oz) curing salt

40g (1½oz) light soft brown sugar

1 rounded tsp ascorbic acid (vitamin C powder)

1 Lay the raw meat on a clean board, skin side down. Thoroughly mix the curing ingredients in a bowl and rub the cure evenly over all the flesh and fat of the meat, working it into all crevices.

2 Transfer the meat to a large plastic container with a rack in the base. Secure the lid and leave the container on the bottom shelf of the fridge for 4–5 days (check your fridge is the correct temperature – 5°C/41°F – to ensure that the curing process is a safe procedure).

3 Intermittently drain off any watery liquid that collects (though leave the curing sediment and rub it back into the meat).

4 To check the bacon is sufficiently cured, cut a thin slice from one end. It should be pink all the way across; if there is still a grey patch in the centre, mix up half quantities of the curing mix, reapply, and put the meat in the sealed container in the fridge for another 24 hours.

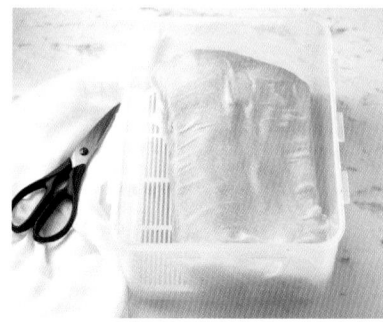

5 Wash the cured bacon in cold water, dry with kitchen paper, wrap in clean muslin, and put back on its tray in the container in the fridge, uncovered, for 4–5 days to dry out (keep away from other food). It will darken slightly and become firm to the touch. To check it is ready to eat, slice a piece and fry it. If it seems too salty, soak the whole joint in cold water in the fridge for 24 hours, then dry, re-cover in muslin, and refrigerate for 3–4 more days.

6 Wrap in greaseproof paper, store in the fridge, and slice as required. To freeze, pack slices into convenient-sized portions and freeze for 2–3 months.

This recipe transforms a cheap cut of pork into gloriously succulent potted meat. Buy good-quality or organic rare breed pork, and there should be sufficient fat for this recipe; a little lard has been included to cover the finished dish if necessary.

Pork rillettes

MAKES 4–6 SERVINGS (1 SMALL PRESERVING JAR)

TAKES 3½ HOURS, PLUS STANDING AND CHILLING TIME

KEEPS 1 MONTH, REFRIGERATED

INGREDIENTS

1 tbsp rosemary, chopped

1 large garlic clove, crushed

¼ tsp ground cloves

2 tsp sea salt

Freshly ground black pepper

500g (1lb 2oz) piece fat belly pork

1 bay leaf

60g (2oz) lard, if necessary

1 Mix the rosemary, garlic, cloves, salt, and a good grinding of black pepper together in a small bowl. Rub this mix all over the meat, place it in a covered container in the fridge, and leave to stand for 24 hours.

2 Place the meat in a casserole dish. Add the bay leaf and 250ml (8fl oz) of boiling water. Cover tightly with foil, then the lid, and place in a low oven at 150°C (300°F/ Gas 2). Cook for 3 hours until meltingly tender. Check the meat after 1½ hours of cooking and add a spoonful or 2 of water, if necessary.

3 Remove the pork from the oven, spoon off any fat and reserve it. Tip the meat and juices into a sieve, cover, and leave to drain and cool. If there appears to still be plenty of fat on the juices, spoon it off and reserve with the other fat. Reserve the juices too.

4 When cool enough to handle, discard the rind and bones and put the meat on a board. Use 2 forks to shred the meat and pack it into a warm sterilized jar. Add the reserved juices. Melt the spooned-off fat or the lard (or a mixture of both) and pour over the top of the meat. Seal and, when cold, store in the fridge for up to 1 month. Once the jar is opened, eat within 2 days.

Originally from Gascony, France, this delicacy can also be made with goose, chicken, or game birds. If you prefer, use a mixture of olive and sunflower oil instead of goose or duck fat, but ensure when cooking and storing the duck that it is completely submerged in oil.

Duck confit

MAKES 4 SERVINGS

TAKES 2¾ HOURS, PLUS CHILLING TIME

KEEPS 2 WEEKS, REFRIGERATED

INGREDIENTS

4 duck leg portions

2 tbsp sea salt

8 black peppercorns, lightly crushed

2 large garlic cloves, crushed

¼ tsp ground allspice

1 tsp dried thyme

2 bay leaves, torn into pieces

340g (12oz) jar or can of goose or duck fat

A little lard, if necessary

1 Put the duck portions in a large container with a sealable lid. Mix the salt, peppercorns, garlic, allspice, thyme, and bay leaves together and rub all over the meat. Cover with a lid and chill for 24 hours in the fridge.

2 Wash the duck thoroughly under cold water and pat dry on kitchen paper (this is very important, or the finished dish will be too salty). Pack the meat tightly in a medium-sized flameproof casserole dish. Add the goose or duck fat and heat through until the fat melts – about 10 minutes. If necessary, add a little lard so that the meat is completely covered.

3 Cover the casserole with a lid and cook in a very low oven at 150°C (300°F/Gas 2) for 2½ hours until the meat is meltingly tender.

4 Remove the casserole from the oven and leave until fairly cool. Carefully transfer the duck to a suitable container that can be kept in the fridge and pour all the fat over to cover it completely. Cover with a lid and, when completely cold, store in the fridge.

5 To serve, carefully take the duck out of the fat, scraping off any excess. (The fat can be stored in the fridge and reused up to 3 times for making confit.) Heat a large heavy-based frying pan and fry the duck, skin sides down first, until crisp and golden, then turn it over, turn down the heat, and cook until piping hot right through – about 10 minutes in all.

Making sausages

Home-made sausages are additive- and preservative-free, taste succulent, and are full of flavour. Keep the ingredients cold to ensure good hygiene and success (only cold meat forms sausages properly), and invest in a sausage maker.

Toulouse-style sausage

MAKES APPROX 1.1KG (2½LB)

TAKES 30–45 MINUTES, PLUS SOAKING TIME

KEEPS 1–2 DAYS UNCOOKED, 4–5 DAYS COOKED (2 MONTHS UNCOOKED, FROZEN)

INGREDIENTS

1m (3ft) hog casings

1kg (2¼lb) lean pork (e.g. from the shoulder), chilled until very cold in the fridge

150g (5½oz) streaky bacon or pancetta

½ small glass white wine (if the sausage is cooked immediately) or very cold water (if stored)

10g (¼oz) fine sea or rock salt

2 garlic cloves, crushed to a smooth paste with a pinch of salt

1 level tsp finely ground white pepper

> **SAUSAGE-MAKING TIP**
> Have the seasonings measured and the equipment cleaned and laid out before you start to make the sausages.

1 Wash the casings in warm water and soak them for at least 2 hours in cold water, then rinse. Keep them in the bowl of water in the fridge until needed.

2 Mince the pork and the bacon coarsely in a mincer (or chop the bacon finely) when you are ready to make the sausages.

3 Put all the ingredients in a large bowl and mix them with your hands, or use a food mixer with a dough attachment. Put in the fridge for 2–3 hours to firm up.

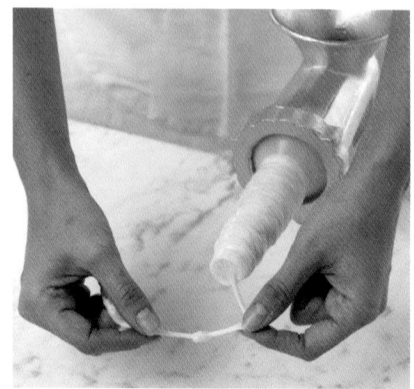

4 Keep a bowl of cold water nearby to rinse sticky fingers. Fit the length of wet casing over the nozzle of the sausage maker. Tie a knot in the end of the casing.

5 Gradually fill the casing with the meat, using your hand to support the weight of the sausage as it appears out of the nozzle. Push the meat into the centre of the casing and squeeze out any air pockets with your hand.

6 Curl the filled casing into a coil and tie the other end of the casing in a knot. Cut off any excess casing at either end.

7 Put the sausage on a clean plate. Use a sterilized cocktail stick to prick it along its length to smooth out any remaining air pockets. Keep uncovered in the fridge overnight to firm up and let the flavours permeate.

Pork sausage
For the best results, cook and eat Toulouse sausage immediately or add, sliced, to cassoulets.

Chorizo sausages are usually dried, but are also delicious fresh. They are simple to make, either as sausages or meatballs. Fresh chorizo are best eaten as soon as possible: simply fry, bake, or add to casseroles, pasta sauces, and other savoury dishes.

Fresh sweet chorizo

SPECIAL EQUIPMENT
MINCER, SAUSAGE MAKER

MAKES APPROX 1KG (2¼ LB)

TAKES 20 MINUTES,
PLUS SOAKING AND CHILLING TIME

KEEPS 3–4 DAYS, REFRIGERATED
(3 MONTHS FROZEN)

INGREDIENTS

1m (3ft) hog casings

1kg (2¼lb) pork shoulder, freshly minced
(p312)

15g (½oz) sea salt

2 garlic cloves, crushed and mashed

15g (½oz) sweet smoked paprika

1 tsp chilli powder

½ tsp fine white pepper

1 Wash the casings in warm water and soak them for at least 2 hours in cold water, then rinse. Keep them in the bowl of water in the fridge until needed.

2 Put the rest of the ingredients in a large bowl and mix with your hands, or use a food mixer with a dough attachment. Put in the fridge for 2–3 hours to firm up.

3 Fill the casings with the meat mixture (pp312–13). Twist the casing at regular intervals to form a link of sausages. To make meatballs, simply form the meat into small balls using cold, wet hands (instead of feeding it into hog casings). Arrange on a tray.

4 Put the sausages or meatballs in the fridge (hang the sausages up, if possible) and leave for 24 hours for them to dry, firm up, and allow the flavours to marry. Keep refrigerated until ready to cook.

Unlike many bought sausages, home-made sausages rate among the best. British bangers differ from continental sausages in that they include a certain amount of rusk or breadcrumbs and different seasonings. Use good-quality bread for this recipe.

Traditional British sausage

SPECIAL EQUIPMENT
MINCER, SAUSAGE MAKER

MAKES 10–12 SAUSAGES

TAKES 45 MINUTES,
PLUS STANDING AND SOAKING TIME

KEEPS 3–4 DAYS, REFRIGERATED
(3 MONTHS FROZEN)

INGREDIENTS

1m (3ft) hog casings

150g (5½oz) stale, good-quality white
   bread, such as sour dough

1kg (2¼lb) pork shoulder,
   freshly minced (p312)

15g (½oz) sea salt

½ tsp mace

½ tsp nutmeg

½ tsp dried rosemary

¼ tsp cloves, freshly ground

1 Wash the casings in warm water and soak them for at least 2 hours in cold water, then rinse. Keep them in the bowl of water in the fridge until needed.

2 Put the bread in a very low oven and leave until biscuit-dry but not coloured (leave the door ajar if necessary). To crumb, whizz briefly in a food processor to get fine crumbs, or roll over the bread with a rolling pin.

3 Put the pork and all the dry ingredients into a large clean bowl and mix. Add 150ml (5fl oz) of icy cold water and, using cold, wet hands, mix everything together very thoroughly. Put back in the fridge and leave overnight for the flavours to marry and the mixture to firm up.

4 Fill the casings with the meat mixture (pp312–13). Twist the casing every 10cm (4in) to form a link of sausages. Each sausage should weigh about 85g (3oz).

5 Put the sausages or meatballs in the fridge (hang the sausages up, if possible) and leave for 24 hours for them to dry, firm up, and allow the flavours to marry. Keep refrigerated until ready to cook.

Smoking, using the smoke from the embers of a smouldering fire, is probably the earliest-known method of preservation. Food may be cold-smoked (the traditional method, in which food is smoked at very low temperatures for 24 hours or longer and remains uncooked), or hot-smoked – covered in this section. Although it is unsuitable for long-term storage, hot-smoking fish, meat, and certain vegetables is easy to do at home – there is even a variation of the technique where food can be smoked in a wok – and keeps food beautifully moist while simultaneously cooking it.

The best ingredients for...
Smoking

Traditionally, only hand-reared meat and fish caught fresh from the wild were smoked. Today, a wider range of foods can be smoked, but the golden rule remains: buy the best quality you can.

Prawns
Choose prawns carefully and avoid any that smell fishy. Avoid intensively farmed tiger prawns and select organically farmed or sustainably caught cold water prawns.

Mackerel

Fish
A wide range of fish are delicious smoked in a domestic smoker (pp320–21) or a wok (pp328–29). Oak is the traditional wood used to smoke fish, but experiment with other light-flavoured wood chips. Avoid intensively farmed fish.

Haddock

Coley

Trout

Salmon

Mussels

Inexpensive and in plentiful supply, with sweet flesh and juices, mussels are delicious smoked. Choose local seasonal wild or farmed (rope-grown).

Peppers

Smoking adds an interesting flavour to peppers (and chillies) but don't smoke them for long as, like other vegetables, they may acquire a slightly bitter tang.

Garlic

Smoked garlic is very popular (and can be made into a tasty garlic butter). New season's dried garlic is best; choose fat cloves.

Potatoes

Freshly cooked potatoes, peeled and sliced, are good to smoke with whichever meat or fish you are smoking, or on their own. Smoke lightly for a short time.

Eggs

The humble hard-boiled egg is transformed by smoking. Buy the best eggs you can. Pickled smoked eggs are extra good, too.

Pheasant

Smoking enriches the natural taste of all game and pheasant is ideal to use. Smoke whole birds and finish by cooking in the oven, or smoke individual breasts with the skin on.

Chicken

Good-quality chicken breasts have firm flesh and maximum flavour. Chicken is an ideal meat to smoke; keep the skin on for added succulence (pp320–21). A whole chicken can be smoked then oven-cooked.

OTHER INGREDIENTS

VEGETABLES
Jerusalem artichokes (cooked)
Sweetcorn (cooked)

NUTS
Almonds
Peanuts
Pine nuts

FISH
(buy sustainably sourced)
Cod
Eel
Herring
Octopus
Pollack
Razor clams
Salmon trout
Shark
Tuna

MEAT
(buy free-range or organic)
Beef (tender cuts e.g. sirloin, rib-eye, or fillet steak)
Hamburgers
Leg of lamb
Loin of lamb (chops)
Pork chops
Sausages
Spare ribs
Tenderloin of pork

POULTRY
(buy free-range or organic)
Boneless quail
Duck breast
Goose breast
Turkey breast

GAME
Grouse
Partridge
Rabbit
Vension

Hot smoking in a smoker

Lean poultry, game, and fish are well suited to hot smoking. Brining the meat first helps to dry it out before smoking, and improves its flavour. Smoking steams food while cooking it, resulting in succulent meat whether eaten hot or cold.

Hot-smoked chicken breasts

MAKES 4 CHICKEN BREASTS

TAKES 45 MINUTES, PLUS STANDING TIME

KEEPS 2–3 DAYS, REFRIGERATED (2–3 MONTHS FROZEN)

INGREDIENTS

4 chicken breasts with skin on

For the brine

200g (7oz) fine sea salt dissolved in 1 litre (1¾ pints) boiling water, then left to cool

2 level tbsp light wood chips, e.g. oak

HOT-SMOKING TIPS

Only hard woods are suitable as wood chips for smoking.

Wood chips should not be in direct contact with food, and you need very few: 1 level tbsp produces a light flavour; 2 tbsp gives a medium flavour, and 3 tbsp gives a heavy flavour.

Use oven gloves: on a medium heat, the inside temperature is equivalent to 190°C (375°F/Gas 5).

Open a window and turn on the extractor fan when hot-smoking indoors.

Smoked food keeps perfectly in the smoker for a few minutes once off the heat, if required.

1 Lay the chicken in a shallow dish, stab each a few times with a clean skewer, pour over the brine to completely submerge the meat, and leave for 2 hours in the fridge.

2 Remove the chicken from the brine, rinse briefly, pat dry, and transfer to a tray lined with kitchen paper. Refrigerate, uncovered, for 4–8 hours for the cure to permeate it.

3 Sprinkle the chips in the centre of the smoker base tray. Set the rack over the tray, arrange the chicken on top, insert the tray into the smoker, and close the lid.

4 Set the smoker over a moderate heat. When the first wisps of smoke appear, turn the heat down slightly, smoke the chicken for 20–25 minutes, then check if it is cooked.

Smoked chicken
Cooking times for smoking vary slightly depending on the heat source, the thickness of the chicken, and how full the smoking tray is. Serve hot with rice and a spicy relish or chutney, or with salad, potatoes, and walnut and coriander pesto. Or serve cold, sliced thinly for salads or sandwiches.

All types of sausage taste superb and are extra succulent if hot-smoked. If you want a "traditional" finish, gently fry the sausages for five minutes once smoked, turning them so they brown evenly. Serve with polenta or mash and home-made tomato ketchup (p262).

Hot-smoked sausages

SPECIAL EQUIPMENT
STAINLESS STEEL SMOKER

MAKES 3–4 SERVINGS

TAKES 30 MINUTES

KEEPS 2–3 DAYS, REFRIGERATED

INGREDIENTS

450g (1lb) home-made (p312), or similar
   good-quality sausages

For smoking

1 level tbsp oak, cherry, or, for a stronger
   smoke flavour, hickory wood chips

1 Place the wood chips in the centre of the base of a smoker (p15), insert the drip tray, then position the wire rack on top of the tray.

2 Wipe the sausages (but don't prick them) and arrange on the wire rack. Ensure there's space around each sausage so the smoke can penetrate evenly. Insert and close the lid.

3 Turn on the extractor fan, open the window, and set the smoker over a moderate heat. As soon as you begin to smell smoke, or wisps of smoke appear (about 2–3 minutes), turn the heat down slightly and smoke thin sausages for 10–12 minutes, thick sausages for 15 minutes, and Toulouse-type or extra-thick sausages for 20 minutes.

4 Turn off the heat, wait until there are no wisps of smoke, open up the smoker, and cut open 1 sausage to check it is cooked through with no signs of pink in the centre. If not quite cooked, smoke for another 5 minutes, or until cooked. If you want to release the fatty juices from the sausages, prick them once they've cooked, allowing the juices to drip into the tray. Serve, or leave to cool and then refrigerate.

Smoking brings out the best in venison, enhancing its natural gamey flavour and keeping it moist and succulent. Here the meat is marinated first, then smoked. Serve this lovely warming winter dish with lightly steamed cabbage or root vegetable purée (p68).

Smoked venison with juniper berries

SPECIAL EQUIPMENT
STAINLESS STEEL SMOKER

MAKES 4 SERVINGS

TAKES 20 MINUTES, PLUS MARINADING TIME

KEEPS EAT IMMEDIATELY

INGREDIENTS

4 venison loin steaks (approx 225g/8oz each and of even thickness, approx 2cm/¾in thick)

For the marinade

1 tbsp juniper berries

250ml (8fl oz) red wine

4 tbsp ruby port

2–3 tsp caster sugar

1–2 pinches of salt to taste

For smoking

1 level tbsp oak or cherry wood chips

1 Put all the marinade ingredients in a large, deep dish and stir to dissolve the sugar. Place the venison steaks in the marinade, cover, and refrigerate overnight. Turn occasionally to ensure even marinating.

2 Put the wood chips in the centre of the base of a smoker (p15) and place the drip tray on top. Sit the wire rack over the drip tray and arrange the venison steaks on it, making sure there's space around each of them. Insert and close the lid.

3 Turn on the extractor fan, open the window, and set the smoker over a moderate heat. As soon as you begin to smell smoke, or wisps of smoke appear (about 2–3 minutes), turn the heat down slightly. For medium-rare venison smoke for 10–12 minutes; if you prefer well-cooked venison, smoke for 15 minutes. Turn off the heat, wait until there are no wisps of smoke, open up the smoker, and insert a knife through the centre of 1 steak to check the venison is cooked to your liking; if not, smoke for another 5 minutes.

4 While the meat is smoking, pour the marinade into a saucepan and cook on a medium-high heat until the liquor has reduced by at least half and started to thicken – about 15 minutes. Check the seasoning and then strain to remove the juniper berries. Serve the venison steaks immediately on hot plates with a little of the sauce.

Home-smoked garlic is more delicate than the smoked garlic you can buy, and is easy to do. Experiment with different flavoured wood chips, if you wish (p21). Use to make smoked garlic butter or mayonnaise, add to soups, or serve with barbecued meat.

Hot-smoked garlic

SPECIAL EQUIPMENT
STAINLESS STEEL SMOKER

MAKES 4 BULBS

TAKES 35 MINUTES

KEEPS 2 WEEKS

INGREDIENTS

4 large whole garlic bulbs, dried

1 tbsp olive oil

For smoking

2 level tbsp oak wood chips

1 Place the wood chips in the centre of the base of a smoker (p15), insert the drip tray, then position the wire rack on top of the tray.

2 Brush the garlic bulbs with the olive oil and arrange them on the wire rack. Ensure that there is sufficient space around each garlic bulb so the smoke can penetrate them evenly. Insert and close the lid.

3 Turn on the extractor fan, open the window, and set the smoker over a moderate heat. As soon as you begin to smell smoke, or wisps of smoke appear (after 2–3 minutes), turn the heat down slightly and smoke the garlic for 30 minutes.

4 Turn off the heat, wait until there are no wisps of smoke, open the smoker, and remove the garlic bulbs. Once cooled, store in a tightly sealed container in the fridge, or in a cool, dark place.

These tuna steaks are marinated before smoking to give extra flavour. Vary the flavoured wood chips depending on whether you like a mild or rich smoke flavour (p21). Garnish with chopped coriander.

Hot-smoked marinated tuna

SPECIAL EQUIPMENT
STAINLESS STEEL SMOKER

MAKES 4 SERVINGS

TAKES 30 MINUTES,
PLUS MARINATING TIME

KEEPS 3–4 DAYS, REFRIGERATED

INGREDIENTS

4 tuna steaks, approx 175g (6oz) each

For the marinade

1 medium-sized organic orange, washed

2.5cm (1in) piece of fresh root ginger, finely chopped

1 large garlic clove, peeled and finely chopped

2 tsp Thai fish sauce (nam pla)

½ tsp five-spice powder

2–3 tsp vodka (optional)

For smoking

1 level tbsp alder (for a light flavour) or pecan wood chips

1 Lay the fish in a shallow dish. Squeeze the juice from the orange into a bowl, finely zest quarter of the rind and add to the bowl, along with the ginger, garlic, Thai fish sauce, five-spice powder, and vodka (if using). Mix well and taste, adding a little extra fish sauce or other seasonings if needed.

2 Pour the marinade over the fish, turn the steaks over making sure both sides are well coated, cover with cling film, put in the fridge, and leave to marinate for 8–12 hours, turning the fish over halfway through.

3 Arrange the wood chips in the base of a smoker (p15). Place the drip tray on top, scatter over the remaining orange rind, cut into pieces, over the tray, and pour in 60ml (2fl oz) of water. Position the rack on top of the drip tray, lay the fish steaks on top, pour over the marinade, and seal the lid.

4 Turn on the extractor fan, open the window, set the smoker over a low heat, and smoke for 20 minutes. Turn off the heat, wait until there are no wisps of smoke, open up the smoker, and insert a knife into the centre of 1 steak to check the tuna is cooked through; if not, smoke for another 5 minutes. Then serve, or cool and refrigerate for up to 4 days.

Salmon and white fish both benefit from gentle smoking, as the fish effectively steams in the smoker. Dry-salting the fish first is also beneficial (p298). Serve hot with mayonnaise, or make a kedgeree and add the cooked fish to the rice for the last five minutes.

Hot-smoked fish

SPECIAL EQUIPMENT
STAINLESS STEEL SMOKER

MAKES 4 SERVINGS

TAKES 15–50 MINUTES,
PLUS SALTING TIME

KEEPS 2–3 DAYS, REFRIGERATED

INGREDIENTS

Approx 60g (2oz) fine sea salt

4 fish steaks (approx 175g/6oz each)
   of an even thickness

Pinch of light soft brown sugar (optional)

3–4 bay leaves, 1 tsp coriander seeds, or
   1 star anise (optional)

For smoking

1 level tbsp alder or beech (for a light
   flavour), or oak (for a richer flavour)
   wood chips

75ml (2½fl oz) water, white wine, or cider

1 Dry-salt the fish first: put the salt on a clean plate, dip the fish into the salt, coating it thickly on all sides, shake off the excess and transfer to a clean plate. Sprinkle the fish with a pinch of sugar, if using (this adds a subtle sweetness), and refrigerate for 5 minutes for thin steaks and up to 30 minutes for very thick steaks (p298).

2 Rinse the fish under running water, dry with kitchen paper, cover with cling film, return to the fridge, and leave for 2–3 hours to allow the salt to permeate evenly.

3 Place the wood chips in the centre of the base of a smoker (p15), insert the drip tray, pour in the water, wine, or cider, and add the flavourings (if using). Position the wire rack on top of the tray, arrange the fish on the rack leaving space around each one for the smoke to penetrate evenly, and slide on the lid.

4 Turn on the extractor fan, open a window, and set the smoker over a moderate heat. As soon as you begin to smell smoke, or wisps of smoke appear (after 2–3 minutes), turn the heat to low and smoke thin fillets for 8–10 minutes, medium-thick fillets for 12–15 minutes, and thick fillets for 15–20 minutes.

5 Turn off the heat, wait until there are no more wisps of smoke, then check the fish is cooked through (the flesh should be opaque); if not, smoke for another 5 minutes or until cooked. Serve immediately or, if storing, wrap in cling film and keep in the fridge. Reheat, wrapped in foil, in the oven, or use cold in salads.

Hen, duck, bantam, and quail's eggs acquire an attractive pale brown tint when smoked, and are quite a delicacy. Serve hot with spiced rice pilafs or kedgeree, or cold with mayonnaise and salads. Smoked quail's eggs can also be served as canapés.

Hot-smoked eggs

SPECIAL EQUIPMENT
STAINLESS STEEL SMOKER

MAKES 4 SERVINGS

TAKES 30–35 MINUTES

KEEPS 2–3 DAYS, REFRIGERATED

INGREDIENTS

4 very fresh, good-quality hen, duck, or
  bantam eggs, or 8–12 quail's eggs

For smoking

1 level tbsp wood chips, e.g. apple, maple,
  oak, or pecan

1 Place the eggs in a saucepan of boiling water, bring back to the boil, and cook until hard-boiled (this will take approximately 2½ minutes for quail's eggs, 5 minutes for bantam eggs, 7 minutes for hen's eggs, and 8 minutes for duck eggs). Plunge into cold water, then peel off the shells.

2 Place the wood chips in the centre of the base of a smoker (p15), insert the drip tray, and position the wire rack on top of the tray. Lightly oil the wire rack with a brush, then arrange the shelled eggs on the rack, leaving space around each one for the smoke to penetrate evenly. Pour 60ml (2fl oz) of water into the drip tray and insert and close the lid.

3 Turn on the extractor fan, open a window, and set the smoker over a moderate heat. As soon as you begin to smell smoke, or wisps of smoke appear (after 2–3 minutes), turn the heat down to low and smoke the quail's eggs for 10 minutes, bantam eggs for 12 minutes, hen's eggs for 15 minutes, and duck eggs for 20 minutes.

4 Turn off the heat, wait until there are no more wisps of smoke, then remove the eggs and serve, or place on a plate, cover with cling film, and keep in the fridge.

Quail's eggs
These tiny, vitamin-rich eggs are more
nutritious than hen's eggs and make
delightful canapés and starters. Avoid
intensively reared quail's eggs.

Instant smoking in a wok

A wok with a lid makes an admirable instant smoker. It must be well sealed to stop smoke escaping and used over a low heat. Fish and shellfish are perfect for instant smoking. Serve hot or cold with salad and horseradish sauce (p268).

Instant smoked fish

MAKES 2 WHOLE TROUT OR OTHER FISH

TAKES 15–20 MINUTES, PLUS INFUSING TIME

KEEPS 2–3 DAYS

INGREDIENTS

1 tbsp light wood chips, such as apple

2 fresh whole organic trout or mackerel, gutted and cleaned with heads on

4 fennel fronds or 6–8 sprigs tarragon (optional)

HOT SMOKING WOK TIPS

The wok needs to be well sealed to prevent too much smoke escaping (a foil collar pressed around the edge of the lid usually prevents this).

The wok is best used over a low heat on a hob, or outside on a barbecue. Keep separate woks for smoking.

A wok with a clear lid enables you to see the food cooking so that you can control the cooking and smoke levels more accurately: keep the lid firmly closed during cooking and turn the heat slightly up or down to control the amount of smoke.

1 Line the inside of the wok with a double sheet of kitchen foil. Place the wood chips in the centre of the foil (so it will smoke evenly) and place the wok rack inside the wok.

2 Wipe the insides of the trout and make 2 or 3 slashes on each side of the fish. Stuff the insides of the fish with the herbs if you are using them.

3 Place the fish on the rack and put the lid on. Put a foil collar around the edge of the lid to keep the smoke in. Cook over a low heat for 10–15 minutes. Then turn off the heat and leave the sealed wok for 15 minutes to allow the flavours to infuse the fish.

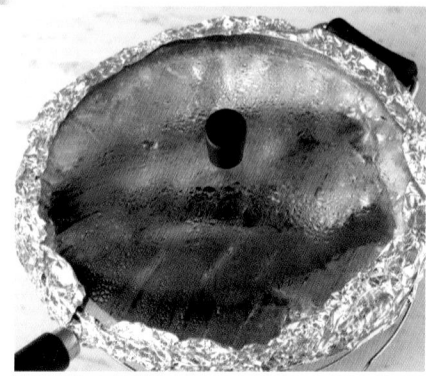

**Instant
hot-smoked trout**
If you are eating the smoked fish
immediately, serve it with salad and
a fresh tomato salsa. Otherwise
leave to cool, transfer to a plate,
cover, and store in the fridge.

Mussels are inexpensive, sustainably produced, and in plentiful supply. They cook fast when smoked in a wok, which gives them a subtle smoked flavour and sweet, flavoursome cooking juices. This recipe makes a great starter or sauce for pasta.

Smoked mussels in fresh tomato sauce

MAKES 4 STARTER SERVINGS OR 2 MAIN COURSE SERVINGS

TAKES 40–45 MINUTES

KEEPS EAT IMMEDIATELY

INGREDIENTS

1 level tbsp beech or alder wood chips

750g (1lb 10oz) prepared mussels in their shells (cleaned, with beards removed)

1–2 tbsp olive oil for frying

2 large shallots, finely diced

2 garlic cloves, finely diced

1 400g can chopped tomatoes or passata

6 ripe tomatoes (approx 450g/1lb), skinned, deseeded, and cut into small, bite-sized pieces (plunge the whole tomatoes into boiling water for 30 seconds to make their skins easier to remove)

Salt and freshly ground black pepper

A few sprigs of parsley, chopped

1 Wrap the wood chips in kitchen foil to form a flat parcel. Pierce several holes in the top of the parcel with a sharp knife to allow the smoke to escape. Place in the bottom of the wok, then insert the wire wok rack.

2 Spread the mussels out evenly on the wok rack, put the lid on tightly and seal the join with a strip of kitchen foil. If there are too many mussels to fit in 1 layer on the rack, cook them in 2 batches.

3 Turn on the extractor fan and open the window. Smoke over a high heat for 5 minutes until the mussels have opened. Turn off the heat, wait for the smoke to subside, and remove the mussels, setting them to one side (discard and throw away any that haven't opened). Remove the parcel of wood chips carefully and reserve any juices.

4 Wash and dry the wok. Set over a gentle heat, add the olive oil, and lightly fry the shallots and garlic for 5 minutes or until softened but not coloured. Add the mussels and toss with the garlic and shallots for 2–3 minutes, then add the canned tomatoes, stir thoroughly, bring to the boil, and simmer on a moderate heat, for 5–10 minutes. Add the fresh tomatoes and, for a smokier flavour, add the reserved cooking juices (taste these first, and use as a seasoning, adding as much or as little as you want). Toss, season to taste, and serve with a garnish of parsley.

Ripe peppers, like garlic and cooked potatoes, can be smoked successfully (other vegetables develop a bitter tang). Light smoking in a wok gives them a subtle flavour that complements their natural sweetness, and they are then finished off in the oven.

Smoked peppers stuffed with citrus couscous

MAKES 4 SERVINGS

TAKES 45 MINUTES–1 HOUR

KEEPS EAT IMMEDIATELY

INGREDIENTS

1 level tbsp oak wood chips

4 medium ripe red or yellow peppers

125g (4½oz) couscous

60g (2oz) pine nuts, toasted or smoked on a piece of kitchen foil and smoked with the peppers for the same length of time

½ tsp dried chilli flakes or 1 tsp finely chopped fresh chilli

2 sprigs of coriander, chopped

Juice of 1 lemon and 1 lime

Salt and freshly ground black pepper

1 Wrap the wood chips in kitchen foil to form a flat parcel. Pierce several holes in the top of the parcel with a sharp knife to allow the smoke to escape. Place in the bottom of the wok, then insert the wire wok rack.

2 Slice the tops off each of the peppers and reserve. Cut out the seeds inside without piercing the flesh.

3 Put the peppers cut side down on the wok rack and place the tops, stalks facing upwards, next to them. Put the lid on tightly and seal the join with a strip of kitchen foil. Turn on the extractor fan and open the window. Smoke over a moderate heat for 10–12 minutes until the peppers start to soften. Turn off the heat, wait for the smoke to subside, and remove the peppers.

4 Put the couscous in a bowl, add 200ml (7fl oz) of boiling water or hot stock, cover with cling film, and leave for 4 minutes until the water is absorbed and the grains are soft. When the peppers are ready, fluff up the couscous, stir in the pine nuts, chilli, coriander, lemon and lime juice, and season to taste. Spoon the couscous into the peppers, place the lids on top, put in an oiled, snug-fitting ovenproof dish, and cook in a hot oven (220°C/425°F/Gas 7) for 10 minutes until heated right through. Serve immediately with a crisp salad or as a vegetable accompaniment.

Brewing and wine-making

are an art that has been handed down and enjoyed for centuries. It has become a popular pastime and has many attractions: the results are refreshingly pure and natural, as well as delicious to drink, it is environmentally friendly, and the resulting brews are far cheaper than their bought equivalents. Like all preserving methods, brewing **beer** and **cider** and making **wine** all rely on particular chemical reactions, and certain procedures, such as sterilizing all equipment, must be followed meticulously to obtain consistent results.

The best ingredients for...

Brewing and wine-making

Hops, fruits, vegetables, herbs, wild berries, and plants from the hedgerows all provide a rich and varied harvest from which to make beers, ciders, and wines – a grand finale to the preserving season.

Hops
'Fuggles' and 'Golden' are popular varieties of hops to grow for making beer (pp346–47). They are prolific scramblers and can reach 5m (16ft).

Grapes
Successful wine can be made from any grapes (pp338–39). Chardonnay and other grape varieties are easy to grow and are long-lived, so are worth growing to make your own wine.

Plums
'Victoria' plums are good to use for wine, as are those growing wild in hedgerows (mix with elderberries if you like). Pick when ripe and their sugar content is highest.

Damsons
The damson season is short – from August to September. Pick when ripe and freeze overnight first to release their rich flavour.

Crab apples
These apples can be used instead of other apple varieties to make lovely country wines. Freezing them first helps to break down their pectin content, which would otherwise hinder fermentation.

Beetroots
These root vegetables produce earthy wines (traditionally ginger, cloves, and cinnamon were added when cooking the beetroots before fermentation). Dark-coloured varieties will ensure a deep red claret colour.

Rhubarb

Use firm, freshly picked stalks and crush them before chopping. Ferment with an organic lemon and raisins (to supply sugar) and leave the wine for six months to mature.

Apples

Cider can be made with any apples, but a good cider apple such as 'Brown's Apple' (which is much sharper, and higher in tannins) is worth finding. Use windfalls.

Pears

Use cider pears for perry and other varieties for country wines (you can blend them with apples). Chop but do not peel or core, and then leave the wine for 12 months to mature fully.

Elderflowers

These clusters of pretty, star-shaped flowers make gorgeous, light, refreshing summer wines, with a heady muscat flavour. Use to flavour gooseberry and other summer wines, too.

Parsnips

An excellent root vegetable for making winter wine in January and February once the frosts have converted some of its starch to sugars. All varieties of parsnip are suitable.

Elderberries

Gather the ripe bunches of berries in autumn and strip them from their stalks using a fork before fermenting into wine.

Brewing cider

Cider can be made with any apples, including windfalls. Generally, the sweeter the apple, the sweeter the cider, so cooking apples will make a drier cider than dessert varieties. Sterilize all brewing equipment before use.

Cider

MAKES APPROX 4 LITRES (7 PINTS)

TAKES 1–1½ HOURS, PLUS FREEZING, STRAINING, BREWING, AND STORING TIME

KEEPS 6 MONTHS

INGREDIENTS

3.5kg (7–8lb) apples, or 4 litres (7 pints) apple juice

5g (⅛oz) champagne yeast

100g (3½oz) unrefined cane sugar

TIPS ON BREWING

▪ Scrupulous hygiene and sterilization are essential at every stage of brewing to keep out unwanted rogue yeasts and other microbial contaminants.
▪ Don't use baker's yeast.
▪ Check your brew regularly to see if it is still fermenting, and don't rush the brewing process.
▪ Make sure the fermentation process is complete before bottling, or bottles may explode.
▪ Use screw caps, metal caps, or corks to seal your bottles. Use a corking machine for corking and a capping machine to attach metal caps.
▪ Store corked bottles sideways to ensure the corks keep moist (dry corks shrink and let in too much air, which spoils the brew).

1 Ensure that the fruit is in good condition and, if using windfalls, cut away any badly bruised parts. Put all the apples in the freezer overnight to soften them by breaking down their fibrous cell walls.

2 Leave the apples to thaw thoroughly and then process them in small batches using a food processor. You want to reduce the apples to a pulp. If you have an electric fruit juicer, simply juice the fresh apples instead.

3 Strain the pulp through a jelly bag or a clean, muslin-lined sieve suspended over a large clean bowl. Leave to strain until you have 4 litres (7 pints) of juice. Measure the gravity of the strained juice (or bought juice, if using) with a hydrometer. If it is not in the range of 1,035–1,050, gradually dilute with water until it falls within this range.

4 Add the sugar to the juice, stir well, and then pour the juice into a demijohn using a sterilized funnel.

5 Add the yeast. Leave for 2 days at room temperature (15–25°C/59–77°F) with some cotton wool in the top of the demijohn as a seal.

6 When the frothing has reduced, fit the sterilized airlock and pour water into it. The cider should start to fizz. Leave to ferment for 2 weeks or longer until the airlock has stopped bubbling.

7 Siphon the cider using a sterilized siphon into sterilized bottles, leaving 2cm (¾in) of space at the top. Seal the bottles and leave for approximately 3 months in a dark place (a cupboard is fine) at room temperature.

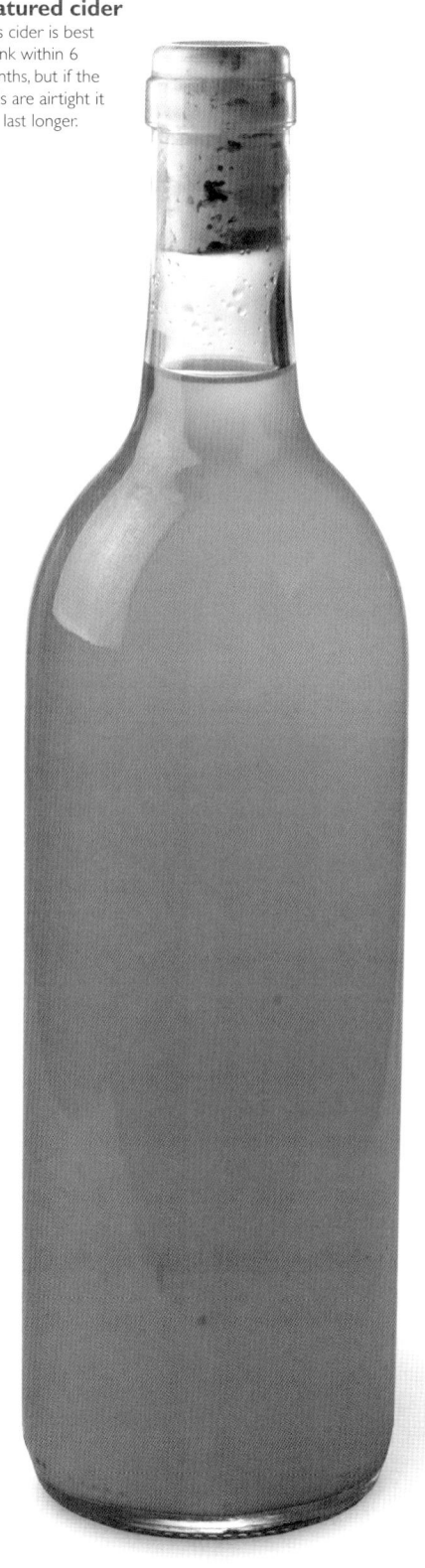

Matured cider
This cider is best drunk within 6 months, but if the seals are airtight it can last longer.

Making wine

Grapes contain the right amount of sugar and acids to make wine. Add yeast and other wine-making ingredients and use sterilized equipment (all available from a home-brew shop or online) to avoid complications such as mould.

Simple grape wine

MAKES APPROX 4.5 LITRES (1 GALLON)

TAKES 2 HOURS, PLUS FERMENTATION AND STORING TIME

KEEPS APPROX 2 YEARS

INGREDIENTS

5kg (11lb) ripe white grapes, washed, with stalks removed

1 Campden tablet

1 tsp pectolase

Up to 1kg (2¼lb) unrefined cane sugar

1 tsp tartaric acid or 1 tsp potassium carbonate

1 sachet hock wine yeast

HOW WINE IS MADE

Wine is made when the natural sugars in fruit or vegetables ferment with yeast (which converts the sugar to alcohol). These natural sugars usually need to be supplemented with extra sugar. All wines need a primary (aerobic) fermentation, which can be violent, followed by a second, quieter (anaerobic) fermentation, and maturing time in the bottle before drinking. Red wines are fermented with their skins, white wines are fermented without.

1 Put the grapes into a sterilized bucket or container. Using a sterilized plastic potato masher, mash the grapes well. Add the Campden tablet and pectolase and leave for 24 hours.

2 Dissolve 100g (3½oz) of the sugar in 50ml (2fl oz) of hot water, allow to cool, and add to the grapes. Repeat the process until a gravity of 1,090 can be read on your hydrometer. Use a litmus paper to test the acid level (the ideal level is 3–3.4 pH). If it is not acidic enough, add the tartaric acid; if it is too acidic, add the potassium carbonate instead.

3 Pour some of the grape mixture into a sterilized muslin cloth suspended over a sterilized bowl. Strain the grape mixture in batches to collect all the juice.

4 Pour the juice into a sterilized demijohn using a sterilized funnel. Add the yeast and attach the sterilized airlock. Leave to ferment at 21–24°C (70–75°F) for 3–4 months. Fermentation is complete when the bubbles have stopped and the water in the airlock is level. (To ensure fermentation is finished, move to a warm place for 24 hours to see if the bubbling has truly ceased.)

5 Being careful not to disturb the sediment (which spoils the flavour), siphon off the clear liquid, using a sterilized siphon, and bottle into sterilized bottles, leaving 2cm (¾in) of space at the top, and seal. Store in a cool, dark place, ideally a cellar. The wine can be drunk immediately, but is better left for 6 months. Like commercial wine, its keeping qualities will vary, but it can last years.

This is a lovely dry, deep red country wine. Use traditional red beetroot varieties such as 'Detroit' or 'Boltardy'. Avoid leaving the wine in bright sunlight, as the colour can fade. If lacking in body, add a tot of brandy just before bottling. Serve as a light claret.

Beetroot wine

SPECIAL EQUIPMENT
FERMENTING BIN, SIPHON,
2 DEMIJOHNS, AIRLOCK

MAKES APPROX 4.5 LITRES
(1 GALLON)

TAKES 2½ HOURS,
PLUS BREWING AND STORING TIME

KEEPS 2 YEARS

INGREDIENTS

1.5kg (3lb 3oz) beetroots,
  peeled and topped

1kg (2¼lb) unrefined cane sugar

Strained juice of 3 lemons

1 cup of cold black tea

1 tsp wine yeast

1 tsp yeast nutrient

1 Put the beetroots in a large pan, add 3 litres (5¼ pints) of water, bring to the boil, and simmer for 15 minutes. Then remove the beetroots.

2 Strain the liquid into a 10 litre (2¼ gallon) sterilized fermenting bin. Add the sugar and stir until dissolved. Add 4.5 litres (1 gallon) of water and leave to cool to 20–25°C (68-77°F).

3 Add the rest of the ingredients. Cover the bin with a clean tea towel and leave at room temperature (15–25°C/59–77°F) away from direct sunlight. Leave to ferment for 1 week or until fermentation has slowed down.

4 Using a sterilized siphon, transfer the liquid into another sterilized demijohn, fit a sterilized airlock, pour a little water into it, and leave at room temperature until fermentation is complete, there are no air bubbles in the airlock, and the wine has cleared – approximately 2 months.

5 Using a sterilized siphon, transfer into sterilized bottles, leaving 2cm (¾in) of space at the top. Seal the bottles and leave in a cool, dark place for 4–6 months before drinking.

An excellent pale yellow dessert wine to make with a glut of fruit or windfalls. (Plums, if used instead, make a fruity red wine.) If made with very ripe fruit, the wine can be a little sweet, so you may want to use less sugar if this is the case. Served chilled.

Greengage wine

SPECIAL EQUIPMENT
FERMENTING BIN, MUSLIN, SIPHON, DEMIJOHN, AIRLOCK

MAKES APPROX 4.5 LITRES (1 GALLON)

TAKES 2 HOURS, PLUS FREEZING, BREWING, AND STORING TIME

KEEPS 2 YEARS

INGREDIENTS

2kg (4½lb) greengages

Juice of 1 lemon

1 tsp pectolase

1 tsp wine yeast

1.5kg (3lb 3oz) unrefined cane sugar

1 Wash the fruit, drain, and put in the freezer overnight, then defrost (this destroys the pectin that would otherwise turn the wine cloudy).

2 Stone and mash the defrosted fruit and add the lemon juice. Place in a sterilized fermenting bin or other suitable container and cover with 3.5 litres (6 pints) of boiling water. When cool, add the pectolase. Leave for 24 hours at room temperature (15–25°C/59–77°F).

3 Add the yeast to the fruit mash, cover, and leave for 4–5 days at room temperature (15–25°C/59–77°F) somewhere dark.

4 Strain the pulp through a muslin cloth into a clean, sterilized container to remove the skins. Put the sugar into a large jug and add enough hot water to cover, stirring until it has dissolved (add extra warm water, if necessary). Stir the dissolved sugar into the mash, mixing well.

5 Using a sterilized siphon, transfer the liquid into a sterilized demijohn and fit a sterilized airlock. Pour a little water into the airlock and leave to ferment at room temperature for 2 months.

6 When there are no air bubbles in the airlock use a sterilized siphon to transfer the wine into sterilized bottles, leaving 2cm (¾in) of space at the top. Seal and store the bottles in a cool, dark place for 6 months before drinking.

This classic kitchen gardener's or allotment grower's wine is quite a dry, hock-style white wine to serve chilled. Use fresh, not end-of-season, pods (freeze them through the season if you don't have enough at one time), or use mangetout or sugarsnap pea pods.

Pea-pod wine

SPECIAL EQUIPMENT MUSLIN, SIPHON, 2 DEMIJOHNS, AIRLOCK

MAKES APPROX 4.5 LITRES (1 GALLON)

TAKES 2 HOURS, PLUS BREWING AND STORING TIME

KEEPS 6 MONTHS

INGREDIENTS

1.8kg (4lb) pea pods

1kg (2¼lb) unrefined cane sugar

1 tbsp wine yeast

2 tea bags

30g (1oz) raisins

1 Put the pea pods and 5 litres (8¾ pints) of water in a preserving pan or a large saucepan over a moderate heat and simmer until soft. Remove from the heat, add the sugar, and stir until it has dissolved. Leave to cool to 37°C (98°F), then add the rest of the ingredients.

2 Cover and leave for 1 week at room temperature (15–25°C/59–77°F) away from direct sunlight.

3 Strain the liquid through a muslin cloth into a sterilized container, then use a sterilized siphon to transfer it into a sterilized demijohn. Fix a sterilized airlock, pour a little water into it, and leave the liquid to continue to ferment at room temperature (15–25°C/59–77°F) for 6 months until fermentation is complete.

4 To help the wine to clear, use a sterilized siphon to transfer it into another sterilized demijohn after 2 months, and then again after another 4 months.

5 When fermentation is complete, use a sterilized siphon to transfer the wine into sterilized bottles leaving 2cm (¾in) of space at the top. Seal and store the bottles in a cool, dark place. The wine is best drunk after 6 months.

Pea pods
Peas (and mangetout and sugarsnap peas) are picked when tender, but if you are picking pods for wine, pick them when they are more mature but not old and tough.

Low in alcohol and distinctively floral in bouquet, this bubbly wine tastes instantly refreshing. It is easy to make, is ready to drink in only two weeks, keeps for many months, and is perfect to serve at summer barbecues and parties.

Elderflower champagne

SPECIAL EQUIPMENT
FERMENTING BIN

MAKES APPROX 4.5 LITRES
(1 GALLON)

TAKES 1 HOUR,
PLUS CHILLING, BREWING,
AND STORING TIME

KEEPS 3 MONTHS

INGREDIENTS

1.25kg (2¾lb) unrefined cane sugar

8 large elderflower heads

4 organic lemons, washed and 2 cut
    into slices

4 tbsp white wine vinegar

1 Put the sugar into a large sterilized bucket or fermenting bin. Boil 8 litres (1¾ gallons) of water and pour it over the sugar to dissolve it. Leave to cool.

2 Shake the elderflower heads to remove any insects and add to the sugar solution with the juice of 2 lemons, the lemon slices, and the vinegar. Cover with a clean cloth and leave for 1 day.

3 Strain through a fine sieve or muslin cloth into a clean, sterilized bucket, squeezing the flowers as you do so to release more flavour.

4 Using a sterilized funnel, transfer into sterilized bottles, leaving 2cm (¾in) of space at the top. Seal and store the bottles in a cool, dark place. They are ready to drink in 10–14 days.

For wine-making, it's best to use parsnips that have been touched by a frost, which helps bring out their natural sugars. If using shop-bought parsnips, buy them during the cold winter months. Serve this white, full-bodied wine as you would a dry sherry.

Parsnip wine

SPECIAL EQUIPMENT
MUSLIN, FERMENTING BIN, SIPHON, DEMIJOHN, AIRLOCK

MAKES APPROX 4.5 LITRES (1 GALLON)

TAKES 2 HOURS, PLUS BREWING AND STORING TIME

KEEPS 2 YEARS

INGREDIENTS

1.8kg (4lb) parsnips, well washed and scrubbed, but not peeled, and chopped

1kg (2¼lb) raisins, washed and chopped

1.5kg (3lb) unrefined cane sugar

Juice and rind of 1 organic lemon, washed

25g (scant 1oz) wine yeast

1 tsp yeast nutrient

1 tsp pectolase

1 Campden tablet

Parsnips
Parsnips grow best in light soils and need a long growing season to produce large sweet roots. They have long been a home-brewer's favourite.

1 Put the parsnips in a preserving pan or a large saucepan. Add 4.5 litres (1 gallon) of water, bring to the boil, and cook for 10–15 minutes or until the parsnips are soft, but not soft enough to fall apart.

2 While the parsnips are cooking, put the raisins in a medium saucepan, cover with 1 litre (1¾ pints) of water, bring to the boil, and simmer for 5 minutes. Strain through a muslin cloth and collect the juice in a clean, small saucepan.

3 Add the sugar and juice and rind of the lemon to the raisin juice and simmer for 45 minutes, stirring occasionally. Leave to cool. Meanwhile, strain the parsnip liquid through a muslin cloth into a sterilized fermenting bin. When the raisin juice is hand-hot (21°C/70°F), add it, the yeast, yeast nutrient, pectolase, and Campden tablet to the bin. Cover with a clean tea towel and leave for 10 days to ferment somewhere warm (15–25°C/59–77°F).

4 Use a sterilized siphon to transfer the wine into a sterilized demijohn. Fix a sterilized airlock, pour a little water into it, and leave the must to continue to ferment at room temperature (15–25°C/59–77°F) for 6 months until fermentation is complete or until fermentation has ceased and the wine has cleared.

5 Using a sterilized siphon, transfer into sterilized bottles, leaving 2cm (¾in) of space at the top. Seal and store the bottles in a cool, dark place for 6 months before using.

Pectolase is used with wines made from high pectin fruit to help make them clear. Without it, the wine would need clarifying several times. (Campden tablets purify the wine.) Crab apples make strong-tasting wines, which vary in colour and flavour.

Crab apple wine

SPECIAL EQUIPMENT
FERMENTING BIN, 2 DEMIJOHNS, JELLY BAG, AIRLOCK, SIPHON

MAKES APPROX 4.5 LITRES
(1 GALLON)

TAKES 2 HOURS,
PLUS BREWING AND STORING TIME

KEEPS 2 YEARS

INGREDIENTS

2.5kg (5½lb) crab apples, washed, with stalks removed

1 tsp citric acid

1 tsp pectolase

1½ Campden tablets

500g (1lb 2oz) raisins, washed and chopped

25g (scant 1oz) champagne yeast

1 tsp yeast nutrient

675g (1½lb) unrefined cane sugar

1 Put the crab apples into a thick, clean plastic bag, a few at a time, and crush them with a rolling pin (but not hard enough to crush the seeds). Transfer the crushed apples into a sterilized fermenting bin. Top up the fermenting bin with 3 litres (5¼ pints) of cold water and add the citric acid, pectolase, and 1 Campden tablet. Cover the bin with a clean tea towel and leave for 1 day somewhere warm (15–25°C/59–77°F).

2 Add the raisins, yeast, and yeast nutrient to the fermenting bin. Cover tightly and leave to ferment for 1 week.

3 Fit a sterilized funnel in the neck of a sterilized demijohn, line it with a sterilized jelly bag, and strain carefully in small batches into the demijohn. In a saucepan boil 1.5 litres (2¾ pints) of water and dissolve the sugar in it. Allow to cool and then add to the demijohn, topping up with extra boiled, cooled water if the demijohn is not full. Place the remaining half crushed Campden tablet in the sterilized airlock. Attach a bung and the airlock to the demijohn and fill the airlock with water.

4 Leave for 3 months, then use a sterilized siphon to transfer the wine into another sterilized demijohn. Leave for a further 12 months, leaving 2cm (¾in) of space at the top. Seal and store the bottles in a cool, dark place for 6 months before drinking.

Brewing beer

Home-brewed beers are not difficult to make and can taste impressively good, although their alcoholic strength varies, so treat them with respect. This brew is roughly 5–6 per cent alcohol by volume. Sterilize all equipment before use.

Beer from hops

MAKES APPROX 14 LITRES (3 GALLONS)

TAKES 1 HOUR, PLUS BREWING AND STORING TIME

KEEPS 6 MONTHS

INGREDIENTS

60g (2oz) dried hops

1kg (2¼lb) malt extract

750g (1lb 10oz) unrefined cane sugar

20g (¾oz) ale yeast

THE NATURE OF HOME-BREWING

Part of the appeal and fascination of brewing your own alcoholic drinks lies in the unexpected. As brewing is a natural process, the results can never be reliably predicted, and even the most experienced home brewers have failures – but also sensational successes.

For this reason, treat the recommended storage times as a guide: each brew (beer, cider, or wine) will mature, reach perfection, then deteriorate at a different rate to the next. Sampling a brew regularly is the only sure way to track its progress.

1 Thoroughly clean a preserving pan, or 2 very large saucepans. Fill with 7 litres (1½ gallons) of water, bring to the boil, add the hops, and boil for 25–30 minutes until the water has changed colour.

2 Sterilize a fermenting bin, rinse it thoroughly, and pour in the malt extract and sugar. Position the bin away from direct sunlight and draughts in a room with a temperature of 15–25°C (59–77°F).

3 Strain the hop liquid through a nylon sieve, or a colander lined with clean muslin, into the bin.

4 Check the temperature of the liquid is below 18°C (65°F), then sprinkle in the yeast.

5 Stir the mixture (called wort) until the sugar dissolves. Pour in 6 litres (1.3 gallons) of water. A hydrometer is not essential, but if you have one, the gravity should be roughly 1,030. Put the lid on the bin and leave for 1 week or until there is no more gurgling and bubbling. The hydrometer reading should now be 1,000.

6 Place 1 level tsp of sugar into each sterilized bottle. Siphon the beer using a sterilized siphon, into the bottles, ensuring that none of the sediment is siphoned in, and leaving 2cm (¾in) of space at the top. Seal and leave the bottles in a cool, dark place for 10 days, after which the beer will be ready to drink.

Home-brewed beer
Beer brewed from hops tastes satisfyingly smooth and velvety, and is comparable in alcoholic strength to pub ales.

Index

Page numbers in *italics* indicate recipes. Page numbers in **bold** indicate step-by-step instructions and "best for…" ingredients information.

Acknowledgments

Lynda Brown is an award-winning food writer and author, and frequent broadcaster. She is a kitchen garden expert, and life-long supporter of organic food and farming, and organic gardening. In 2009, her garden was featured on BBC2 Gardeners' World. Her beliefs that "you are what you eat" and that good cooking is about fresh unadulterated food, cooked simply, using foods produced in the best ways possible, are what inspire her. She has written several books including *Organic Living* (Dorling Kindersley).

In 1992, Lynda won the prestigious Glenfiddich Cookery Writer of the Year Award. She is also a lifetime member of the Soil Association and Garden Organic.

Lynda Brown would like to thank: all the contributors, Andrew Roff, Will Hicks, Jane Lawrie, Jan Stevens, and the production team at DK; Peter Denyer (www.kilnerjarsuk.co.uk); Dr. Colin May (adviser to Certo Ltd.); Jeremy and David Trehane (blueberry producers); Melanie Humphries (Tiptree Preserves); Anne Theakstone and Patrick Good (Silver Spoon); Gill Della Casa and Andrew Farmer (www.birchesmill.co.uk); a very special thanks to my editor Susannah Steel; and to Carolyn.

Dorling Kindersley would like to thank:
Tim Young and Christine Williams at the Soil Association (www.soilassociation.org), Nicky Collings for art directing the photoshoot, food stylist Jane Lawrie, prop stylist Sue Rowlands, Anna Burges-Lumsden and Jan Stevens for recipe testing, Sue Morony for proofreading, Sue Bosanko for the index, Clive Husselbury for the smokers (www.cookquipe.co.uk), and Wares of Knutsford for the jam and preserving jars (www.waresofknutsford.co.uk).

And the following recipe contributors:
Carolyn Humphries for her freezer jams, bottled delights, and salting and charcuterie recipes.

Heather Whinney for her sweet and savoury preserves, and preserving in oil recipes.

Graham Waddington, James Swift, and Mitchel Troy at Trealy Charcuterie for their recipes on pages 304–309 and 312–15. www.trealyfarm.com

Michael Leviseur at the Organic Smokehouse for his smoking recipes on pages 298, 320, and 328. www.organicsmokehouse.com

Richard Muirhead at The Old Smokehouse, Brougham Foods for his smoking recipes on pages 323–24 and 330–31. www.the-old-smokehouse.co.uk

Andy and Dave Hamilton for their brewing and wine-making recipes on pages 336–47. www.selfsufficientish.com

And the following for their recipes taken from the DK and Soil Association websites:
Christine Bailey for her Cranberry and apricot chutney (p176), Mary Baldwin for her Cucumber pickle (p204), Fi Bird for her Gooseberry and raspberry jam (p109), Joanne Downes for her Plum and squash chutney (p186), Gloria Wilding for her Plum and rum jam (p108), and Kay Wilkinson for her Rhubarb and vanilla purée (p70).

All images © Dorling Kindersley
For further information see: **www.dkimages.com**